The Home Equity Management Guidebook

$ $ $ $ $ $ $ $ $ $

How to Achieve Maximum Wealth with Maximum Security

Enjoy the book.

Also by Roccy DeFrancesco, JD, CWPP, CAPP, MMB

The Doctor's Wealth Preservation Guide

Wealth Preservation Planning: A "Team" Approach

The Home Equity Management Guidebook

$$\$\ \$\ \$\ \$\ \$\ \$\ \$\ \$$$

How to Achieve Maximum Wealth with Maximum Security

By: Roccy DeFrancesco, JD, CWPP, CAPP, MMB

The Home Equity Management Guidebook

By: Roccy DeFrancesco, JD, CWPP™, CAPP™, MMB™

TriArc Advisors, LLC
3260 S. Lakeshore Dr.
St. Joseph, MI 49085
269-216-9978
313-887-0532 (fax)

ISBN-10: 0-9770770-9-8

ISBN-13: 978-0-9770770-9-0

This book is dedicated to all readers
who have ever purchased an educational or self-help book
only to find out that it turned out to be a sales book
for the author or his/her team.

This book is a comprehensive and authoritative
book on the subject of Home Equity Management.
This book does not use fuzzy math and does not
ignore the realities of the tax code.

I hope you enjoy reading this book as much as I enjoyed writing it.

Roccy DeFrancesco, JD, CWPP, CAPP, MMB

Table of Contents

The Home Equity Management Guidebook

How to Achieve Maximum Wealth with Maximum Security

Acknowledgements

As this is my first general public book (vs. one for advisors or specifically for physicians), I have a list of people to thank for helping me put it together.

Always at the top of my list is my wife Kara who, for reasons few can understand, has been married to me for over twelve years. I'd also like to thank my two children, Lauren and Mitchell. I'm lucky to have a family who understands my passion to spend time on projects such as this book.

On the technical side of the book, I have several people to thank as this book covers several different subject matters (mortgages, financial planning, tax, estate planning, insurance, etc.)

In alphabetical order, I'd like to thank the following people for their contributions to this book:

Todd Batson, Gordon Bell, Jeff Cohen, Marcia DeFrancesco, Roccy DeFrancesco, Sr., Mike Duncan, Dennis Haber, Steve Jackson, Trace Kirkpatrick, Jason Ruggerio, Joseph Stella, John Steinke, and Mike Tivolini.

I will save my biggest acknowledgement for the two unnamed authors of the two most prevalent books in the marketplace which cover the Home Equity Harvesting topic.

If these two unnamed authors would have written quality books with real math and attention to the Internal Revenue Code, I would never have been motivated to create this book (one that is needed to give consumers an unbiased look at the concepts discussed).

<u>Foreword</u>

This book is dedicated to readers who are looking for understandable answers to the following questions:

1) How do you build a tax-free retirement nest egg in the most efficient and most economic manner possible?

2) How do you build a tax-free retirement nest egg in the most efficient and least risky manner possible?

3) What is the difference between a sales book and an educational book?

4) Does it make sense to pay off your home mortgage early, and, if not, why not?

5) What is Equity Harvesting and why is it such a hot topic in the insurance, financial, and mortgage marketplaces?

6) How can you pay off your current home mortgage years earlier without changing your lifestyle?

7) What is the 1% Cash Flow Arm (CFA) mortgage and is it right for you?

8) Is cash value life insurance a good financial tool to build wealth for retirement?

9) Does it make financial sense to over-fund a qualified retirement plan or IRA?

10) How can you use Home Equity Management to remove money from your IRA tax free in retirement?

11) What is a Reverse Mortgage, and is it something you or your parents should consider after reaching 62 years of age?

12) What are the laws that govern your ability to use Home Equity Management to your benefit as a tax-favorable/wealth-building tool?

WHY YOUR ADVISORS WILL NOT KNOW MANY OF THE TOPICS COVERED IN THIS BOOK (OR IF THEY KNOW THE TOPICS, WHY THEY LEARNED THEM FROM BIASED SOURCES)

Why advisors do not know many of the topics covered in this book is a very common question I receive when educating clients on the concepts revolving around Home Equity Management. The main reason local advisors do not know many of the topics covered in this book is because there is no formal educational body in the country that educates on them.

Only recently did I decide to create the <u>Master Mortgage Broker</u> (MMB™) certification course to teach advisors about the concepts covered in this book. Before the MMB™ course, there was no non-biased association, society, or educational institution educating on these topics.

Honestly, before I was forced to review the marketing books in the marketplace on Home Equity Management, I didn't know much about the topic. I say "forced to" because I had multiple requests from advisors who had taken one of my certification courses to review the sales books in the marketplace and comment on whether they were technically accurate.

My journey to create this book started when I read the two obviously biased educational/sales books in the marketplace, which covered the concept of Home Equity Management. When I read both books, I was shocked at the technical flaws in the books and obvious attempts to sell readers without giving full disclosure of all the important issues.

When I started receiving calls every week from many of the 100,000+ advisors who receive my weekly newsletter touting the most prominent books, asking me if I had read the book, and even calls recommending that I read the book and incorporate the teachings into one of my educational courses, I finally had enough.

I said to myself, advisors who "sell" clients based upon the sales books in the marketplace on Home Equity Management are going to provide inaccurate and/or incorrect advice to their clients; and many will eventually get sued by them after they figure out that the advice was either not in their best interest or simply wrong.

Not many advisors in the country have the ability to right a wrong or an injustice that is happening to the American public. Not many advisors can choose to shut their lives down for several months while devoting themselves to writing a for-public education book.

Having said that, my business model affords me just that opportunity. As you will read in the upcoming pages, I can allocate the time to write a new book when needed; and that's just what I did to create this book. What you are reading is the final outcome of my research and writings on how to use Home Equity Management the "correct" way to build maximum wealth for retirement (or if you choose to pay off your house early, how to use a simple plan to accomplish that goal).

I hope you enjoy reading the book as much as I enjoyed writing it.

About the author

My name is **Roccy DeFrancesco, Jr, JD, CWPP™, CAPP™, MMB™**; and I am an attorney, licensed to practice law in Michigan and Indiana.

I've already told you a little bit about why I decided to write this book, and you'll read more stories in the book which will further elaborate on why I devoted time to this project.

As with any book or educational program, I believe it is vitally important for you to know the details of the author's background. Why? When you are reading a book which is supposed to help you alter your life to build wealth in a tax-favorable manner where your decisions will affect you for the rest of your life, don't you think you should know something about the person who wrote the book? I think so.

Therefore, if you will indulge me, I will give you the not-so-brief history of my professional career and will let you determine for yourself my credibility as an author.

Let me start a discussion about my background by going back to my fourth year of undergraduate studies at Embry Riddle Aeronautical University in 1992. In 1992, I was a commercial pilot looking to graduate undergrad in 1993 and start looking for a job. As it turned out, the airline industry was in a tailspin (pun intended), and you could not find a job anywhere (and if you found one, it was a very low-paying job). Actually, to get a job, you had to pay the airlines for your own training (which usually exceeds $10,000).

Thinking that flying would be a fun career, but not the only possible one, I contacted my parents and asked them what they would think if I decided not to work as a pilot and instead went to law school?

To my surprise, they were very supportive of the move; and so in 1993, I started law school at Valparaiso University School of Law.

While in law school, I decided that I wanted to be a personal injury attorney (you see them typically on the back of your phone books). I had family friends who did that type of law, and they seemed happy and made more money than other attorneys in my home town. Therefore, when taking elective courses in law school, I concentrated on personal injury courses.

When I graduated from law school (similar to the airline industry), personal injury law was on the downswing due to "tort reform." Therefore, few firms were hiring in the area where I wanted to live.

As it turned out, I could not find a job that I wanted; and so in 1996, I ended up coming back to my home town of St. Joseph, Michigan, to practice law with my father, Roccy M. DeFrancesco, Sr., J.D. My areas of practice were business law (setting up corporations), real estate law, a little personal injury law, and a heavy emphasis on estate planning and divorce law.

I was truly amazed at how much Roccy, Sr., knew and was more than happy to make virtually no money while learning as much as I could from him.

As it turns out, I've got one of those personalities where I'm always searching for that next challenge in life. The next challenge was to still become a personal injury attorney. After a year or so of working with Roccy, Sr., I found out that our local personal injury firm in town was hiring (a rare occasion). The firm was founded by a long-time family friend who after an interview process hired me to be their new associate in the summer of 1997.

During that summer, I blew out my knee playing with my dog in the yard and had it operated on by another long-time family friend, Dr. Sterling Doster, and his new sports fellowship-trained surgeon, Dr. Gregory Fox. Most people stop me when I'm going through the twisted story of why I do what I do for a living and ask why I tell people I blew my knee out. The answer is simple—blowing my knee out and having it operated on ended up being a life-altering event as you will read.

On one of the follow-up visits with the doctors who fixed my knee (their office was in Bloomington, Indiana, which was four hours south of where I lived at the time), we all went out to dinner. After a few glasses of wine, the doctors asked me if I wanted to come down to Bloomington to run their medical practice. They said their office manager was getting in over her head and that they'd double my salary to come run their practice.

I told them I could not possibly entertain accepting their offer, as I just took a new job with the local personal injury law firm in town. After dinner, I went home and continued to work at the law firm. As it turned out and through no fault of the new employer, I really didn't enjoy the personal injury work I was doing.

Therefore, after working at the new firm for a few months, I called the doctors back and asked them if they were serious about me running their medical practice. They said they had a few glasses of wine that night and sort of remember the conversation. They asked for a few days to talk about it and a week later called me and told me to come down to Bloomington, Indiana, to run their medical clinic.

When I told the attorneys who hired me at the personal injury firm that the medical practice was going to double my salary, they laughed a bit and wished me well. I didn't expect them to match that offer; and as I said, they were long-time family friends and they simply wanted the best for me.

When I moved down to Bloomington, Indiana, in January of 1998, my wife was pregnant with our first child and things were moving quickly. The lady who was supposed to train me took six weeks of sick time and then quit. I learned on the fly how to run the medical practice, which took a good six months.

As it turned out, I was a <u>terrible manager of people; but I was a whiz with the finances</u>. Understand that I came out of a litigation practice where I went to war every day with other attorneys on behalf of my clients (especially the divorces I used to work on). Then suddenly I ended up running a medical clinic with thirteen female employees who worked under an office manager who really did not give much direction.

Needless to say, I did a very poor job of managing the staff the first six months. The finances of the office, on the other hand, were another matter. Since I had no faith in the previous office manager, I decided to shop every vendor the medical practice used to see if I could save the office some money.

As it turned out, I saved the four-physician medical office over $35,000 in expenses my first year. On what? Health insurance, malpractice insurance, office supply purchasing, outside professional help, collections expenses, overtime, and I successfully helped negotiate a very difficult purchase of the medical office building the practice rented.

After about six months, I had things in the office the way I wanted them from a financial point of view. While I did not always get along with the staff, I have to give them their due in that most of them were top-notch and did a tremendous job in their particular specialty. What that left me with, however, was a dilemma.

After fixing the office financially, and because the staff did not require much oversight from me, I had a tremendous amount of free time on my hands. I could run the medical office for what I needed to do as a manager in two to four hours or less each day. Remember that in the practice of law I used to have 25+ clients all wanting something from me, and now I was running a medical office with less than 20 employees. If I didn't come to work for weeks on end, the office would run just fine.

The physicians at the medical office knew I would get to the point of being bored and thought I would open up a small legal practice out of the medical office or that I would play golf every day. Instead of doing either, I decided to research in extraordinary detail "advanced" planning for high-income/net-worth clients (which were my physician employers).

People wonder how I was able to create three advanced education/certification courses with over 1,200 pages of text and two books by the age of 37. It's really not that I'm any brighter than anyone else or anyone reading this book. It's that, due to the extraordinary circumstances of my employment at the medical practice, I was able to spend two-and-a-half years researching: asset protection, income, estate and capital gains tax planning/reduction, corporate structure, advanced estate planning, long-term care, disability and life insurance, annuities, mortgages, on the list goes on and on.

After my research on a topic, I would write an article on it and get it published in any number of places including, but not limited to the following: Orthopedics Today, Physician Money Digest, Physician's News Digest, MomMD, American Urological Association Newsletter, Today in Cardiology, The Rake Report by PriceWaterhouseCoopers, The CPA Journal, CPA Wealth Provider, Strategic Orthopaedics, General Surgery News, the Indiana Bar Journal, the OH CPA Newsletter, Financial Planning Magazine, and Insurance Selling Magazine.

Then I started doing educational seminars for the following organizations (not an exhaustive list): Indiana State Medical Association, Ohio State Medical Association, Academy of Medicine of Cincinnati, Mid-America Orthopaedic Association, the MI, OH, IN, and KY CPA Societies, Professional Association of Health Care Office Management (PAHCOM), BONES, the American Academy of Medical Management, TX Medical Group Management Association (TX MGMA), Texas Medical Association Insurance Trust (TMAIT), the Michigan Orthodontics Association, the National Funeral Home Directors Association, the Society of Financial Service Professionals, the National Association of Insurance and Financial Advisors, and more.

After awhile, you have enough content from articles and speaking engagements to write a book; so I wrote my first book, The Doctor's Wealth Preservation Guide.

MOVING ON FROM THE MEDICAL PRACTICE

While at the medical practice, I started two separate consulting companies—one company where I would provide advice to physicians and one company to work with advisors who wanted help with their physician clients.

As it turned out, I made enough money from the side consulting businesses to allow myself to try consulting full time. By then my wife was pregnant with our second child; and since the family didn't visit us much in Bloomington, Indiana, we also wanted to move back to Michigan so we could be closer to the entire family.

That's just what we did in the spring of 2000. My wife, daughter, and soon-to-be son moved back to my home town of St. Joseph, Michigan, where I worked with my two companies to help physicians with asset protection, estate and tax planning, and advisors who had physicians or other high-income/net-worth clients who needed help.

The good news is that I was making a good living with my two consulting companies. The bad news is that after awhile I became miserable. I don't want to sound like I was crying with a loaf of bread under my arm; but I was traveling a lot to visit clients and advisors around the country, as well as doing several seminars, and I was getting worn out. It's not that I didn't enjoy it; but with two young children, I was looking for a business model that would let me go to the kids' ball games, go to the pool, and work in the yard (although I despise yard work).

THE LIGHT BULB GOES ON

I was in Las Vegas in 2004 giving a seminar for the National Society of Accountants (NSA) when the light bulb finally went on for me. A friend of mine, Lance Wallach (who introduced me to the NSA), and I were out to dinner in between the days of the seminar; and I was complaining to him about how I was making decent money but that I was really getting worn out. I basically had made the decision that I needed to do something else, and I was even considering going back to practicing law (it's hard to even type that and see it in print).

Lance told me to stop complaining and then off the cuff said: "Roccy, what you need to do is to create your own Roccy-certification course. You need the school of Roccy."

Of course, he was making fun of me, which I'm sure I deserved; but he was onto something and didn't know it. Lance had heard me speak many times and read my book <u>The Doctor's Wealth Preservation Guide</u>. As someone "in the industry," he knew that the topics I dealt with in my book and speak about at seminars are fairly unique and that other advisors who have or want to have high-income/net-worth clients would like to learn these topics.

Like the day I decided to take the job running the medical practice, that day in Vegas was again one of those days in your life you look back on and see it as life altering.

I went home from the Vegas NSA seminar and thought about putting my own educational program together. I figured I could put the program together with no problem. I had a lot of content and some of the best experts in the country who were nice enough to let me bend their ear on advanced-planning topics. The question was: Could I make a living doing "education"?

I said to myself that it really didn't matter as I didn't want to continue traveling like I was, no matter how much money could be made. Therefore, I told my wife that I was changing courses; and I hoped for everyone's sake it would work out. I decided to put together what I now call the only "advanced" education/certification courses in the country where I educate CPAs/EAs/accountants, attorneys, financial planners, mortgage brokers, security traders, etc., advanced planning for high-income/net-worth clients.

I formed my own educational institute with an educational board of some of the country's best experts in their fields.

The three courses are the Certified Wealth Preservation Planner (CWPP™), Certified Asset Protection Planner, (CAPP™), and Master Mortgage Broker (MMB™). Each course requires advisors to read over hundreds of pages of text, take a lengthy multiple-choice/true-false test and pass an essay test. The essay test confirms to me that the advisors who take the courses not only understand the material, but can apply it in the "real world."

I rolled the CWPP™ and CAPP™ courses out in 2005 and have had a nice steady flow of advisors sign up to take the courses online or in person. In 2007, I finally rolled out the MMB™ course (which educates more fully on Home Equity Management).

I'm proud to say that the reviews from those who have taken the courses have been tremendous. I image that is the case not so much because I'm that great of a writer of the material, but because the material is practical and usable in the real world (vs. esoteric educational material), and because the majority of the topics in the courses are new to those who take them. No other entity in the country provides unbiased education on asset protection, which is the foundation of the three certification courses.

My travel has been severely curtailed as I only put on about six in-person seminars a year; and I get to do what I've found I'm best at, which is to help other advisors fashion solutions for their clients. Therefore, it seems that the move from full-time consulting to educating advisors and working with their clients has turned out to be a good move for me, my family, and those who have taken my courses.

RECENT NEWS

As the certification courses continue to get traction nationwide, I am always searching for the next challenge. I found that next challenge when I decided to form a new society called the Asset Protection Society (APS™) (www.assetprotectionsociety.org).

I finally got tired of all the asset-protection "scammers" in the marketplace who were luring unsuspecting clients to do business with them only to have the clients find out that the services they purchased were worthless and usually far too expensive.

I formed the APS™ with a handful of other like-minded advisors with one overriding goal and that was to form an organization that would protect the public. It's a tough chore and one that will take time to accomplish, but I believe it is a worthwhile cause.

The APS™ is a place where the public can receive baseline education on how to protect assets from creditors (like the personal injury attorneys I used to work for). In addition, the APS™ will "Rate" advisors on their knowledge of what I call "global asset protection."

My definition of global asset protection is that anyone or anything that can take your money is a creditor. Think about that for a second. Who is your number one creditor every year? The IRS. Is the stock market a creditor? Sure. Did you lose money in the stock market in 2000-2002 when it lost nearly 50% of its value? What about the costs of long-term care? Is that an expense that will take your money in retirement? Absolutely.

Because advisors have knowledge in different areas, the APS™ gives out either an A, AA, AAA, G, or O Rating. G stands for global and O stands for offshore.

I wanted to create a Society that would set the "standard of care" in the industry for how to provide asset-protection advice, and I wanted the public to feel comfortable going to the Society to look for help from "Rated" advisors. I believe the APS™ is such a place, and I look forward to having it grow over the coming years with the help of all of its members and State Representatives.

If you are interested in asset-protection or finding an advisor who can help you, please check out the Society on the web.

THE END

By the end, I mean that the end of my overly long summary of my background. I probably made this section of the book too long, but I figure if you are not interested in the whole story, you can flip through it or skip it. I know that when I talk with people these days, they seem interested in the whole story so I thought I would put it in the book.

The end of the story is really the beginning of this new book, The Home Equity Management Guidebook.

As you now know, the reason I felt compelled to write this book is because of the other books in the marketplace that deal with this subject matter in a pure sales manner vs. a full-disclosure educational manner. Throughout the book, I will point to where this book differs from the sales books, and I'll let you decide for yourself who is making an attempt to sell you and who is making an attempt to educate you on the topics so you can make an informed decision on what is best for you.

HELP FROM THE AUTHOR

Invariably when you write books, you have a segment of readers who want to get in touch with the author to ask questions. I understand that, and I will do my best to accommodate the inquiries. You can always e-mail me directly at info@thewpi.org. I am usually fairly timely with my responses. I will be able to give you a brief response, but then I will probably forward you the name and contact number of an advisor in your local area who has taken one of The Wealth Preservation Institute's certification programs. That way I know you'll be working with an advisor who knows the subject matter and has agreed to abide by the Ethics Code of the Institute.

For those of you who believe you need more comprehensive planning (asset protection, estate, and tax planning), you should consider using the C.A.L.M. Plan. It is a platform I put together for the advisors to use who have taken a certification course. C.A.L.M. stands for Comprehensive Asset Liability Management. You can read about the C.A.L.M. Plan at http://assetprotectionsociety.org/client/?a=PG:818.

Again, thank you for buying this book; and I hope it helps you better understand how to manage the equity in your home to reach your retirement goals.

Roccy M. DeFrancesco, Jr., JD, CWPP™, CAPP™, MMB™
Founder: The Wealth Preservation Institute
www.thewpi.org
Co-Founder: The Asset Protection Society
www.assetprotectionsociety.org
3260 S. Lakeshore Drive
St. Joseph, MI 49085
269-216-9978

Chapter 1
Sales Books vs. Educational Books

Have you ever read a book where in the Foreword you read quotes that were so enticing that you just had to buy the book?

What if you read the Foreword of a book and saw the following quotes from the author touting how wonderful his/her book is?

"What if I told you I'm about to share insider secrets that, before now, only the very wealthy among us knew?"

"What if I told you these secrets will absolutely transform you into a millionaire?"

"What if this proven system could be set up so that you could just implement it once to be wealthy?"

"Then, what if I showed you how to recycle it every three to five years to double or triple your wealth?"

"What if I said it doesn't involve effort, concentration, or budgeting?"

"In front of you is an empowering starter kit to becoming a millionaire, stocked with insights and opportunities you may not have known existed."

My guess is that, if you read the Foreword of a book with the above quotes, you'd want me to tell you the name of it and you'd wish you bought that book instead of mine.

Generally speaking, most of the American public has the intelligence to know the difference between reading a book that is trying to "sell" them a concept and one that is trying to educate them on a concept.

With that said, if readers buy books that are "sales" books and never read anything with substance or details (or learn either from their advisors), there is no frame of reference to allow a reader to understand that the sales books are NOT an authoritative guide for how to grow wealth, but are, in fact, very clever sales books drafted for very specific reasons.

WHAT IF THE FOREWARD TO A BOOK STATED THE FOLLOWING?

What you will learn in this book is the **truth** about how to build wealth using the equity in your home.

What you will learn will be based on the law and real-world illustrations, not hypothetical situations crafted a certain way so that the outcome is always positive for the reader.

What you will learn is that the concept of Equity Harvesting is not for everyone, and you may find out after reading this book that you can use the concept to build wealth in a tax-favorable manner or not.

WHICH BOOK WOULD YOU RATHER READ?

Many would say the first book because it seems to state that readers of the books can become "millionaires," whereas the second book says that you may be able to use the concept and you might not.

I'll tell you what I'd like. I'd like a concept that doesn't require work, risk, or a lot of money and can turn me into a millionaire in the very near future. Unfortunately, this concept does not exist and no "book" can give you that magical concept.

As I indicated, most people can tell when they are being "sold" a concept; and that's really what's happening with some books in the marketplace that deal with the concept of Home Equity Harvesting.

Let's be realistic. If it was easy to become a millionaire with a few "secrets" you can read about in massively published for-public (vs. trade) books, wouldn't one of your neighbors or friends already be a millionaire? Would you see the gurus who have written these books on CNBC or other financial-based television shows?

SELLING SYSTEMS

You are going to learn some "secrets" by reading this book, which will be very enlightening. You are going to learn the secrets of the authors who write for-public books not necessarily to educate the public but to create a national referral source for advisors who buy into their selling systems.

Am I saying that some of the books in the marketplace were not meant to educate the public on the concept of Equity Management? Not necessarily. The books are meant to give the public baseline education on certain concepts in a manner so the public gets hot and bothered about what they've read and, therefore, want to seriously consider implementing the concepts discussed in the books.

In other words, the books were designed to give you enough select information so you want to pick up the phone and ask for help from the author and his/her "TEAM."

Would you be interested to know that the biggest market for the Equity Management books is the advisor market looking to learn new concepts to sell products? Would that give you reason to read such books with a more cautious eye?

Think of the following and ask yourself which author would you rather be?

Author 1—He/she writes a book that will sell for $19.95 and will sell 100,000 copies. The author receives a $50,000 up-front signing bonus to write the book and then 15% of the revenue from gross sales. If the book did, in fact, sell 100,000 copies, this author would make $299,250 on the book sales (15% of the gross) and the $50,000 signing bonus for a total of $349,350.

Not bad, but the authors of get-rich-quick-and-easy books want to become millionaires themselves by writing the books.

Author 2—The same as author one, except the author then creates a seminar to teach advisors how to use the concepts in the book. Assume that, if the advisors who attend these seminars and learn how to sell to the public the concepts in the book, they then will believe they can double their income from attending the training. Do you think advisors would flock to such seminars? Absolutely.

Assume the author charges advisors $5,000-$8,000 to attend these training seminars and that 1,000 advisors a year go through the training programs.

Would more advisors want to attend the seminars and become part of the "TEAM" if they knew that they would receive sales leads from the author? Leads? Yep, leads. What if the author was bright enough to set up a referral system to funnel general public readers of the book who contacted the author for help to "approved TEAM" members who are trained in the teachings of the book? Would that help the advisor pull the trigger to pay $5,000-$8,000 for the training?

How much would the second author make? Between $5,000,000 - $7,000,000 more a year just doing the training.

Finally, what if the concepts in the book revolved around the sale of life insurance, and the author was also able to have some of the "TEAM" member advisors licensed under him/her to sell life insurance?

I will not be getting into the commissions of life insurance in this book; but what I will tell you is that, if the sales force of "TEAM" members is productive, the amount of money the author can make from override commissions on the sales force would be in excess of the amount of money he/she would make from the training and the book sales.

My point is that any book that hopes to accomplish what author two is trying to accomplish better be really good and be written in such a way that the lay reader will have few or no hesitations when making the decision to pick up the phone and contact the author or a local "TEAM" member for help.

ARE YOU FOR SALE?

You might be shaking your head after reading the previous few paragraphs. You might be thinking to yourself, how could anyone be so clever as to pull off such a marketing plan based on a "for-public" book?

Don't believe me? The following will shock you. The following is an <u>actual e-mail</u> (names deleted) I obtained from a "TEAM" member of one of the authors in the marketplace who has a book on Home Equity Management.

"Hello TEAM members!

*****(The lead will go to the first person who e-mails me, and if I Do not respond to you then someone else received the Lead.)*******

I am happy to announce that we have a new Lead in your area!

-They are from Payson, AZ

-He is 66

-They have read (*name of the book omitted*) several times -He is retired
-Their home is worth $300,000 -And they owe $0 on it -They have $450,000 -They also have $25,000 in various non-qualified accounts

Possible total repositionable assets of at least $500,000.

Possible Target Premium of at least $25,000

Purchase this lead for (first come first serve-FCFS): $1000

or

"Guarantee" if no case is closed is $1250 (guarantee means that if the lead does not do a plan we will reimburse you $750 of that $925, in the form of credit to be used on (*name of book omitted*), brochures, refresher courses, other leads, etc.)

Lead to end Friday September 16th at 8:00am (MST)

If you have any questions please contact me.

*****(BTW "first come first serve" is the first person who e-mails me, and if I do not respond to you then someone else received the Lead.)*******"

When I received the above e-mail from a TEAM member of the author, it vindicated my writing of this book. I knew a book like this one was needed to better educate and protect the public, but I never knew that readers were for sale.

I need to interpret the above e-mail for readers who do not know the insurance industry and to reinforce exactly what is going on.

A general public reader of a book on Home Equity Harvesting contacted the author for help. The author's team took the potential client's information and created a profile.

The profile was then e-mailed to all the "TEAM" members (those who had paid big bucks to be trained on what is in the book) telling "TEAM" members that there is a lead and asking them if they want to buy it. Yes, that's right—the potential client is basically being auctioned off to the first "TEAM" member to e-mail back.

Also, most readers will not know what is meant in the e-mail when the writer says there is a "<u>Possible Target Premium of at least $25,000</u>."

Life insurance agents are paid on a percentage of "target" premiums. With many insurance companies, agents can get paid over 100% of target. So what the e-mailer is saying is that this lead could be worth a first-year life insurance commission of $25,000.

Pretty slick, but if the client actually knew what was going on, do you think he would be pleased? Do you think he would want to work with such a "TEAM"? Would you? I don't think so.

The ironic thing about the "TEAM" structure is that the vast majority of advisors who tout the virtues of the book (in an effort to generate sales of existing or potential clients) are not on the "TEAM."

Those non-"TEAM" members are handing out the book to clients in an effort to facilitate sales not knowing that, IF their clients happen to call the author for help, the author is going to put the lead on the auction block and the non-"TEAM" advisor who gave the client the book is going to have a "TEAM" member contacting his/her potential client.

If the non-"TEAM" advisor knew what was going on, do you think the advisor would be handing out the book? I don't think so.

THE COLD WATER GUY

I want readers to know that I have a certain reputation in the "industry." By industry, I mean the financial planning, accounting, and legal communities.

My reputation, as I've been told by others, is that I'm just about the only one who tells the downside to concepts. Some people say that I'm the **cold water guy** because by telling the downsides to concepts I am throwing "cold water" on the sale's process.

I like to think of myself not as the cold water guy but instead as the "**full disclosure**" guy.

EVERY topic has pros and cons. There is NO MAGIC way to become a millionaire. There is NO EASY way to become a millionaire. If there was, everyone would be doing it.

Remember my question: If these sales books on this topic are so powerful and work for everyone, why is one of your neighbors or family members not a millionaire because of the concepts in the books?

The honest answer is that the concepts covered in guru books on Home Equity Management can work to help many clients build wealth. While the books in the marketplace lack full disclosure and use fuzzy math (which will be detailed in this book), the concepts when used properly for the "right" client do work and can work very well.

This book will go into chapter and verse (literally) on many Home Equity Management concepts, and you will not have to wonder if the concepts are right for you; you will know because the material will give you the details to feel confident when making the decision to move forward or not with the concepts discussed.

A CONFESSION BY THIS AUTHOR

As you may have read in the About the Author section to this book, I myself have three training courses for advisors that are administered through The Wealth Preservation Institute ("WPI").

The WPI has the following professional designations: Certified Wealth Preservation Planner (CWPP™), Certified Asset Protection Planner (CAPP™), and Master Mortgage Broker (MMB™). You can read about all three designations at www.thewpi.org.

The CWPP™, CAPP™, and MMB™ are what I consider the only "advanced" certification courses in the "industry." The foundation of each certification is asset protection. It is my opinion that you cannot have a proper financial or estate plan without incorporating asset protection. You cannot have a proper Home Equity Management plan without incorporating asset protection.

I have multiple confessions to make, which explain why I decided to write this book. The following are my reasons for writing this book. They are reasons, but also confessions to readers, so you will know my self-interested reasons for putting this book together.

1) I got sick and tired of hearing advisors (life insurance, financial planners, CPAs/EAs/accountants) touting the virtues of books in the marketplace that sell the concepts of Home Equity Management. This is by far the number-one reason I decided to write this book.

I have over 100,000 advisors who receive my e-newsletters every week. I travel around the country giving seminars to advisors as well. Therefore, I have many discussions with advisors on a variety of topics, including Home Equity Management.

I said to myself, if I heard another advisor tell me how wonderful these other books are and how they can be used to sell clients and make money based on the concepts in these books, I would write my own unique "full-disclosure," for-public book on the topic. After saying that to myself, it took less than a few days to receive my next call from an advisor touting one of the sales books covering Home Equity Management.

With the recent revelation that at least one author is selling leads, I know I made the right decision to put forth a full-disclosure book for the public and professionals in the industry to read.

2) Speaking honestly, I knew that writing such a book and telling the truth about the hypocrisy in the industry would create significant press, specifically in the advisor marketplace. Since my core business is to have advisors learn about and take my courses, the press would do nothing but help make advisors aware of my educational institute and the CWPP™, CAPP™, and MMB™ certification courses.

3) I also knew that this book would sell a number of copies to the general public, and, as such, would allow me to make readers aware of the concept of asset protection. Most people with wealth are not asset protected; and any way I can make them aware of the concept and tell them that there are simple ways to protect their assets, I like to take the opportunity.

Additionally, this book will allow me to tell readers about the new Asset Protection Society (dedicated to protecting the public from asset protection scammers) and advocate that readers check out the Society at www.assetprotectionsociety.org.

4) Money? I'm sure I'll make some money from the actual book sales. I can tell you that, after paying for and selling a few thousand of my other book, The Doctor's Wealth Preservation Guide, self-published authors do not make a living from selling books. Again, the money I'll make on this book will be when advisors read it, learn about my certification courses, and eventually take one (or buy other services I offer advisors through The WPI).

SUMMARY

It is my hope after you read this chapter that you can't wait to get started on the substantive parts of this book. I hope you take from this chapter that I will do my best to give you real math and real-world examples and will try to stay away from "selling" you on the concepts in the book.

If you feel the contrary, please e-mail me with your thoughts, as I take these issues very seriously. My vision with this book is to have it be seen as an authoritative book on the pros and cons of Home Equity Harvesting, along with a separate section to the book for those who want to pay off the debt on their home years early using the <u>Home Equity Acceleration Plan</u> (H.E.A.P.™).

Chapter 2
The Laws That Govern Equity Harvesting

You may find it odd that in the second chapter of this book I am going to explain to you the laws that govern <u>Equity Harvesting</u>. Odd because I have not explained fully what Equity Harvesting is and generally speaking most people find a discussion of the law to be rather boring.

As you read in the previous chapter, this book is not a "sales" book; it is an educational book.

I, the <u>Wealth Preservation Institute</u>, the <u>Asset Protection Society</u>, and those advisors affiliated with all three are not about "hiding the ball" so sales can be made to an under- or uninformed consumer.

As you will glean (if you have not already) from reading this book, I have significant disdain for "marketers" who write books, put on seminars, and sell to consumers concepts they know or should know are not technically sound and are intentionally or unintentionally misleading.

The biggest flaw with those who market the Equity Harvesting concept that you'll read about in this book revolves around the interest deduction on <u>Home Equity Debt</u> (which includes home equity loans, lines of credit, AND refinances of home mortgages).

Let me ask you a few questions, and let's see what your answers are.

1) If you remove $25,000 of equity from your home through a refinance or home equity loan, is the interest on the new debt always deductible as an interest expense on your personal tax return?

<u>Answer</u>: False.

2) If you remove $125,000 of equity from your home through a refinance or home equity loan, is the interest on the new debt always deductible as an interest expense on your personal tax return?

<u>Answer</u>: False

My guess is that 99% of the non-CPA/EA/accountant readers answered yes to at least one of the above questions. If you answered yes, I wouldn't blame you. The general public has been conditioned to believe that all interest on a personal residence is 100% tax deductible as an itemized expense on a personal tax return.

FYI, most CPAs/EA/accountants do not know the information in this chapter as it pertains to Code Section 264(a) (discussed in detail in the coming pages).

When you answered yes to one of the earlier questions, you probably thought of the typical way people use money when removing equity from a home—that way being to use the money to improve the home by refinishing a basement, kitchen or bathroom, or adding on a room to the house.

What if the question was: Can you remove equity from your home through a refinance or home equity loan and invest it in the stock market? Or invest in real estate? Or reposition the money into cash value life insurance? If you repositioned the borrowed funds in any of these places, would that affect your ability to write off the interest?

The answer is **yes,** and that is the reason this chapter is needed as a vital part of this book.

STRAIGHT FROM THE IRS

This material is going to do something you'll never see in public books covering Equity Harvesting or sale's programs. Much of the following material is straight from the IRS web-site which summarizes <u>IRC Title 26 Section 163</u>.

THE HOME MORTGAGE INTEREST DEDUCTION

As you'll learn in great detail, the concept of Equity Harvesting revolves around removing equity from a piece of property (for this book I will assume the property is a personal residence) and repositioning the borrowed funds into a tax-free retirement vehicle (cash value life insurance).

As you can imagine and as will be discussed in great detail later, the concept becomes much more powerful if you can write off the interest on the borrowed funds (meaning that the cost of borrowing funds is less than the actual interest expense due to the income-tax write off).

The ability to write off the interest on a loan taken against a personal residence will depend on whether the debt is considered **Home Acquisition Debt** or **Home Equity Debt**. The IRS defines both as follows:

HOME ACQUISITOIN DEBT (HAD)

Home Acquisition Debt is a mortgage taken out after October 13, 1987, to buy, build, or substantially improve a qualified home (a main or second home). The debt must be secured by that home.

If the amount of the mortgage is more than the cost of the home plus the cost of any substantial improvements, only the debt that is not more than the cost of the home plus improvements qualifies as Home Acquisition Debt. The additional debt may qualify as Home Equity Debt (discussed later).

Home Acquisition Debt limit. The total amount you can treat as Home Acquisition Debt at any time on your main home and second home cannot be more than **$1 million** ($500,000 if married filing separately). This limit is reduced (but not below zero) by the amount of your grandfathered debt (discussed later).

Refinanced Home Acquisition Debt. Any secured debt used to refinance Home Acquisition Debt is treated as Home Acquisition Debt. However, the new debt will qualify as Home Acquisition Debt only up to the amount of the balance of the **old mortgage** principal just before the refinancing. Any additional debt is not Home Acquisition Debt but may qualify as Home Equity Debt (discussed later).

Mortgage that qualifies later. A mortgage that does not qualify as Home Acquisition Debt because it does not meet all the requirements may qualify later. For example, a debt that is used to buy a home may not qualify as Home Acquisition Debt because it is not secured by the home. However, if the debt is later secured by the home, it may qualify as Home Acquisition Debt after that time. Similarly, a debt that is used to buy property may not qualify because the property is not a qualified home. However, if the property later becomes a qualified home, the debt may qualify after that time.

Mortgage treated as used to buy, build, or improve home. A mortgage secured by a qualified home may be treated as Home Acquisition Debt even if the proceeds are not actually used to buy, build, or substantially improve the home. This applies in the following situations.

1. The home is purchased within 90 days before or after the date the mortgage is taken out. The Home Acquisition Debt is limited to the home's cost plus the cost of any substantial improvements within the limit described below in (2) or (3). (See Example 1.)

2. A home is built or improved, and the mortgage is taken out before the work is completed. The Home Acquisition Debt is limited to the amount of the expenses incurred within 24 months before the date of the mortgage.

3. A home is built or improved, and the mortgage is taken out within 90 days after the work is completed. The Home Acquisition Debt is limited to the amount of the expenses incurred within the period beginning 24 months before the work is completed and ending on the date of the mortgage. *(See Example 2.)*

Example 1

You bought your main home on June 3 for $175,000. You paid for the home with cash you got from the sale of your old home. On July 15, you took out a mortgage of $150,000 secured by your main home. You used the $150,000 to invest in stocks. You can treat the mortgage as taken out to buy your home because you bought the home within 90 days before you took out the mortgage. **The entire mortgage qualifies as Home Acquisition Debt because it was not more than the home's cost.**

Example 2

On January 31, John began building a home on the lot that he owned. He used $45,000 of his personal funds to build the home. The home was completed on October 31. On November 21, John took out a $36,000 mortgage that was secured by the home. The mortgage can be treated as used to build the home because it was taken out within 90 days after the home was completed. The entire mortgage qualifies as Home Acquisition Debt because it was not more than the expenses incurred within the period beginning 24 months before the home was completed. This is illustrated by Figure C.

Figure C.

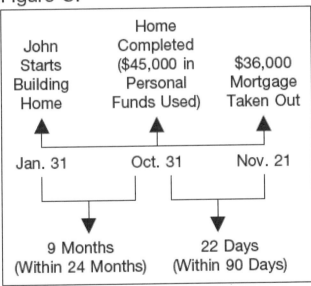

Date of the mortgage. The date you take out your mortgage is the day the loan proceeds are disbursed. This is generally the closing date. You can treat the day you apply in writing for a mortgage as the date you take it out. However, this applies only if you receive the loan proceeds within a reasonable time (such as within 30 days) after your application is approved. If a timely application you make is rejected, a reasonable additional time will be allowed to make a new application.

Cost of home or improvements. To determine your cost, include amounts paid to acquire any interest in a qualified home or to substantially improve the home.

The cost of building or substantially improving a qualified home includes the costs to acquire real property and building materials, fees for architects and design plans, and required building permits.

Substantial improvement. An improvement is substantial if it:

- Adds to the value of your home,

- Prolongs your home's useful life, or

- Adapts your home to new uses.

Repairs that maintain your home in good condition, such as repainting your home, are not substantial improvements. However, if you paint your home as part of a renovation that substantially improves your qualified home, you can include the painting costs in the cost of the improvements.

HOME EQUITY DEBT (HED)

If you take out a loan for reasons **other than to buy, build, or substantially improve a home**, it may qualify as Home Equity Debt. In addition, debt incurred to buy, build, or substantially improve a home, to the extent it is **more than** the Home Acquisition Debt limit (discussed earlier), may qualify as Home Equity Debt.

Home Equity Debt is a mortgage taken out after October 13, 1987, that:

- Does not qualify as Home Acquisition Debt or as grandfathered debt, and

- Is secured by your qualified home.

Example:

You bought your home for cash 10 years ago. You did not have a mortgage on your home until last year when you took out a $20,000 loan secured by your home to pay for your daughter's college tuition and your father's medical bills. This loan is Home Equity Debt.

Home Equity Debt limit.   There is a limit on the amount of debt that can be treated as Home Equity Debt. The total Home Equity Debt on your main home and second home is limited to the smaller of:

- **$100,000** ($50,000 if married filing separately), or

- The total of each home's fair market value (FMV) reduced (but not below zero) by the amount of its Home Acquisition Debt and grandfathered debt. Determine the FMV and the outstanding home acquisition and grandfathered debt for each home on the date that the last debt was secured by the home.

Example:

You own one home that you bought in 1999. Its FMV now is $110,000, and the current balance on your original mortgage (Home Acquisition Debt) is $95,000. Bank M offers you a home mortgage loan of 125% of the FMV of the home less any outstanding mortgages or other liens. To consolidate some of your other debts, you take out a $42,500 home mortgage loan [(125% × $110,000) = $95,000] with Bank M.

Your Home Equity Debt is limited to $15,000. This is the smaller of:

- $100,000, the maximum limit, or

- $15,000—the amount that the FMV of $110,000 exceeds the amount of Home Acquisition Debt of $95,000.

Debt higher than limit.   Interest on amounts over the Home Equity Debt limit (such as the interest on $27,500 [$42,500 - $15,000] in the preceding example) generally is treated as personal interest and is **not deductible**. But if the proceeds of the loan were used for investment, business, or other deductible

31

purposes, the interest may be deductible. The limit on writing off interest if it qualifies as an investment is the income generated by the investment (which with a life insurance policy is typically ZERO).

Part of home not a qualified home. To figure the limit on Home Equity Debt, you must divide the FMV of your home between the part that is a qualified home and any part that is not a qualified home.

Fair market value (FMV). This is the price at which a home would change hands between a seller and a buyer, neither having to sell or buy, and both having reasonable knowledge of all relevant facts. Sales of similar homes in your area, on about the same date your last debt was secured by the home, may be helpful in figuring the FMV.

GRANDFATHERED DEBT

If you took out a mortgage on your home before October 14, 1987, or you refinanced such a mortgage, it may qualify as grandfathered debt. To qualify, it must have been secured by your qualified home on October 13, 1987, and at all times after that date. How you used the proceeds does not matter.

Grandfathered debt is not limited. All of the interest paid on grandfathered debt is fully deductible home mortgage interest. However, the amount of your grandfathered debt reduces the $1 million limit for Home Acquisition Debt and the limit based on your home's fair market value for Home Equity Debt.

There is more to learn about grandfathered debt that has been omitted from this book due to space issues.

If you have grandfathered debt, please contact The WPI (info@thewpi.org) for further information you can read to make sure you are compliant when using the planning techniques in this book.

WHAT YOU NEED TO KNOW FROM THE PREVIOUS INFOMATION

1) If a married couple buys a new home, they can write off the interest on the mortgage taken out to purchase that home up to a $1,000,000 Home Acquisition Debt (HAD) limit (with certain phase out limits that will apply to high income readers).

Why is this important?

a) If you are married and buy a home where the loan is more than $1,000,000, you need to know that you will not be able to write off the interest on debt which exceeds $1,000,000 (most clients think that ALL home acquisition debt is deductible).

b) What's equally important to understand is that, if you sell a home that has significant equity and buy a new home where the new home has sizable debt, all of the interest is deductible up to $1,000,000 of debt.

Example:

Assume a married couple has lived in a home for 10 years. The couple bought the home for $400,000, paid off the debt on the home over the last 10 years, and is going to sell the house for $1,000,000 (after realtor fees).

IF the couple then buys a new house worth $1.25 million and takes out a home loan for $1,000,000, all of the interest on the home is deductible.

Why is this important? As you will read in detail in the following material, if you want to implement an Equity Harvesting strategy using the **current** $1,000,000+ house with no debt, the interest deduction would be limited to $100,000 of Home Equity Debt (IF the debt can be structured properly). With this example, the couple could sell the home, invest the $1,000,000 net proceeds anywhere (including cash value life insurance), and buy a new home with $1,000,000 of debt and write off all the interest on the new home loan.

c) Following up on the previous example, it is vitally important to understand that on Home Equity Debt you can only write off debt up to $100,000. Also, the Home Equity Debt cannot be deducted to the extent it exceeds the fair market value (FMV) of the home.

Example:

Assume Mr. Smith (age 45) has a home that was purchased 10 years ago for $300,000. Today the home is worth $700,000, and the client has $200,000 of debt on the home. Assume Mr. Smith ran into a stock jockey (a stock broker who is looking to capture money under management) who understands the concept of harvesting a home's equity to build wealth. Assume the advisor told Mr. Smith to refinance his home and remove $300,000 of equity for repositioning into stocks and mutual funds to grow his wealth (ignore the fact that it is a potential Securities violation for the advisor to make this recommendation).

It is vitally important for the advisor to disclose to Mr. Smith that he will only be allowed to write off debt on $300,000 worth of the $500,000 debt because of the $100,000 limit on the deduction for Home Equity Debt.

DISSALOWANCE OF THE HOME MORTGAE INTEREST DEDUCITON

It's funny how nearly everyone thinks that, if you take out Home Equity Debt, the interest on that debt is always deductible. As you've already read, that is not the case. Interest on Home Equity Debt (See IRC Title 26, Section 163) is limited to $100,000 of new equity debt up to the FMV of the home.

While the issue rarely comes up by sales people pitching Equity Harvesting, the next issue that needs to be dealt with is: Can a normally valid deduction on Home Equity Debt be "disallowed" for any reason?

Again, nearly everyone who is asked this question will say that there are no restrictions on what you can do with the money obtained through removing equity from a home. For purposes of this material, the really big question is:

Does the disallowance of the interest deduction apply when you reposition equity into a **cash value life insurance policy** (classic Equity Harvesting)? You will learn later why cash value life is the preferred tool used to build wealth when using Equity Harvesting.

Most readers will be surprised to learn that, if you reposition equity from a home through Home Equity Debt (vs. Home Acquisition Debt) and move that money directly into a cash value life insurance policy where you contemplate borrowing from the policy ("tax-free retirement income"), the interest on the Home Equity Debt is **NOT deductible**.

Why is this important? Because it changes the financial viability of Equity Harvesting (which when sold the vast majority of time is sold on the concept of writing off the debt on Home Equity Debt).

Few advisors (CPAs/EAs/accountants) and virtually no non-advisors are familiar with the following Code Section. This Code Section is not discussed by sales people in the Equity Harvesting world because it is harmful to the sale of the concept.

Again, I know reading IRS Code Sections is not terribly interesting; however, it is vital to the understanding of proper Home Equity Management. Also, if you are a non-advisor, you can have a little fun asking your local CPA/EA/account if they are familiar with this code section (which most won't be).

Title 26 Section 264 deals with the disallowance of an interest deduction when the borrowed funds are used to fund insurance contracts.

Title 26 – Internal Revenue Code
 Subtitle A **- Income Taxes**
 Chapter 1 – Normal Taxes and Surtaxes
 Subchapter B - Computation of Taxable Income
 PART IX - ITEMS NOT DEDUCTIBLE

Section 264. Certain amounts paid in connection with insurance contracts

(a) General rule

No deduction shall be allowed for—

(1) Premiums on any life insurance policy, or endowment or annuity contract, if the taxpayer is directly or indirectly a beneficiary under the policy or contract.

(2) Any amount paid or accrued on indebtedness incurred or continued to purchase or carry a **single premium life insurance**, endowment, or annuity contract.

(3) Except as provided in subsection (d), any amount paid or accrued on indebtedness incurred or continued to purchase or carry a life insurance, endowment, or annuity contract (other than a single premium contract or a contract treated as a single premium contract) **pursuant to a plan of purchase which contemplates the systematic direct or indirect borrowing of part or all of the increases in the cash value of such contract** (either from the insurer or otherwise).

(4) Except as provided in subsection (e), any interest paid or accrued on any indebtedness with respect to 1 or more life insurance policies owned by the taxpayer covering the life of any individual, or any endowment or annuity contracts owned by the taxpayer covering any individual.

Paragraph (2) shall apply in respect of annuity contracts only as to contracts purchased after March 1, 1954. Paragraph (3) shall apply only in respect of contracts purchased after August 6, 1963. Paragraph (4) shall apply with respect to contracts purchased after June 20, 1986.

(b) Exceptions to subsection (a)(1)

Subsection (a)(1) shall not apply to—

(1) any annuity contract described in section 72 (s)(5), and

(2) any annuity contract to which section 72 (u) applies.

(c) Contracts treated as single premium contracts

For purposes of subsection (a)(2), a contract shall be treated as a single premium contract—

(1) if substantially all the premiums on the contract are paid within a period of 4 years from the date on which the contract is purchased, or

(2) if an amount is deposited after March 1, 1954, with the insurer for payment of a substantial number of future premiums on the contract.

(d) Exceptions

Subsection (a)(3) shall not apply to any amount paid or accrued by a person during a taxable year on indebtedness incurred or continued as part of a plan referred to in subsection (a)(3)—

(1) if no part of 4 of the annual premiums due during the 7-year period (beginning with the date the first premium on the contract to which such plan relates was paid) is paid under such plan by means of indebtedness,

(2) if the total of the amounts paid or accrued by such person during such taxable year for which (without regard to this paragraph) no deduction would be allowable by reason of subsection (a)(3) does not exceed $100.

(3) if such amount was paid or accrued on indebtedness incurred because of an unforeseen substantial loss of income or unforeseen substantial increase in his financial obligations, or

(4) if such indebtedness was incurred in connection with his trade or business.

For purposes of applying paragraph (1), if there is a substantial increase in the premiums on a contract, a new 7-year period described in such paragraph with respect to such contract shall commence on the date of first such increased premium is paid.

INTERPRETING THE ABOVE CODE SECTION

The previous Code Section needs a little interpretation. On its face, 264(a)**2** simply states that, if you borrow money (Home Equity Debt) and reposition the borrowed funds into a single premium life or annuity contract, the interest is **NOT deductible**.

Side Note:

I know I'm putting the cart before the horse a bit, but what you need to know now as you are reading through to this part of the book, is that Equity Harvesting revolves around funding cash value life insurance as a tax-favorable/wealth-building tool.

I wanted to lead with this chapter before I moved onto a full explanation of Equity Harvesting to drive home the point to readers that this book is NOT about selling you a concept; it's about educating you on the proper way to build wealth using Home Equity Management. By putting a somewhat negative aspect to Equity Harvesting (that most of the advisors who sell the concept ignore) in the early part of the book, it should drive home that point.

Many advisors in the Equity Harvesting marketplace who have read 264(a)**2** say the way around this issue is to place the borrowed funds into a CD or money-market account where the funds would then be used over a five-seven year period to pay life insurance premiums. While not discussed in this chapter (see the chapter on Life Insurance), when funding a cash value life insurance policy for tax-favorable retirement income, the premiums are typically paid into the policy over a five-seven year period to keep the costs of the policy down and to maximize cash values).

If Code Section 264(a)**3** did not exist, using the tactic discussed in the previous paragraph would be sufficient to allow you to fund cash value life insurance with borrowed funds and take the interest deduction on your personal tax returns.

Unfortunately, 264(a)**3** makes the issue of writing off interest on a loan when the proceeds are used to fund life insurance very difficult.

264(a)3 states that if "…..any amount paid or accrued on indebtedness incurred or continued to purchase or carry a life insurance, endowment, or annuity contract (other than a single premium contract or a contract treated as a single premium contract) **pursuant to a plan of purchase which contemplates**

the systematic direct or indirect borrowing of part or all of the increases in the cash value of such contract (either from the insurer or otherwise).

While not described in great detail yet in this book, the concept of Equity Harvesting has as its foundation the ability of a reader to borrow money and use that money to fund cash value life insurance so the money in the policy can grow tax free and be removed tax free in retirement.

How is the money removed from a life insurance policy in retirement? Through **systematic borrowing** from the life insurance policy. It's like the IRS had an Equity Harvesting sales person on staff when they drafted Section 264(a)3.

Is there any way you can write off the interest on a loan when the money is used to fund life insurance as an investment/retirement vehicle? The answer is no with a big caveat—that caveat being that there are three ways to borrow money where life insurance can be funded and where the interest on the borrowed money should still be deductible.

The three potentially viable ways to deal with this Code Section are:

1) You can pay four-out-of-seven life insurance premiums with non-borrowed funds.

2) You can use "other" funds to purchase the life insurance and use the borrowed funds for other needs (or as part of the premium in accordance with 264(a)).

3) You can reposition the borrowed funds into an LLC which can then purchase as one of its investment a life insurance policy (which with fairly simple accounting procedures which still allows you to affectively have access to the cash values income-tax free).

1) You can pay four-out-of-seven life insurance premiums with non-borrowed funds.

This is directly from the code:

(d) Exceptions

Subsection (a)(3) shall not apply to any amount paid or accrued by a person during a taxable year on indebtedness incurred or continued as part of a plan referred to in subsection (a)(3)—

(1) if no part of 4 of the annual premiums due during the 7-year period (beginning with the date the first premium on the contract to which such plan relates was paid) is paid under such plan by means of indebtedness,

The four-out-of-seven rule has been around seemingly forever. You don't hear it talked about much by those who sell the Equity Harvesting concept due to the fact that most people do not want to follow this rule or can't follow this rule.

Most people don't want to follow it because they see Equity Harvesting as a new way to build wealth without taking away from their other wealth-building tools.

Many people can't comply with this exception because they simply do not have the funds. Many people who implement the Equity Harvesting concept use the borrowed funds as their sole source of funds available to build wealth and, therefore, couldn't comply with this rule if they wanted to.

Having said that, most people don't want to or can't use this exception; it is truly the only exception that I know for a fact the IRS will respect.

As you will learn in the chapter where I discuss how to use cash value life insurance as a tool to build wealth, reposition other non-borrowed funds into such a vehicle can make much more sense than you would imagine. As such, when people are educated on the benefits of cash value life (at least those with other funds), many will opt to comply with the four-out-of-seven rule.

2) Use other money to purchase the cash value life insurance

It sounds simple enough and will be easy to understand through an example.

Example:

Mr. Smith, age 45, has $250,000 in a brokerage account he has been building for years. He is like most Americans in that his average rate of return on his portfolio is less than 3% (for information as to why Americans averaged less than 3% from 1984-2002 (one of the biggest "bull" runs our stock market has ever seen) when the S&P 500 averaged over 12%, see Chapter 3 on Traditional Wealth Building for the number which supports the statements in this paragraph).

Mr. Smith likes the concept of EH and wants to borrow $100,000 of Home Equity Debt out of his home to reposition for wealth building purposes. He understands Section 264(a) and so, before implementing an EH strategy, he takes $100,000 from his brokerage account (after any capital gains taxes are due) and funds a Single Premium Immediate Annuity (SPIA). This SPIA's sole purpose is to pay five annual premiums into an indexed equity life policy in the amount of $20,000 (plus any investment returns minus income taxes on the income from the SPIA).

After the SPIA has been funded, Mr. Smith can then borrow money from his home through Home Equity Debt and invest that money in any way he sees fit. Mr. Smith might use the money to buy real estate or start a new business or whatever. What Mr. Smith will not do with the money is fund a life insurance policy.

As stated, this is a simple way to posture yourself to have a good chance of writing off the interest on Home Equity Debt deductible under Section 264(a).

What's the problem with this solution? Many readers who will want to use Equity Harvesting to build maximum wealth in a tax-favorable manner will not have outside funds available to fund a SPIA/cash building life insurance policy without the borrowed funds.

Like many things in life, the Equity Harvesting concept is another one of those the rich-get-richer topics. That's just life. Those with money typically have more options, and the Equity Harvesting concept is no exception.

3) The use of an LLC for investment purposes

The use of an LLC is not the easiest to explain and will not be fully explained in this book. However, you will learn the basic structure so you can determine if it is one you would like to look into further. If you would like to look into it further, I recommend you contact an advisor who has the **CWPP™** (Certified Wealth Preservation Planner) or **CAPP™** (Certified Asset Protection Planner) designations issued by the <u>Wealth Preservation Institute</u> (<u>www.thewpi.org</u>). Such advisors have been schooled in the multiple uses of the LLC structure described below and should be able to help you with it.

When implementing the EH structure, you will first create a multi-member Limited Liability Company (LLC). Other members might include a spouse, majority age children, or a trust for the benefit of the children and/or spouse.

The other members will contribute 10% of the money that will ultimately be contributed to the LLC, and you will contribute 90%.

In the $100,000 Equity Harvesting example from earlier, Mr. Smith will fund the LLC with the borrowed funds as a contribution. The other member (let's use a trust for the children's benefit as the other member) will contribute $11,000 to the LLC as a contribution.

Mr. Smith will be the managing member of the LLC and have a 90% interest in the LLC, and the trust will be the non-managing member and will have a 10% interest in the LLC.

As the managing member of the LLC, Mr. Smith makes the decisions about where the money in the LLC is invested. Mr. Smith could make the decision that some or all of the money in the LLC could be used to fund a cash building life insurance policy.

Let's assume Mr. Smith did, in fact, buy a cash value life insurance in the LLC (which could be on his life or on one of the beneficiaries of the trust). What happens?

The life insurance policy is funded over five years to maximize cash values and minimize insurance costs.

Mr. Smith as the managing member can have the LLC take tax-free loans from the life insurance policy owned by the LLC at any time.

Mr. Smith could wait until age 66-90 to have the LLC borrow money from the LLC.

Then through a special allocation, the LLC can transfer that money to Mr. Smith income-tax free (which Mr. Smith can use as tax-free retirement income).

Again, this material does not go into detail on the LLC structure which allows for the special allocation to come out to Mr. Smith tax free. You can look for a local attorney who can help you with this structure or find a CWPP™ or CAPP™ advisor who can help you.

The LLC structure is an "advanced" structure that few in the country are familiar with and, as stated, this material is not meant to make you an expert in the topic.

What you need to know about the LLC structure is that it is a viable option when trying to deal with the 264(a) problem of not being able to write off the interest on HED. Because the borrowed funds go into a multi-member LLC where the funds and life insurance can be used for many different purposes (estate planning, other business ventures), the interest on the Home Equity Debt should be deductible.

Summary on options 1), 2), and 3) for how to write off the debt on HED when using the Equity Harvesting concept.

Option 1) is the option that is in the code, and those who understand this topic know it will work when attempting to write off the interest.

Option 2) is simple, but many readers will not have significant other monies which can be used to fund the life insurance policy.

Option 3) while it sounds complicated is really not, but there is an up-front cost to create the LLC and a small fee to maintain it every year.

The caveat with 2) and 3) is that the options are what I and the experts I talk to think will work to allow you to write off the interest.

Right now the interest deduction has not had much litigating in the Home Equity Management arena. Anyone who can read and speak English can understand that 264(a)3 prevents the deduction if the borrowed funds are repositioned into cash value life insurance with the contemplation of borrowing from the policy.

Having said that, 95% of the advisors telling clients to build wealth using Equity Harvesting do not know 264(a)3 exists and so they are telling clients incorrectly to write off the interest (or they simply "don't give advice" on the issue at all).

Sadly, a small percentage of the advisors who do know 264(a)3 exists intentionally ignore it because to disclose it is harmful to their selling life insurance and/or mortgages.

The driving force behind my writing this book is that small percentage of advisors in the marketplace who are intentionally giving bad advice so they can profit by their client and their client's advisors' ignorance.

Please take this chapter for what it's worth. I know it's a bit dry, but it is something you have to understand before implementing an Equity Harvesting strategy to build wealth for retirement.

You'll be happy to know that, even if you do not write off the interest on Home Equity Debt when building wealth tax favorably through Equity Harvesting, the concept still works very well and much better than what most of you are doing right now to build your wealth.

ALTERNATIVE MINIMUM TAX (AMT)

The AMT is a nasty little tax that many readers will not be familiar with. The reason many readers have not felt the bite of the AMT is because Congress seems intent on passing band-aid bills to temporarily exempt most tax payers from paying the tax. The AMT is a tax law that has been on the books for many years and, when passed, did not include an adjustment for inflation.

What that means is, if Congress does continue to keep passing band-aid bills temporarily raising the income level of a tax payer to fall under the AMT, literally 15 million or more Americans could be affected by the tax.

Deciding how to deal with the AMT in this book was a tough chore since I don't know if Congress will finally fix the AMT problem or keep passing band-aid bills. If Congress keeps passing band-aid bills on an annual basis, it would be impossible to take into account those changes in this book.

Therefore, I'll simply tell you how the AMT can affect you in terms of Home Equity Management and what the tax rate is.

The AMT <u>does not</u> affect Home Acquisition Debt. It only affects clients who have Home Equity Debt.

The AMT is a separate/additional tax you pay in addition to normal federal and state income taxes.

Technically speaking, the AMT does not affect your ability to deduct Home Equity Debt. However, if you have Home Equity Debt and fall under the AMT, you may be required to pay an additional AMT at the 26-28% tax rate.

The tax you pay is based on your interest deduction for Home Equity Debt. If you had a $5,000 annual interest expense for Home Equity Debt used in conjunction with Equity Harvesting, your AMT would be 26-28% of that $5,000.

The AMT was designed to tax the ultra-wealthy; and so long as Congress keeps passing band-aid bills, many readers will not have a problem with this tax.

Finally, as you'll find out when reading the chapter on Equity Harvesting, the concept works well to grow your wealth in a tax-favorable manner whether you write off the interest on Home Equity Debt or not.

Chapter 3
Traditional Wealth Building

I'd like to give a special thanks to Jeff Cohen of Jeffrey M. Cohen & Associates. Jeff helped write the material in this chapter under the title, INVESTMENT RETURNS FROM 2000-2002. I appreciate his help and contribution to the book.

Before moving into the material on Home Equity Management as a way to build wealth for you and your family, I wanted to discuss how Americans typically build wealth.

The following are the typical ways Americans will build wealth for retirement:

1) **Invest** extra money after taking it home from work (and paying income taxes) **in the stock market** (stocks and mutual funds typically).

2) **Invest** money tax-deferred into an employer's **401(k) plan** at work or in an individual **IRA**.

If you are a business owner, you have the additional option of contributing a decent amount of money annually for yourself into a profit sharing plan or defined benefit plan (which also requires contributions for employees if any).

3) **Invest in real estate** (rental properties).

4) **Do nothing**. Most Americans "do nothing" (or very little) for a variety of reasons. Some people don't have extra money to invest and need every dollar just to meet their monthly expenses. Many Americans have extra dollars to invest but, because many choose to spend that money on "wants" (vs. needs), they either build very little wealth or none at all.

Many of you may have read the book, Millionaire Next Door. It's an interesting read and will really make you think. The book tells readers that many people in this country became millionaires by not spending their money on items that they "want" and instead buying items that they "need" while investing the remainder of their money wisely.

For the most part, we Americans are an instant gratification society. We see something on TV, and we want it. If we have extra dollars to invest (that would help us retire with security and wealth), many times we instead spend that money on a new car (we love to have the newest, nicest car) or on a new flat-screen HD TV, computer, furniture, and on and on and on.

Americans are a "keep up with the Joneses" society. If our neighbors just bought something shiny and new, we need something shiny and new (and bigger and better than our neighbors if possible).

The <u>Millionaire Next Door</u> tells stories about how many millionaires never purchased a new car (always bought a used one). The book tells how many millionaires resoled their shoes instead of throwing them out and buying new ones.

I am not here to judge readers on the American dream of living life to the fullest and buying nice things, which does make many people happy. Instead, I wrote this book to help readers understand Home Equity Management so that they can understand how to build wealth using the equity in the home in a manner that is not painful or life altering when it comes to cutting back on items that the readers may want to purchase.

For those of you who currently invest your money in the stock market (or for those of you who are thinking about it), this chapter will truly blow your mind when it illustrates how poorly the American investor does when investing his/her money.

In the following pages, I will point out the problems with investing your money the "American way," which is investing it in equity markets (stocks and mutual funds). In Chapter 6, I will discuss funding qualified retirement plans and post-tax brokerage accounts vs. funding cash value life insurance as a safer and more tax-favorable tools when using Home Equity Management. I believe you will find that discussion very interesting as well.

1) INVESTING "AFTER-TAX" MONEY IN THE STOCK MARKET (stocks and mutual funds typically)

When I say "after-tax," I am talking about money you take home from work, pay income taxes on, and have what's left to invest.

Before getting into the details of this section of the material, we need to have a little discussion about how taxes affect money invested outside of a qualified plan or IRA (typically in the stock market). Many readers will know the following taxes and how they affect annual investment rates of return, but, even so, putting them down on paper will help crystallize how damaging these taxes can be when trying to grow wealth for retirement purposes. The following discussion will be limited to stocks and mutual funds.

SHORT-TERM CAPITAL GAINS TAXES

If you invest your money into stocks and mutual funds and you sell either within 12 months of their purchase, there is a short-term capital gains tax due IF you, in fact, had a gain when selling the assets. The tax you owe on the gain is at your **ordinary income tax bracket**. See the following income tax brackets to determine how much you would pay when incurring short-term capital gains taxes on the sale of your investments.

Married Filing Jointly or Qualifying Widow(er)

If taxable income is over-	But not over-	The tax is:
$0	$15,650	10% of the amount over **$0**
$15,650	$63,700	**15%** for amounts over $15,650
$63,700	$128,500	**25%** for amounts over $63,700
$128,500	$195,850	**28%** for amounts over $128,500
$195,850	$349,700	**33%** for amounts over $195,850
$349,700	no limit	**35%** for amounts over $349,700

Remember that we have a progressive income tax system here in the United States. You will pay a tax of $1,565 on your first $15,650 of income. If you earn $63,700, you will pay taxes at the 15% rate on income between $15,650 and $63,700 which would equal $7,207.50. Therefore, the total income taxes due on your first $63,700 of income would be $1,565 + $7,207.50 = $8,772.50.

Therefore, if you "actively" traded stocks, let's say with your online E-Trade account, or you have a money manager who "actively" traded your money in an account for you (actively meaning buying and selling stocks within 12 months), you would pay ordinary income taxes on the gains.

The above chart does NOT take into account state income taxes which range from zero to nearly 10% in California.

For example, if you had $10,000 actively traded where you sold the stock with gains this year of 12%, at the end of the year, you would calculate the capital gains taxes due on that gain. If you were in the 35% income tax bracket, your gain would be reduced by 35% (meaning your effective return for the year is not 12% but instead is 7.8%).

If you also live in a state with a state income tax (using California as the worst example which has a 9.3% income tax as its highest bracket), your 12% return in the previous paragraph now returns you only 6.7%. You can do the math on the money you've invested based on your own tax bracket.

Side note:

You have to be very careful when reading books on Home Equity Management when they discuss income taxes. Many of the books in the marketplace use what I call "fuzzy math" so they can manipulate the outcome of examples to fit their needs (which is to make readers think using Home Equity Management is a "can't miss" proposition).

With Home Equity Management concepts, you will incur more debt. If that debt is properly structured, the debt can be deductible for you in your current income tax bracket. If you are in the 35% bracket, the income tax saving (at the federal level) would be 35 cents on the dollar. As you will read in upcoming chapters, when creating a new deductible home interest expense, the cost of the borrowed money is 35% less expensive for readers in the 35% income tax bracket (44.3% if you live in California).

Obviously, if you are in a lower tax bracket, the numbers need to be adjusted accordingly. This is one of the dilemmas with writing a book for the general public. Readers of all tax brackets will be reading the book. I try very hard in this book to give you real math vs. fuzzy math; and, as you will read, I do create a variety of examples so readers of varying amounts of wealth and income can determine if growing wealth through Home Equity Management makes financial sense.

LONG-TERM CAPITAL GAINS TAXES

If you buy and hold investments for **more** than 12 months before selling them, you will pay a long-term capital gains tax. Today that rate is 15% (although it is scheduled to increase in 2011 should Congress not act to extend the lower rate).

This tax is only incurred when you sell your investments. Therefore, if you do what many professional money managers will tell you to do (which is buy and hold quality stocks or mutual funds), you would not have an annual tax bill like you would with an actively traded account or with stock or mutual funds that create dividend income (discussed below).

STATE CAPITAL GAINS TAXES

As stated in the section about short-term capital gains rates (which are taxed at your ordinary income tax rates), many states have their own state capital gains tax due on investment gains. Again, those who live in California are punished the most. The California short- and long-term capital gains tax rate is 9.3%.

DIVDEND (NON-QUALIFIED) TAXES

If you own stock that pays a dividend (income to the stock holder), that dividend is taxed at your ordinary income tax bracket. If you earn $100,000 a year as your calculated income for tax purposes, you would be in the 25% income tax bracket. Therefore, any dividend received from stocks you own would also be taxed in the year received at the 25% rate.

If you are in the 35% income tax bracket, the dividend is reduced by a 35% income tax. If you live in the sunny state of California, you have the added pleasure of paying state taxes as well on your dividends at the 9.3% rate.

If a dividend is considered "qualified" the tax rate today is 15% not the ordinary income tax rate. Explaining qualified dividends is outside the scope of this book.

While all this talk about taxes might not excite you, or it may even depress you, it is vitally important for you to understand the impact taxes have on your investments that are not tax deferred.

Too often you will read in books on Home Equity Management where the examples in the books discuss a "side fund" that grows at 8% annually. The 8% annual rate of return is not defined as net or gross and somehow magically grows at 8% annually without capital gains taxes, dividend taxes, money management fees, or mutual fund expenses.

To my knowledge, there is no such magical investment that grows at 8% annually without having to deal with taxes and expenses. In order to earn a "net" 8% rate of return on an actively managed account (depending on the variables with annual taxes and other expenses), you would typically need to earn in excess of 11% pre-tax/pre-expense in the equity markets).

Needless to say, taxes and other expense will affect how your money grows; and as you will learn in other chapters of this book, there are tax-favorable tools you can use that allow your money to grow tax free and come out tax free in retirement.

REAL WORLD ILLUSTRATIONS/FORWARD TESTING

As stated in the preceding paragraphs, many books on Home Equity Management use "fuzzy" math when projecting how much money you can grow in a post-tax "side fund" or "safety fund."

I'd like to show you a side fund example from one of these books and then show you what happens in the real world. In this example, we are getting a little ahead of ourselves in that it is an Equity Harvesting example; but because you need to understand the math sooner rather than later when it comes to post-tax investing, now seems as good a time as any to show you the math.

Example: Assume you own a $400,000 home with $200,000 of debt on it and you decide to remove $100,000 of equity from the home to reposition elsewhere in an effort to help you build wealth for retirement (for now, trust me that Harvesting Equity from your home is a good financial decision).

The other books will show you how you will reposition the borrowed fund into a "side fund" where it is put under a magical spell and is allowed to grow without taxes and expenses at 8% annually (compound growth).

	Start of Year	8.00%	Year End
Year	Balance	Growth	Balance
1	$100,000	$8,000	$108,000
5	$136,049	$10,884	$146,933
10	$199,900	$15,992	$215,892
15	$293,719	$23,498	$317,217
20	$431,570	$34,526	$466,096
25	$634,118	$50,729	$684,848
30	$931,727	$74,538	$1,006,266

Doesn't the above chart look wonderful? By removing only $100,000 of wealth from your home and repositioning it into the magic side fund, you would have over $1,000,000 of wealth after 30 years. The sales pitch with Equity Harvesting is not important at this point in the book. What is important is that you understand when you read "sales" books or are pitched concepts directly by advisors sometimes the math is intentionally fuzzy to make the sale happen.

When you invest or reposition money in the stock market, there are expenses: dividend taxes (at your ordinary income tax rate due in the year earned), capital gains taxes, mutual fund expenses, and money management fees. Let's play with these fees a little and see how they affect how money grows in the "real world."

For the following example, let's take a very conservative 20% blended annual capital gains/dividend tax rate on the growth and a 1.2% mutual fund expense on only 50% of the same $100,000 invested in the previous example (FYI, the average annual mutual fund expense charge is in excess of 1.2%). How much less would you have inside your fund when adding in some real world expenses? The gross rate of return in the following example is 8% leaving 5.8% as the net return after taxes and expenses.

Year	Start of Year Balance	5.80% Growth	Year End Balance
1	$100,000	$5,800	$105,800
5	$125,298	$7,267	$132,565
10	$166,101	$9,634	$175,734
15	$220,191	$12,771	$232,962
20	$291,896	$16,930	$308,826
25	$386,951	$22,443	$409,394
30	$512,961	$29,752	$542,713

The above numbers should be startling. When using conservative assumptions, you would end up with $542,713 instead of the $1,006,266 earned with money growing in the magical 8% no tax/no fee side fund.

Now let's run the same example and add in an additional money management fee of .6% on the invested money (which is a very conservative fee and lower than the industry standard). The following net return you'll notice is now 5.2%.

Year	Start of Year Balance	5.20% Growth	Year End Balance
1	$100,000	$5,200	$105,200
5	$122,479	$6,369	$128,848
10	$157,813	$8,206	$166,019
15	$203,339	$10,574	$213,912
20	$261,999	$13,624	$275,623
25	$337,581	$17,554	$355,135
30	$434,967	$22,618	$457,585

Now the returns after 30 years have dipped down to $457,585 instead of the $1,006,262 from the magical side fund.

I make some bold assumptions in my book and in the certification courses that I put together for the Wealth Preservation Institute. I assume that, when readers of my material are confronted with simple math, they can make up their own minds about who is trying to give them unbiased and "correct" math and who is trying to sell them something using fuzzy math.

The previous examples of fuzzy math vs. real world math are extremely important as you **critically think** about how you want to build wealth and who you end up trusting to help you build your wealth. With the information provided to you in this book, you will be armed to sit down with a qualified advisor and map out your future and path to building tax favorable wealth for retirement.

One last comical note about the previous charts; you will learn in the following material that, when the American public invested in mutual funds from 1997-2001 (one of the biggest bull runs in the history of our country's stock market), the average rate of return over that period of time was less than 2.7% annually. While any savings is better than doing nothing, earning 2.7% on your money as it grows is not really the most effective way to build your wealth and retirement nest egg.

INVESTMENT RETURNS FROM 2000-2002

It's funny (sort of) when you think about it. If I asked you in 1999 what you thought the stock market's average return would be over the next 10-20 years, what would you have said (remember that 1999 was before the "crash" of 2000-2002).

Most readers would have said approximately 12% annually.

Let's look at a little five-year window from 1999-2003 and see what the best performing stock index returned.

The following are the returns from the Standard & Poor's 500 index:

21.04% (1999)

-9.10% (2000)

-11.88% (2001)

-22.09% (2002)

14.71% (2003)

After the stock market crash, are you still of the opinion that the stock market will average double-digit returns on a consistent basis?

How did your investment portfolio perform (tax-deferred or not) in 2000-2002? Millions of Americans lost billions of dollars when the stock market tanked between 2000 and 2002.

Many people saw 2000 as an "adjustment" and did not remove their money from the equity markets.

When 2003 finally ended, however, many lives were changed (and not for the better); and after 2002, the American investors seemed to readjust their thinking - that the equity markets will not be averaging anywhere near 12% annually for any extended period of time.

Depending on whom you ask, there are many who believe the stock market will be flat over the next ten years (5-6% annual returns). There are many who believe over the next 10 years that the stock market will average a rate of return of around 1-2%, and there are some who still believe the stock market will go back to its glory days of 12%+ a year returns.

I'll be the first to admit that I am not a professional money manager. I do not profess to be an expert on where to invest money in an active and unprotected brokerage account. After you read the following material, you'll understand how difficult it is for money managers to predict how the stock market will perform over a given period of time.

I have no idea what the stock market will do over the next 12 months, 5 years, 20+ years. As of the writing of this book, the sub-prime lending market is in a tail spin. The U.S. dollar is very weak, China is a growing concern, global warming is a menace that no one knows how to deal with, and we will always live with the threat of another U.S. tragedy like 9-11. All of the previously listed variables will have an effect on the stock market. I'm just not sure when and how.

WHAT ARE YOUR INVESTMENT GOALS THESE DAYS?

Did the dismal investment returns of 2000-2002 serve as a wake-up call to you that the stock market actually does go down? My guess is that most readers are of the opinion that the stock market should average 8% or so a year over the next many years. No one has any idea what will actually happen as you will see from the following material, but we do need to make some assumptions in order to have a useful discussion about where your money should be invested or positioned.

MANAGING RISK

We at The WPI suggest that your investment goals should be to **protect principal** and go for **growth** when you can do so in the **least risky** manner possible (or in a manner that meets your risk threshold).

How do you usually manage risk? The typical answer is by sacrificing yield when investing in CDs, money markets, and Treasuries (which are annually taxable investments), or by outsourcing risk when giving money to a stockbroker or money manager, where there is **no principal protection**.

As most people have found out, the vast majority of mutual funds provide no downside protection. Everyone seems to think Merrill Lynch is a great money management firm. Look at what happened to some of their funds in 2001. What kind of protection did their clients receive? The S&P 500 was down 17%, but that would have been much better than what happened with some of the Merrill funds.

Merrill Lynch Mid-Cap Growth Fund –   **-36.6%**
Merrill Lynch Premier Growth Fund –   **-52.6%**
Merrill Lynch Focused Twenty Fund –   **-70.1%**
Merrill Lynch Fundamental Growth Fund – **-19.4%**
Merrill Lynch Global Growth Fund –   **-26.3%**

The following are some of the problems with actively managed mutual funds: There is no downside protection, they underperform the market, are very expensive – (whether the funds go up or down), and lack of consistent results.

STUDIES SHOW THAT MOST MUTUAL FUNDS UNDERPEFORM THE MARKET:

-1,226 actively managed funds with 5-year track record – 1.9% less than S&P 500*

-623 actively managed funds with 10-year track record – 1.7% less than S&P 500*

-406 actively managed funds with 15-year track record – 1.5% less than S&P 500*

-Adjusted for "survivorship bias" – 1.5% worse. "With returns corrected for survivorship bias, the average actively managed fund trails the market by about 3 percentage points per year."**

* Morningstar Principia Pro, data through Dec 31, 2001. Funds identified were all domestic stock funds, excluding index funds and funds holding more than 20% in bonds.

** *The Great Mutual Fund Trap*, Baer and Gensler, 2002.

BACKGROUND

Most financial advisors get their "investment training" from their employers, i.e., their broker/dealers at compliance meetings, company conventions, or training symposiums. These meetings are usually, and at least partially, sponsored by various money management organizations. Consequently, these same meetings consist primarily of presentations made by these money managers and/or compliance officers from the broker/dealer. The result is that, in an environment that supposedly trains financial advisors and provides them a balanced look at investment alternatives, they actually get a completely unbalanced view that, as will be demonstrated, is also inaccurate.

The handout material at these conferences marked "for broker/dealer use only" is an indication that such materials may not be balanced and suitable for distribution to the public. However, they are used to persuade the advisor that these approaches are appropriate. Why should it be proper to use such materials to persuade the "persuaders" but not those they will ultimately advise using that information?

The truth is that they shouldn't; and as a result, most financial advisors are persuaded to give advice that they wouldn't otherwise provide if they were actually given unbiased, truthful training at these meetings. Throughout the balance of this book, you will be introduced, first, to some independent studies about professional money management and, then, to a suggested investment alternative.

THE INDEPENDENT STUDIES

Let's start out by making it clear that **nobody knows the direction that the stock market or any particular stock is going to go**. In fact, if anyone should be able to accurately predict the direction of a particular stock, it would be the analysts at the major brokerage firms. These analysts have limitless resources at their fingertips to aid them in performing their research. However, the independent studies demonstrate that, even with all these resources, they do a terrible job.

Consider this study by Investars.com, a firm that tracks the recommendations of the analysts at the largest brokerage firms. Investars.com found that from 1997-2001, 16 of the largest 19 brokerage firms issued money-losing advice at the same time that the S&P 500 Index was increasing by 60% (*The Industry Standard*, 2001).

Another study by the Haas School of Business at the University of California at Berkley showed that the stocks most recommended by analysts in 2000 fell an average of 48% while the least recommended stocks increased by over 31%.

Another distressing example involved Charles Schwab and was described in an 11/25/03 article in the *Orange County Register*. You may have seen the television ads being run by Schwab offering clients their free, independent ratings on over 3,500 domestic stocks. Well, the Schwab ratings cost nothing because that's apparently what they're worth. The article reported that from May 2002 to October 2003, Schwab's "F" rated stocks performed the best and their **"A" rated stocks performed the worst!**

The point is that there is no amount of research and no stock-picking strategy that can consistently forecast the direction a stock is going to move. This book review from Publishers Weekly says it all:

> *"The eternal truth is simple: **you can't beat the market**. Well, technically, you can beat the market, but not profitably, because the transaction costs of your brilliant trading will eat up the extra returns. You can also beat the market by pure luck-but you can't deliberately beat the market, because you can't predict future stock prices. You can't predict them by divining Wall Street's crowd psychology; or by charting trends in stock prices; or by doing lots of research on companies' business prospects. You can't predict them from hemlines or Super Bowl winners.*

*In fact, according to the efficient market theory, which states that all knowable information about a stock's value is already reflected in its share price, you can't predict them at all. Malkiel, a Princeton economist and professional investor, backs it all up with statistics, charts and studies. Standing by his notorious claim that "a blindfolded chimpanzee throwing darts" at the NYSE listings could pick stocks as well as the Wall Street pros, **Malkiel advises investors to "buy and hold" a diversified portfolio heavy on index funds that passively mirror the market, which usually out-perform actively managed funds.***"

The point is that, if nobody really knows what direction stocks are going to go, why would we pay someone to guess on our behalf? The answer is that maybe we shouldn't (especially not with all of our invested dollars). As we review the specific problems associated with using mutual funds or variable annuities, it will be clear why recommending professional managers may, in fact, be an inappropriate course of action (at least for all or most of the money you have to invest or reposition elsewhere).

CHRONIC UNDERPERFORMANCE

According to the MotleyFool.com (2004): "Though you would think that mutual funds provide benefits to shareholders by hiring "expert" stock pickers, the sad truth of the matter is that over time, the vast majority - **approximately 80% of mutual funds underperform the average return of the stock market**." That's compared to the S&P 500, the benchmark stock market index that most equity-based mutual fund managers are paid to beat. So if one invests in mutual funds, they have an 8 in 10 chance of underperforming the market.

Nearly everyone at some time or another has been to Las Vegas or a local casino. If you played any of the games with your own money, everyone seems to understand that Vegas wasn't built with the lavishness it has because the house loses.

Let's use some Vegas analogies to understand what kind of game we might be playing when actively investing in the stock market. What are the odds of beating the Las Vegas house? 46%

if you play craps, 48% if you play blackjack, 44% if you play roulette, and **20% if you are in actively traded mutual funds instead of index funds** (meaning that you have a 20% chance of beating the indexes if you are invested in mutual funds).

"The average actively managed stock mutual fund returns approximately 2% *less per year* to its shareholders than the stock market returns in general" ("What's Wrong," 2004). And that doesn't take into account those mutual funds that have closed due to merger or poor performance, argue Baer & Gensler, authors of *The Great Mutual Fund Trap* (2002). If you consider this "survivorship bias," the numbers are even worse. The bottom line is that S&P 500 unmanaged stock market index beats the average mutual fund by approximately 2-3% per year after all fees and expenses (Baer & Gensler, 2002).

Peter Lynch ran the Fidelity Magellan Fund for 15 years and had an outstanding record. He was certainly the exception when compared with today's fund managers. Discussing himself and a handful of other successful money managers in his classic book, *One Up On Wall Street* (Lynch, 1989), Lynch says frankly:

> *"These notable exceptions are entirely outnumbered by the run-of-the-mill fund managers, dull fund managers, comatose fund managers, sycophantic fund managers, timid fund managers, plus other assorted camp followers, fuddy-duddies and copy cats hemmed in by the rules."*

Peter Lynch, one of the few bright spots in the business, clearly is not a fan of most mutual fund managers.

NO DOWNSIDE PROTECTION

Investing your hard-earned nest egg in the equities market can be treacherous (pre- or post-tax investing). From 2000 – 2002, we saw the S&P 500 get cut almost in half in less than three years and the NASDAQ did even worse ("At long last," 2004).

Many financial experts believe that the rough ride on Wall Street is not over. They cite examples like:

- High unemployment levels
- Huge federal budget deficits
- The war on terrorism
- Homeland security issues

Your $100,000						
	S&P 500			NASDAQ		
	% Loss	$ Loss	Balance	% Loss	$ Loss	Balance
2000	- 10.1%	- $10,000	$89,900	- 39.3%	- $39,300	$60,700
2001	- 13.0%	- $11,687	$78,213	- 21.1%	- $12,808	$47,892
2002	- 23.4%	- $18,302	$59,911	- 31.5%	- $15,086	$32,806
Total Loss	- 40.1%	- $40,089		- 67.2%	- $67,194	

Honestly, for most clients with large mutual fund or stock portfolios and for their advisors, isn't it difficult to sleep sometimes when they know the client's wealth can be significantly diminished in another three-year run like 2000-2002?

While we all pray that there is no future 9-11 tragedy waiting for us, the fact of the matter is that most experts predict there will be another 9-11 type attack. When that happens, even the "best" stocks and mutual funds will feel the effects irrespective of the stock or mutual funds real value (absent the attack).

The problem is you don't get any downside protection when you buy big, well-known mutual funds. Take a look at the 2001 results for some of Merrill Lynch's well-known funds. If you had invested in their Mid-Cap Growth fund, you would have lost over 36% in one year. If you had invested in their Premier fund, you would have lost over 52%. And with their Focus Twenty fund, you would have lost over 70%.

Another simple example of how little we know:

Which of the following companies would you have purchased back in July 2003?

Wal-Mart: One of largest companies in the world; consistent earner; pays dividends.

K-Mart: Just emerging from bankruptcy; big marketing tie to Martha Stewart (who was looking at jail time); no anticipated dividends

-In July 2003, Wal-Mart stock was valued at $56.08

-In July 2003, K-Mart stock was valued at $24.20

Be honest. You would have chosen Wal-Mart all day long.

What happened?

-In July 2004, Wal-Mart stock was valued at $51.76

-In July 2004, K-Mart stock was valued at $76.80

If we are honest, do any of us really know what is going to happen with individual stocks or mutual funds? Not really. We simply know that the market as a whole will go up over time.

MUTUAL FUNDS ARE VERY EXPENSIVE

Mutual funds are loaded with fees. Investors can be charged four types:

1) **Sales Commissions** – clients may pay sales commissions upfront (A funds) or backdoor (B funds).

2) **Expense ratio** – *each year* investors will pay the expenses to run the fund and compensate the fund manager whether he/she "guesses" right or wrong and whether they make or lose money. According to John Bogel (1999), the average management fee charged by actively managed equity mutual funds is 1.55% per year and rising.

3) **12b-1 fees** – reimburses the fund for marketing expenses. Clients pay to help their fund attract the next customer.

4) **Turnover** – clients pay for the transaction costs incurred by the fund to buy and sell securities during the year. Bogel (1999) writes that these costs "are hidden, but nonetheless real."

A 1993 study in the *Financial Analyst Journal* suggests the cost of an average transaction was equivalent to 6/10 of 1% (Bogel, 1999). According to Bogel (1999), "Today the average turnover rate approaches 100% a year." This means that investors owning funds with 100% turnover are paying annual costs of up to 1.2%. High turnover imposes huge costs to individual investors, according to Don Cassidy of Lipper, Inc. (2004). "Investors investing for the long-term are getting slaughtered due to increased costs hurting performance," he says.

Vanguard.com states that owning funds with higher turnover can also mean higher taxes for the investor (Neal, 2/5/04). In a recent Wall Street Journal story (3/16/04), the new chairman of MFS admits that the true costs of trading commissions have been "camouflaged." According to the story, the reason fund companies bundle research into commissions is that "commission payments are subtracted directly from shareholder's accounts, rather than from the management fees paid to the fund companies."

No-load mutual fund owners don't pay a commission to buy in or sell out of the fund and may avoid the 12b-1 fee, but the expense ratio and turnover expenses are still charged by the no-load mutual fund companies. The no-load fund manager doesn't work for free.

And the fees charged on many variable annuities can be even worse. On top of the fees we just discussed, variable annuities add an insurance charge (M&E risk charge).

John Bogle continues to champion the cause of the individual investor against mutual fund fees. Bogle is critical of U.S. mutual funds and maintains that funds risk losing investors if they don't cut the costs of managing portfolios. Recently he called for more disclosure about fees and for reform from within the industry ("Bogle Criticizes," 2003).

When we add the expense ratio, the 12b-1 fee, and the turnover costs, total mutual fund fees that exceed 4% per year are not uncommon (Bogel, 1999). Did you realize that you were paying all these fees? Were you aware of all these fees? Some of these fees are in the prospectus, but most advisors and their clients don't take the time to read the disclosures thoroughly. Unfortunately, hidden fees like turnover and its related transaction costs are not revealed in the prospectus.

CHASING "STAR" FUNDS

And how do you know which funds to pick anyway? Many people use the fund's track record as a basis for that decision. Well, let's see what happens when investors try to chase the "hot funds." A study by the Bogle Financial Centre and the Lipper

Organization looked at the 851 domestic equity funds with over $100 million in assets at the beginning of 1996. They followed these 851 funds for three years to determine the Top 10 performers. The Top 10 were then tracked for the next three years – through 2002. Here's what the study discovered: all of the Top 10 finished in the <u>bottom</u> 10% from 1999-2002 ("<u>Law of Averages</u>," 2003).

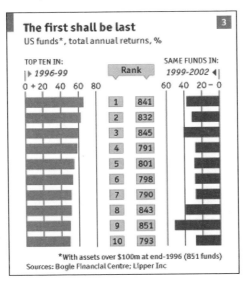

Reporting on "star" funds - those ranked #1 in their category for the previous year - financial columnist Eric Tyson of the *San Francisco Chronicle* reported in 1997 that: "Over the subsequent 3, 5, and 10 year periods, a whopping 80% of these 'star' funds performed worse than the average similar fund." And according to *Morningstar* (2001), since 1987, the least popular funds have annually outperformed 90% of the most popular funds over the following three years.

Compliance requirements to warn investors that "past performance is not an indication of future results" may be some of the only objective information obtained at our training seminars.

The result of chasing "hot" funds has produced disastrous consequences for investors. An independent study performed by DALBAR Associates found that from 1984-2002 ("Law of Averages," 2003):

- The S&P 500 index averaged over 12% per year,

- The average fund averaged under 10% per year,

- *But because of switching to so-called "hot funds," the individual fund investor managed an annual return of just 2.7%.*

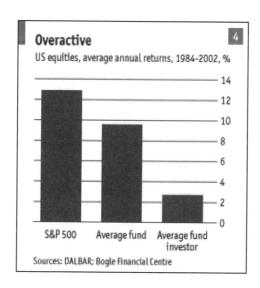

Overactive 4
US equities, average annual returns, 1984-2002, %

Sources: DALBAR; Bogle Financial Centre

It seems almost impossible, but it's true that individual mutual fund investors did so much worse than the funds they invested in. But that's because it is so difficult to know which fund to invest in. Nobody would purposely make a bet in Vegas which had 80% odds of losing, yet almost every U.S. investor makes that same gamble with mutual funds every day.

UNETHICAL BEHAVIOR

Counting on traditional Wall Street types to provide honest, useful advice may not always produce the desired results. As reported by the *Associated Press*, many stock analysts maintained a "buy" rating for Enron stock even as the company was disintegrating (Baldwin, 2001). Stock analysts are the people who recommend stocks to mutual fund managers and recommend stocks to advisors, who, in turn, recommend them to clients.

Fortune Magazine in 2003 reported that "last June, during the height of the recession – when even the most optimistic CEOs were unable to hide the bad news – investment analysts couldn't find a stock they couldn't tout. Of 26,451 buy, hold and sell recommendations, only 213 were sells" (Rynecki, 2002). After a probe by the Securities & Exchange Commission (SEC), Wall Street Brokerages agreed to pay $1.4 billion to victims of tainted research ("SEC," 2003).

Disclosures of **Merrill Lynch** e-mails show that supposedly independent stock analysts were publicly hyping stocks that Merrill Lynch had lucrative investment banking relationships with–while privately "trashing" the stocks. Merrill Lynch was sued by New York State and agreed to pay a $100 million civil penalty to reform its analyst-compensation system and to apologize for failing to address the obvious conflicts of interest (Rynecki, 2002).

The SEC investigated **Prudential Securities** for misleading mutual fund sales practices, and 12 brokers and supervisors were fired (Byrne & Goldstein, 2003).

In a complaint, Massachusetts said **Morgan Stanley** misled regulators who were probing its "mutual fund practices." New York and the SEC are also investigating its mutual fund sales practices ("States," 2003).

Many large institutions are using mutual funds as trading vehicles, dramatically driving up the fund expenses. This practice is contrary to what is disclosed in the funds' prospectuses, according to Don Cassidy of Lipper, Inc. "Lying on the prospectus is tantamount to securities fraud," explains Cassidy. His investigation has shown that this practice is prevalent inside variable annuities and variable life products, in addition to mutual funds (Cassidy, 2004).

Other headlines include:

- "SEC Approves Crackdown on Mutual Fund Ads" (*Reuters*, 9/24/03).
- "7 **Janus** Funds Involved in 'Timing' Deals" (*Denver Post*, 10/1/03).
- "**Putnam** Hit with Fraud Charges" (*IBD*, 10/29/03).

- "Mutual Fund Abuse Widespread" (*IBD,* 10/31/03)
- "Mutual Fund Charges Mounting" (*IBD,* 11/5/03)
- "**Invesco** Accused of Fraud" (*Daily Camera,* 12/3/2003).
- "SEC Finds Mutual Fund Abuses" (*IBD,* 1/14/04)
- "The Fund Scandals Biggest Payout" referring to Bank of America and FleetBoston (*Wall Street Journal, 3/16/04*)

In summary, mutual funds seldom outperform an unmanaged index fund, charge exorbitant fees whether they perform or not, provide no downside protection, are difficult to choose, and along with the rest of Wall Street have been guilty of unethical behavior. So, what is an investor to do?

INDEX APPROACH

The answer: use an indexed approach to investing. With index funds, investors get maximum diversification, pay smaller fees, and know their returns will almost match the market. However, a huge problem with an indexed approach is that investors have **no downside protection**. If the market crashes, so will an index fund.

As stated by Motley Fool: "**80% of mutual funds underperform the indexes**." If that's true, then should all investors invest their money in indexed mutual funds? Personally speaking, I think, if you are going to have your money in the stock market, having a percentage of that money in index funds makes a lot of sense for a few reasons. One of the main reasons to use index funds (besides the historic returns which have outpaced traditional mutual funds) is because the expenses are lower. Since a money manager doesn't have to decide which stocks to purchase, the overall expenses of such funds can be reduced significantly.

Another reason to use index funds is because you don't really need a professional money manager to help you choose your investments. If you know the index fund you are purchasing has a 20+ year history of beating the returns of most mutual funds, there is no need to pay .5%-1%+ every year on the returns to a money manager (which is one reason money mangers don't often use index funds).

BUY AND HOLD

Another reason to use index funds is so you have an investment you can buy and hold. Again, if index funds have outperformed mutual funds 80% of the time over a long stretch of years and we think that will be the case going forward, then we can put our money in an index fund and leave it there for years (maybe until retirement). Doing so will help investors mitigate their annual taxes because index funds usually pay small annual dividends and the investor will not incur a capital gains tax until the index fund is sold 10-20+ years down the road.

Then it's settled, if 80% of the mutual funds don't beat the indexes and if the expenses are lower, let's all just invest in index funds and let our wealth grow. It sounds good in theory, but there are a few problems that prevent this from happening.

1) <u>Index funds are boring</u>. It may sound strange, but most readers will agree with me that our society likes "action" and beating the Joneses. While investing in one index fund and letting money grow quicker than most mutual funds sounds exciting, it's not nearly as exciting as what our neighbor or friend has been telling us lately about their investments in individual stocks or traditional mutual funds.

Roger next door was lucky, I mean smart enough to buy E-Bay stock when it first came out; and he tripled his money in a very short period of time (while your index fund only earned 12-18% a year in a good market).

Bill at work told you about his international growth fund that was up 45% in a given year (he didn't tell you the same fund was down 30% two years in a row the years before the up year).

We all get caught up in the get-rich-quick mentality that drives us to invest money in places that could work out; but as you know from the previous material, usually does not work out (remember the average investor earned less than 3% during the stretch when the S&P 500 earned over 12%).

2) There is <u>NO downside protection</u> with indexes. This is the main problem with investing in any equity market that includes the S&P 500 index (or any other index).

This leads me into a discussion about **how money grows**. How does money grow in the stock market? You've read the statistics in this book about average rates of return. The key word in the previous sentence is average.

When tabling out how money will grow in the future, it is impossible to know which years will be up or down. We simply use the assumption that money over time will average a percentage return (6%, 8%, 10%, etc.). As we already know from the previous material, Americans are professionals at buying high and selling low (how else could the average investor earn less than 3% over a period of time when the S&P averaged over 12% and the average mutual fund averaged over 10%?).

I wanted to show you real world numbers with a few different scenarios to show you how the investment period of your investments can dramatically affect your returns.

For example, let's compare a $10,000 investment over similar 17-year and 20-year time frames. If the $10,000 was invested in an S&P 500 index (minus dividends) in 1972, you will have the following results.

Year	Amount Invested	Average Rate of Return	Ending Balance
1972-2002	$10,000	8.66%	$86,500
1972-1999	$10,000	11.25%	$144,500

The above numbers are totally unrealistic because investors do not buy and hold. Having said that, if an investor would have known the market was going to crash between 2000-2002, he/she would have removed the money from the market and would have been much better off. Unfortunately, none of us know when the market is going to adjust downward or crash; and, therefore, we usually do not remove our money in time to avoid significant down years.

An interesting comparison is one for new investors. This could be a reader who has money in CDs and money market accounts and is finally going to get in the stock market, or it could be a reader who finally decides to start to save money for retirement.

I am going to use a smaller time frame to drive home my point.

Year	Amount Invested	Average Rate of Return	Ending Balance
2000-2006	$10,000	-0.66%	$9,321
2003-2006	$10,000	12.80%	$23,352

IF WE ONLY KNEW

If you knew the market was going to crash between 2000-2002, wouldn't you have removed your money from the market and placed it in a checking account, CDs, or even under your pillow? Any of the three choices would have been safer than leaving your money in the market.

If you only knew, wouldn't you have waited until 2003 to invest money in the market? Look at the difference between an account opened up in 2000 vs. one opened in 2003.

On a $10,000 investment, the investor who started in the market in 2000 ended up with an account balance of $9,321. The investor who waited until 2003 to put money in the market has an account value of $23,352 (which is $14,031 more over a very short time period on only a $10,000 investment).

If we only knew, we would remove our money from the market before a crash or wait until after the crash to invest. The problem is that we don't know, and we never will know when the next crash or market correction will occur. Therefore, it is vitally important that every investor have some money positioned in a wealth building tool/account where there is no market risk of loss (and, ideally, good upside growth potential and tax-free growth and tax-free distributions).

RECOVERING FROM LOSS

Answering the following question is simple. Without thinking about it, please read the following question and just blurt out the answer to yourself.

If the stock market decreases by 10% this year, how much does the market have to go up next year to get the account back to even?

Many readers who answered this question quickly without thinking should have said 10%. It sort of makes sense. If your money goes down 10% this year in the stock market, it needs to go up 10% next year to get back to breakeven.

The problem with the math on this is that after a down year you have less money invested; and, therefore, you need a greater return on your money the following year to get back to breakeven. I think the following chart will really be an eye opener for many who lost money in the market from 2000-2002 (when most readers with money in the market lost 40-50%+ of their portfolio balances).

	Traditional Investing
Amount of Loss	% Gain Needed to Recover the following year.
20%	25%
30%	43%
40%	66%
50%	100%

ALTERNATIVE PLACES TO POSITION YOUR MONEY

If there was a way you could partake in the upswings of the stock market without losing money in down years, would that interest you?

After reading how the average investor earned less than 3% in the biggest bull run in this country's history and after understanding that your money is 100% at risk to market losses, I think your answer should be "yes."

I discuss those alternative places to position your money in Chapter 5 where I discuss equity indexed cash value life insurance.

CDs AND MONEY MARKET ACCOUNTS

There is no section in the book where I will discuss and compare using CDs and money market accounts to grow your wealth. Such investments are not totally useless but are close. The problems with both are that the rates of returns are generally low and what's worse is that the income from both is taxable each year.

Generally speaking, CDs and money market accounts should be used by readers who need access to cash in the short term and by those that want to earn a couple of bucks while they wait to spend the money. They should not be used as a long-term investment tool because there are several other options that provide better potential for growth while guaranteeing principal.

Now it's time to move on to discuss the pros and cons of the bread and butter wealth building tool for most Americans: Qualified Retirement Plans and IRAs.

2) INVEST MONEY TAX DEFERRED INTO AN EMPLOYER'S 401(k) PLAN AT WORK OR IN AN INDIVIDUAL IRA

Large financial institutions and the Federal Government have done a good job over the years of marketing to the general public the concept of planning for your retirement by investing money in a tax-deferred vehicle such as a qualified retirement plan or IRA.

Obviously, the financial institutions are pitching tax-deferred investing to employers and their employees because it a nice way for them to gather literally billions of dollars under management. Think about it—if a medium-sized employer with five owners and 100 employees contributes $44,000 a year for the owners and $1,050 per non-owner employee (3% of pay which equals $99,750), the contribution to the qualified plan each year would be $319,750. If a financial institution had only 1,000 clients nationwide, the company would capture $319,750,000 in contributions each year.

If the financial institution charged just 1/2% as a fee every year on the money being managed, the revenue generated just from the first year's contribution would be $1,598,750 (if taken out at the end of the year). If the institution kept the accounts and they grew every year at only 5%, the revenue over the next five years for the institution would look as follows (and this assumes the institution picks up no new accounts).

Year	Start of Year Balance	Plan Contributions	5.00% Growth	Year End Balance	Institution Fee Generation
1	$319,750,000	$0	$15,987,500	$335,737,500	**$1,678,688**
2	$335,737,500	$319,750,000	$32,774,375	$688,261,875	**$3,441,309**
3	$688,261,875	$319,750,000	$50,400,594	$1,058,412,469	**$5,292,062**
4	$1,058,412,469	$319,750,000	$68,908,123	$1,447,070,592	**$7,235,353**
5	$1,447,070,592	$319,750,000	$88,341,030	$1,855,161,622	**$9,275,808**

Most financial institutions that market services in the 401(k) market have thousands of clients, many of whom are much larger than the above example.

My point is that there are a lot of companies out there marketing to the general public the mantra of investing money through tax-deferred retirement vehicles such as 401(k)s, profit sharing and defined benefit plans, and IRAs. While it can be a nice investment tool to build your wealth for retirement, you still need to **critically think** before putting your money into any vehicle (including a simple 401(k) plan).

IS INVESTING MONEY TAX DEFERRED IN QUALIFIED RETIREMENT PLANS A GOOD OR BAD IDEA?

I'd like you to answer that question for yourself before I give you my opinion on the topic.

Think about what you know or have been told by your financial advisors, the talking heads on television shows, or other sources. You can invest $1.00 now into a "retirement plan," allow it to **grow without paying taxes** (dividend or capital gains taxes) for 10, 20, or 30 years (depending on your age), and receive the money after age 59½ without penalty to use for your retirement.

When you receive the money in retirement, it will be <u>taxed as ordinary income at that time</u>. Is that a good idea?

Most readers of this book will say that it is a good idea. Like many financial topics, **the answer depends**. It can be good or bad depending on your individual circumstances.

As I do in many places in this book, I will point out the intentionally slanted view of other books on various subjects that involve Equity Harvesting.

If you read the other high-profile books on Equity Harvesting, you'll notice that they go out of their way to make investing into tax-deferred qualified plans (401(k), profit sharing plans, and defined benefit plans) or Individual Retirement Plans (IRAs) look like a bad investment.

Why is that? Is the American public so dense that they contribute billions of dollars each year to plans that are not in their best interest?

Are income tax deferred qualified plans or IRAs "tax favorable" because they allow people to grow wealth in a tax-deferred manner, or are they "tax hostile" because the money that comes out of a qualified plan or IRA is all income taxed at your current income tax bracket?

Good question, and depending on how an author wants the answer to come out, you could get a different answer.

INFORMATION ON QUALIFIED PLANS AND IRAS

In order to determine if funding a qualified plan or IRA is a good idea, you have to know what plans you can use and what the limits are when funding each plan.

Let's start with a tool that nearly every reader will be familiar with—the Individual Retirement Account (IRA).

<u>TRADITIONAL</u> AND <u>ROTH</u> IRAs

A traditional IRA is a tool readers can use to allow invested money to grow tax deferred (no annual dividend or capital gains taxes); but when the money comes out in retirement (after age 59 ½), the money is income taxed.

It is important to understand that, while almost anybody can make a contribution to a <u>traditional</u> IRA, only a few are allowed to actually <u>deduct</u> the amount contributed to the IRA. If you are eligible to participate in a retirement plan at work, your ability to deduct IRA contributions is phased out based upon the following income amount:

Year	Single	Married Filing Jointly
2007	$50,000 - $60,000	$80,000 - $100,000

Therefore, if you are married, earn more than $100,000, and are eligible to participate in an employer's retirement plan at work, you cannot take an income tax deduction for funding an IRA.

Roth IRAs are different from non-Roth IRAs. With a Roth IRA, under NO circumstances can you income tax deduct contributions.

On the flip side, a Roth IRA is unique because the money in the IRA is allowed to **grow tax free and can <u>be withdrawn completely tax free</u> in retirement** (after age 59 ½).

<u>Roth IRAs</u> (and <u>Roth 401(k)</u> plans) are very important to understand when talking about Home Equity Management Why? Like cash value life insurance, money in each is allowed to grow tax free and can be removed income tax free (See Chapter 5 for a comparison of the two and which one is best for you).

All IRAs are very limited as wealth building tools due to the amount of money you can contribute each year. See the following chart.

Year	IRA contribution limit	Catch-up (Age 50+)
2006-2007	$4,000	$1,000
2008 and after	$5,000	$1,000

It's tough to "become a millionaire" or substantially increase your wealth when you are limited to contributing $4,000-$5,000 a year to a wealth-building tool.

Roth contribution rules have a couple of unique twists to them. Due to the powerful nature of a Roth IRA, Congress, in all of its infinite wisdom, has decided that those who could most benefit from its completely tax-free build up and distribution are not allowed to utilize Roth IRAs.

Roth Income Limits

Filing Status	Income Range for full contributions	Phase out ranges	No Contributions allowed
Single	$95,000 or less	$95,000- $110,000	Over $110,000.00
Married Filing Jointly	$150,000 or less	$150,000 - $160, 000	Over $160,000.00
Married Filing Separate	N/A	0 - $10,000	Over $10,000.00

Therefore, if you are married and earn over $160,000 as a couple, you can't even use a Roth IRA.

401(K) PLANS

In 2001, the tax laws changed for the first time for 401(k) plans and made these plans among the best retirement plan designs for even the smallest of employers. That's because the law fundamentally altered the way these plans operate by changing the treatment of employer contributions and employee contributions.

The Economic Growth and Tax Relief Reconciliation Act of 2001 greatly expanded and simplified the 401(k) world. Each employer may now contribute up to 25% of the "eligible payroll" in the form of **profit sharing**, **matching contributions,** or combinations of the two. The prior limit was only 15% of the payroll and was **reduced** by salary deferrals, which is no longer the case.

These laws dramatically increased the amount that an employ<u>ee</u> can potentially defer into the plan (an employee can contribute to a 401(k) plan through a payroll deduction). It also allows any participant who is age 50 or older during the plan year to contribute additional "make-up" deferrals. These limits will be adjusted in future years for cost of living.

A strict 401(k) plan is simply a salary deferral plan that allows employees to contribute a portion of their paychecks into an account in a tax-deferred manner and then allows it to grow tax free until withdrawn. How much can an employee contribute from their pay each year?

	Deferral	Catch-up	Total Age 50+
2007	$15,000	$5,000	$20,500

As you'll recall from the limits of traditional tax-deferred IRAs ($5,000 in 2008), a 401(k) plan allows an employee to income tax defer significantly more money each year and thereby grow wealth quicker.

THE NEW ROTH 401(K) PLAN

A new retirement account was signed into law on August 17, 2006. It is a component of a "regular" 401(k) plan; however, the funding of a "Roth" 401(k) plan is funded with **AFTER-TAX** dollars. This is similar to the Roth IRA, but with higher funding limits and no limit on earnings to contribute. Money contributed to a Roth 401(k) plan grows without tax and is **distributed without tax**. (In 2007, the funding limit is $15,500 ($20,500 if over the age of 50)).

PROFIT SHARING PLANS

Profit sharing plans traditionally go hand in hand when an employer offers a qualified retirement plan benefit for the employees. Again, the 401(k) part of the retirement plan is a voluntary salary deferral option for the employee. The profit sharing plan, on the other hand, is usually a discretionary plan the employer funds each year in varying amounts, depending on whether the employer had a good year or bad year (and depending on the makeup of the business and whether the owners in a smaller closely-held business are trying to "max-out" the plan).

Profit sharing plans are non-discriminatory plans with several different ways to test them to ensure that equal or near-equal (non-discriminatory) contributions were made on behalf of the employees.

Many older plans were set up so that the amount of money the employee and owners of the business were able to contribute to the profit sharing plan was contingent on how much money the employees contributed to the 401(k) plan. So, if the employees did not contribute much money annually, the owners were not allowed to max out.

Therefore, to entice the employees to contribute to the plans, employers would create plans with "matching" contributions. For example, if an employee contributed 3% of his/her pay, the employer would match that with a 3% contribution for the employee's benefit.

Combined 401(k) and profit sharing plan contributions cannot exceed $45,000 in 2007.

As with many topics when dealing with wealth building, those readers who own profitable small businesses have more options and ability to grow their wealth.

The material in this book is not meant to give readers literally chapter and verse on qualified retirement plans. Specifically, if you are a small business owner, you can be very creative under the current laws to "legally discriminate" through New Comparability Plans, the Double Advantage Safe Harbor Plan, Cash Balance Plan, Carve-Out Defined Benefit, or 412(i) Defined Benefit Plan.

The following material, like the rest of this book, assumes that readers have (or can find through various measures) money to invest or reposition into different vehicles and that your employers have a retirement plan that you can contribute to or you have the ability to individually contribute to an IRA.

BUILDING WEALTH THROUGH QUALIFIED PLANS/IRAs.

Before you can decide exactly where to allocate the money you have available to grow wealth for retirement, I think it is important for you to look at real-world numbers so that you can understand how money can grow in a qualified retirement plan or IRA.

In the following pages, I will show you through simple charts how much money you can amass using traditional 401(k) plans and IRAs and how much of that you get to keep after taxes.

It is important to remember that you will **not** pay annual dividend and capital gains taxes on your investments in such plans. However, when you take distributions from an IRA or 401(k)/profit sharing plan, all the money is income taxed at your ordinary income tax bracket at the time of distribution. If you take the money out of a 401(k) plan/IRA prior to age 59 ½, you will be hit with a 10% penalty in addition to the taxes paid.

Assumptions: For the following examples, I need to make some assumptions. For the first chart, assume you are able to contribute $10,000 a year through a payroll deduction to a traditional (non-Roth) 401(k) plan every year until retirement. Assume you are 45 years old. Assume the money growing in the 401(k) plan does so annually at 7.5% a year (I know, the average investor in mutual funds in qualified plans will not average anywhere near that as the DALBAR study indicated, but I'm going to give readers the benefit of the doubt for my examples).

I will also assume that you will retire when you are 65 years old and will draw down the account from ages 66-84. Finally, I am going to assume you are in the 25% income tax bracket when contributing to the plan and when removing money from the plan.

These examples will use a lot of assumptions. Again, these examples try to utilize "real world" numbers. Even though the other books on Equity Harvesting seem to have slanted the numbers to fit a predetermined outcome, my examples and illustrations will not. I simply calculate the numbers after giving you a full disclosure of how I put them together and will let you determine for yourself if you believe the numbers are credible.

For our first example, using the above assumptions, how much can you remove from a qualified retirement plan **after tax** from ages 66-84? **$34,984**.

Age	Year	Start of Year Balance	Annual Contrib.	Withdrawal	Growth 7.5%	Year end Balance	Available After-tax
45	1	$0	$10,000	$0	$750	$10,750	$0
50	6	$62,440	$10,000	$0	$5,433	$77,873	$0
55	11	$152,081	$10,000	$0	$12,156	$174,237	$0
60	16	$280,772	$10,000	$0	$21,808	$312,580	$0
65	21	$465,525	$10,000	$0	$35,664	$511,190	$0
66	22	$511,190	$0	$46,645	$34,841	$499,385	**$34,984**
70	26	$458,389	$0	$46,645	$30,881	$442,625	**$34,984**
75	31	$366,823	$0	$46,645	$24,013	$344,191	**$34,984**
80	36	$235,367	$0	$46,645	$14,154	$202,876	**$34,984**
85	41	$46,645	$0	$46,645	$0	$0	**$34,984**

Let's now make the above chart a bit more real world by throwing in a typical 1.2% mutual fund expense annually.

Age	Year	Start of Year Balance	Annual Contrib.	Withdrawal	Growth 6.30%	Year end Balance	Available After-tax
45	1	$0	$10,000	$0	$630	$10,630	$0
50	6	$60,282	$10,000	$0	$4,428	$74,710	$0
55	11	$142,102	$10,000	$0	$9,582	$161,684	$0
60	16	$253,153	$10,000	$0	$16,579	$279,731	$0
65	21	$403,879	$10,000	$0	$26,074	$439,953	$0
66	22	$439,953	$0	$36,968	$25,388	$428,374	**$27,726**
70	26	$389,071	$0	$36,968	$22,183	$374,286	**$27,726**
75	31	$305,226	$0	$36,968	$16,900	$285,159	**$27,726**
80	36	$191,426	$0	$36,968	$9,731	$164,189	**$27,726**
85	41	$36,968	$0	$36,968	$0	$0	**$27,726**

Look at the dramatic difference in the amount of money available in retirement when you simply add into the mix the average mutual fund expense, which would be charged in a typical 401(k)/profit sharing plan or IRA.

Now let's change the income tax bracket to the maximum, which would be 35% for federal taxes. The amount you would have after tax in retirement would be reduced from **$27,726 down to $24,029**. If you throw in a 5% state tax, which many states have, the number would be reduced down to **$22,181** annually in retirement. For those lucky few who are in California and have 9.3% as the highest state income tax, the amount they could remove in retirement from such a plan would be **$20,591**.

With most 401(k)/profit sharing plans, in addition to mutual fund expense, there is usually a "wrap" fee. This fee is part of how a local advisor is paid. If we add in a typical wrap fee of 0.5%, the amount you could remove after tax would be as follows.

$25,149 if you are in the 25% income tax bracket.

$21,795 if you are in the 35% income tax bracket.

$20,119 if you are in the 40% income tax bracket.

$18,677 if you live in CA and are in the highest tax bracket.

What you will read in most marketing material or books (that are postured so that readers come to the conclusion that investing pre-tax in qualified plans or IRAs is a bad idea) is a discussion about readers being in a HIGHER income tax bracket in retirement.

Like I say multiple times in this book, smart authors can manipulate numbers many different ways to reach a predetermined outcome. The higher the tax bracket in retirement, the less it makes sense to use a tax deferred qualified retirement plan to build wealth.

Side note: For the previous examples, I used $10,000 annually as the contribution to a 401(k) plan. As you know from the IRA charts, you are not allowed to contribute that much to an individual IRA., If you want to know what the numbers are if you contribute $5,000 to an IRA instead of $10,000 to a 401(k), simply cut the numbers in half. Due to space issues in this book, I've chosen to use numbers in excess of what can be contributed to an IRA when providing examples for wealth building.

RETIRING IN A HIGHER INCOME TAX BRACKET

The theory goes like this: Income taxes today are at an all time low if you compare today to past years and decades. Now that the Republicans are <u>not</u> holding majorities in the House and Senate and because our national debt is getting out of hand, income taxes will likely be raised in the near future to pay our country's debt and expenses.

This is the opposite of trickle-down economics, which the Republican presidents have made famous over the last several decades. Trickle-down economics, in its basic form, is based on having the lowest possible personal and corporate taxes to stimulate growth and income, which, in turn, should generate more taxes because more people will be working and generating a good income.

This book is not a political commentary. I personally have no idea what income tax rates will be in 5, 10, 20+ years. What I do know is that we've seen quite a variance over the last 30+ years.

Here are the TOP tax brackets for select years from the past.

1965	70% above $200,000
1980	70% above $212,000
1986	50% above $171,580
1988	28% above $29,750
1991	31% above $82,150
1993	39.6% above $250,000
2003	35% above $311,950
2007	35% above $349,700

I actually never looked up the history on personal income tax brackets until I started doing research for this book. After looking at the numbers myself, I found them to be very interesting.

What I can say personally is that I'm glad I was not a working American in the early 80's, 70's and 60's. While I might not be in the top tax bracket myself (something to aspire to), the taxes seem obnoxious.

No one can predict the future. How will terrorism affect our economy? How will a growing China affect the economy? How will oil or lack of oil affect the economy? What politicians will we have in charge in the future and how will their economic ideology affect their stance on taxes.

While it is not technically correct to say that we have lower personal income taxes than at any other time in our country's history, we certainly are in a period in which income taxes are lower on average than any other time in the modern history of our country.

Does that mean taxes will be going up any time soon? Maybe, but maybe not. If you want a guess from this author, I believe income taxes will be going up over the next several years. I don't think they will be excessive because the model of lower taxes has proven to grow our economy; but the tax brackets, in my opinion, will be increasing.

I believe the individual brackets will be raised for all but the lowest income individuals; and, in addition to that, I believe the income you need to qualify for each tax bracket will change. This is a stealthier way to raise taxes—keep rates near the same percentage but lower the annual income needed to jump into the next higher bracket.

As you will find out, the discussion from the Home Equity Management point of view will be a moot one as the conclusion I will ultimately draw in this book is that going out of your way to fund tax-deferred plans may not be in your best financial interest. Having said that, IF you are of the opinion that income taxes will be going up, you will certainly want to read Chapter 6 where I discuss alternatives to funding tax-deferred qualified plans and/or IRAs.

One final thought on the discussion about income tax brackets: if you are not in the highest income tax brackets now, the chances you will be in a higher income tax bracket in retirement are reduced significantly.

If you turn to Chapter 4, you can review charts that I found that were created after surveying the American worker about retirement. What you'll notice from that chapter of the book is that the typical American worker does not believe they will be able to save enough money to retire without lifestyle changes. When you factor in the increasing costs of health-care expenses, the American worker is even less confident they will have enough money to retire on and pay their bills.

Again, keep in mind that those who have written books on Equity Harvesting are moving readers to a particular conclusion. The conclusion drawn in these books is a much easier conclusion to draw if a reader assumes he/she is going to be in a higher income tax bracket in retirement.

My belief is that the vast majority of people reading this book will NOT be in a higher tax bracket in retirement, notwithstanding the fact that I believe income taxes themselves will move higher over the coming years. Why do I draw this conclusion? Because the vast majority of people who are reading this book will not be earning more then $300,000 a year AND will not have sufficient income producing assets in retirement to maintain that higher upper income tax bracket income.

Think about it. When most of the readers of this book retire, they will go from making a living as a full-time employee to making no income from an employer. Readers will instead look to Social Security, stocks and mutual funds, and, yes, their retirement plans/IRAs for income. The vast majority of Americans will not have amassed enough money into any of these vehicles to maintain a level income until death at the same level that was earned when fully employed.

If you are currently one of the few who happen to be in the highest personal income tax bracket, it is more likely that you will amass enough assets to maintain an annual income during retirement that will keep you in the highest tax bracket. Being in the highest tax bracket during retirement is a double-edged sword in that you will have done well to earn and grow that income, but the accumulated wealth will be taxed at the highest personal rate, which will be very painful.

Fundamentally speaking, this book is of more value to a more affluent reader. Why? Because when you learn how to use Equity Harvesting to grow your wealth, the money you will use from your Equity Harvesting plan will be "tax-free" income and not the taxable income you would normally receive from your 401(k) profit sharing plan and/or IRA.

That's not to say that building wealth through Equity Harvesting is not a good—or even a very good—idea for readers who are not in the top personal income tax bracket; however, the numbers I've calculated are what they are, and the benefits of Equity Harvesting, from a pure financial point of view, increase as your wealth/income increases.

ROTH IRAs/401(k) PLANS (a further discussion)

As stated earlier, Roth IRAs and Roth 401(k) plans are a unique animal when it comes to retirement planning. While funding them is done in a **non**-income tax-deductible manner, once the money is inside either of these Roth vehicles, the money is allowed **to grow without taxes** (dividend and capital gains) and can be **withdrawn income and capital gains tax free**--if done so after the age of 59 ½ (and in compliance with the other withdrawal guidelines for retirement funds).

Ask yourself the following question: Will you grow more wealth funding a Roth IRA or 401(k) in a non-deductible manner where the money grows and comes out income tax free or will you grow more wealth income tax deferring money into a traditional IRA or 401(k) where when the money is withdrawn it is fully income taxable at your then income tax bracket?

The answer is... it depends. Would you expect any other answer in an honest book based on real world numbers? Usually the answer always is "it depends." Those sales people or authors who tell you something is ALWAYS better are usually trying to "sell" you something. That is not the case with this book.

Since I know people purchased this book for the "answers" and real math, the real world answer about Roth plans is that the vast majority of readers will in fact be better off using Roth plans over traditional income tax deferred plans.

WHO SHOULD USE A ROTH IRA OR ROTH 401(k)?

-Anyone who will be retiring with the same or higher tax bracket.

-Anyone who will be retiring with a tax bracket within 10% of their current tax bracket.

For example, if you are in the 40% tax bracket and will retire in the 30% tax bracket, using a Roth plan is still a better financial tool than using a traditional tax deferred retirement plan.

Examples are really the best way to show the benefits of a Roth plan and when it is appropriate to use one. The material that follows will illustrate the economics of a Roth 401(k) plan for a reader who is in the 40%, 30% and 15% tax brackets when both contributing to a Roth 401(k) and when removing money from it income tax free in retirement.

A Roth 401(k) plan is being used in the example because I want to illustrate using a $15,000 contribution, which is well in excess of the contribution limit for a Roth and traditional IRA.

For this example, assume the client (Mr. Smith, age 45) contributes $15,000 to a Roth 401(k) plan each year for 20 years and takes distributions from the plan from age 66-85.

Because the annual contribution is nondeductible, the client would have to pay the following taxes on his/her contribution to the Roth 401(k), depending on his income tax bracket:

$15,000 x 40% = $6,000 in taxes

$15,000 x 30% = $4,500 in taxes

$15,000 x 15% = $2,250 in taxes

Assume 7% investment returns over the life of the plan.

The goal of these types of examples is to compare how much money a reader would have after tax each year during retirement with a Roth 401(k) plan and with a traditional 401(k) plan.

For an appropriate comparison between a Roth plan and a traditional tax-deferred plan, we need to address the tax deductibility of the contribution into a traditional tax-deferred plan.

IF Mr. Smith funded a <u>traditional</u> 401(k) plan with $15,000, he would have saved taxes, as shown earlier ($6,000 in the 40% tax bracket, $4,500 in the 30% tax bracket and $2,250 in the 15% tax bracket).

Therefore, to run an apples-to-apples comparison, I will allow:

1) $15,000 to grow tax free and be withdrawn tax free from the Roth 401(k) plan.

2) $15,000 to grow tax deferred in the traditional 401(k) plan (taxable when withdrawn).

3) $6,000, $4,500 and $2,250 to be invested into a taxable <u>side fund</u> for the traditional 401(k) plan. The amounts are different because I'm going to show three different examples for clients in different income tax brackets.

When readers actively invest money in the stock market in taxable side funds, capital gains and dividend taxes must be taken into account. The following are the assumed annual blended tax rates for the side fund.

-25% for the client in the 40% tax bracket

-20% for the client in the 30% tax bracket

-15% for the client in the 15% tax bracket

Finally, to make this more of a real world example, I will also add in an annual mutual fund expense of **.6%** annually on the money as it grows (the average annual mutual fund expense is approximately 1.2%)

How much can this client expect to receive in retirement from his **Roth** 401(k) plan?

$56,541 from the plan income-tax free every year for 20 years (66-85).

If the client instead funded a **regular taxable** 401(k), the following is how much the client could receive from ages 66-85 after-tax:

-$33,925 in the 40% tax bracket

-$39,579 in the 30% tax bracket

-$48,060 in the 15% tax bracket

The **previous numbers must be added to the side account** that the client would have funded with the extra dollars he/she would have saved in income taxes when he/she funded a deductible 401(k) plan.

From the side account, the client could receive the following amounts <u>after taxes</u> from ages 66-85.

-$16,533 in the 40% tax bracket

-$13,206 in the 30% tax bracket

-$7,031 in the 15% tax bracket

<u>Totaling the numbers:</u>

If we add the regular tax-deferred 401(k) **plus the taxable side account**, the client would receive the following from ages 66-85:

-$50,458 in the 40% tax bracket

-$52,785 in the 30% tax bracket

-$55,091 in the 15% tax bracket

Since Mr. Smith would receive **$56,541** from a Roth each year, he would be better off with a Roth regardless of the income tax bracket.

MANIPULATING THE NUMBERS

What if Mr. Smith starts in the 40% income tax bracket and then drops down to 30% income tax bracket in retirement?

He could then take out **$57,642** over the same time period. This is a combination of his taxable 401(k) **and his** taxable side fund.

What if Mr. Smith started in the 30% income tax bracket and then dropped down to the 15% income tax bracket in retirement? **$62,569.**

What if Mr. Smith started in the 40% income tax bracket and then dropped down to the 15% income tax bracket in retirement ? **$66,123.**

What if Mr. Smith started in the 30% income tax bracket and then went **UP** to the 40% income tax bracket in retirement? **$48,434.**

As you can see, the Roth 401(k) plan does slightly worse when a client moves from a 40% income tax bracket to a 30% income tax bracket, much worse with a drop from a 30% bracket to a 15% bracket, and even worse yet when dropping from a 40% bracket to a 15% bracket (because the client is lowering his tax bracket in retirement the Roth is not nearly as helpful).

It is interesting to note what happens when a client moves up in tax brackets in retirement. When a client goes from 30% to 40%, the client does significantly better with a Roth 401(k) plan than a regular 401(k) plan ($56,541 from the Roth and only $48,434 from the traditional 401(k) plus the taxable side fund).

SUMMARY ON ROTH PLANS VS. TRADITIONAL INCOME TAX DEFERRED RETIREMENT PLANS:

Roth plans work better for readers who do not drop in income-tax brackets by more than 10% from the time of funding until the time of retirement. Also, if you remain in the lower tax brackets, using a Roth is nearly a wash.

EMPLOYER MATCHING CONTRIBUTIONS

In other books out in the marketplace on Equity Harvesting, you'll be able to read sections that discuss whether you should use income tax deferred retirement plans to build wealth or instead fund cash value life insurance with your take-home/after-tax income. The conclusions of the other books is that you should fund cash value life insurance policies instead because the money in such policies grows tax free and can be removed tax free in retirement.

So far, I have not given you numbers or come to a conclusion on whether you should be using cash value life insurance instead of a tax-deferred retirement plan. You can see the real math and read my conclusion in Chapter 6.

While I rarely agree with the other authors that have opined on the Equity Harvesting topic, I do agree with them that having an employer match the contributions of the employees in a qualified retirement plan is tough to beat.

What other investment in the world can you put in $1.00 and have an account balance of $2.00 with the employer match? However, the match sometimes comes with a caveat, which is that the employee must "vest" in the match or contribution by the employer. To vest, employees usually need to stay employed for three years or so, depending on the structure of the retirement plan.

I could give you several charts showing you the real-world math. However, because a 100% return on your money in the first year is an obvious benefit you cannot find elsewhere, I'll just state that, if your employer offers a match, you should do everything in your power to contribute to the plan at least up to the amount of the match.

I do want to briefly touch on the qualified plan design your employer may have, which will affect your use of the employer match. In the old days (meaning 8+ years ago), plans were designed so that, IF the employees contributed to a qualified plan, the employee/owners of the business could then put more money away. The problem with these plans is that most employees did not want to or were not counseled to contribute much money to the plan each year.

When the employees didn't contribute, the plan designers threw in the matching concept. If the employer offered to match the employee contributions, the thought was that more employees would contribute more money to the plan, which in turn would allow the employer/owners to put more money away.

A typical matching structure would be dollar-for-dollar up to 3% of pay or fifty cents on the dollar up to 6% of pay (which is the same cost for the employer).

While these plans worked better than the plans without matching, owner/employees still did not typically "max-out" their retirement plans because they still needed larger contributions by the employees.

Because of this problem, the next generation of creative plan designs (for allowing high-income business owner/employees to "max-out") did not hinge on the employees' contributions. With these new plans, employers who simply contributed a percentage of pay on behalf of the employees where the contribution is immediately vested could now meet the discrimination requirements regardless of how much money the employees put into the plans from their own paycheck.

This plan design may cost the employer more money, but that would be made up in larger tax-deductible contributions for the high-income business owners.

Since this is not a qualified plan educational book and because I know this is somewhat confusing, I want to simply conclude by saying that most employers have gotten away from matching contributions for the employees. If you are lucky enough to work for an employer who does match 50 cents or one dollar-per-dollar of contribution up to 3-6% of your pay, I strongly recommend you take advantage of that opportunity before looking into any other options for investing those dollars (that you otherwise take home from work, pay taxes on, and invest.)

QUESTIONS TO ANSWER WHEN CONSIDERING FUNDING AN INCOME-TAX DEFERRED PLAN

Now that you know how much you can contribute to various qualified plans and IRAs, you need to look at the variables that will affect your ability and decision to contribute to such plans.

The following are questions you'll want to answer when deciding if it is a good or bad idea to fund a qualified plan.

1) Do you have money you do not need to take home to live on?

If you don't think you have any extra money to fund into an IRA or 401(k) plan but own a home with a 15-30 year conventional mortgage, then you are still in a position to raise money to grow wealth. To learn more about how to raise money to grow your wealth without changing your lifestyle, please read the chapter on mortgages and read about the 1% Cash Flow Arm mortgage.

Most readers of this book will have the means to income tax defer some amount of money into a qualified plan or IRA if they so choose.

If you have extra money you do not need to take home and pay your bills or buy your toys, then you can choose to income tax defer that money into a qualified retirement plan or IRA.

How do you determine if you have surplus income to defer into a qualified plan or IRA? You can fill out the following form, which will tell you if you have supplemental income that you can defer into such a qualified retirement plan or IRA.

Critical Capital Mass Worksheet

A worksheet to determine how much you can contribute to a tax deferred plan

1) Estimate your annual living expenses (food, clothing, travel, entertainment, automobile, rent, college funding, mortgages (for your mortgage, calculate the costs after subtracting out the tax savings resulting from the income tax deduction on your personal taxes), etc...)

Living Expenses (after tax) $_____(a)

2) Divide your annual living costs by sixty percent (.60) to calculate how much taxable income you need to take home each month to pay your living expenses.

Living Expenses (a) $_____ ÷ .6 = $_____(b)

3) Estimate your "net" practice or business income after all expenses (do not deduct your personal income (this number should be your take-home income before income taxes and matching payroll taxes)).

$_____(c)

4) Calculate your total pre-tax income.

Pre-tax income from medical practice (c) $_____

Any outside pre-tax income (rents, speaking fees) $_____

Spouse's pre-tax income $_____

Total pre-tax income (add the above three) $_____ (d)

5) Subtract living expenses from pre-tax income

Total annual pre-tax income (d) $_____

Minus annual living expenses (b) $_____

"Surplus" pre-tax earnings   (d) - (b) $_____(e)

6) Multiply the "surplus" pre-tax income by 40% (or your current income tax bracket) to calculate estimated annual losses due to unnecessary income taxes.

$_____ (e) X 40% = $_____

2) Does your employer have a retirement plan; and, if so, does the employer make **matching contributions** for money you contribute to the 401(k) plan?

As stated earlier, if your employer has a matching program, you need to strongly consider contributing your own money to the plan up to the amount that the employer will match.

3) **You need to determine if funding a "tax-deferred" qualified plan or IRA is the best investment for you. And, if not, what are better alternatives**?

A good portion of this book revolves around educating readers about the best place to reposition equity removed from their home in an effort to build wealth in the most effective and tax-favorable manner possible.

Many times, the concept of Home Equity Harvesting will require you to take out more debt on your home, which, in turn, will create additional expenses for you. For many readers, they will have surplus income that they can allocate to the new interest expense with Equity Harvesting.

For those who do not have a lot of extra money, one question you'll have to determine is whether it would make more sense to use Equity Harvesting to build wealth OR fund a qualified retirement plan where the money allocated to the plan will be reallocated to pay for interest on a new loan associated with Equity Harvesting.

Besides the concept of Equity Harvesting, I will also discuss and explain with real-world math whether it is a good idea in general to fund cash value life insurance instead of tax deferring money into a qualified retirement plan. I think when you read the chapter on this subject; you will be very surprised at the results.

Reading that part of the book should make for an interesting read. It's sort of like answering the million-dollar question: Is it better to fund a tax-deferred, tax-deductible IRA/401(k) plan, a Roth IRA/401(k) plan, invest in stocks/mutual funds after tax, or position wealth in a cash value life insurance policy. You can find the answer by reading Chapter 6.

3) INVESTING MONEY IN REAL ESTATE

This book was written to deal with certain issues that revolve around Home Equity Management. Along the way, I will discuss important issues that go hand in hand with where to reposition equity removed from the home.

One topic I will **not** be discussing is how to borrow funds from your home so you can re-invest the borrowed funds into commercial properties (rental or appreciating or both).

The world of investing in real estate as a profitable endeavor is a book or multi-book series on its own. The variables when trying to run the math and give real world comparisons with real estate investing are many (many more than when comparing investing money in the stock market, qualified retirement plans/IRAs and when funding cash value life insurance (all of which are dealt with in this book)).

When it comes to borrowing funds from your home so that you can invest those funds into commercial real estate, you need to figure out where in the country you will invest that money. You will need to figure out what kinds of investment property you will invest in (residential rental, commercial rental, vacant lots, etc.) once you figure out where to buy the property. You will also need to figure out what the annual expenses on the property will be (real estate taxes, management fees, insurance, utilities, etc.).

For me, these variables are too great and do not lend themselves to give recommendations in a book that I would write. Therefore, again, I will not be giving counsel as to whether it is a good or bad idea to borrow equity from your home so that you can reposition it into real estate property in an attempt to build the maximum amount of wealth possible for retirement with the least amount of risk.

4) DO NOTHING

I give multiple seminars around the country each year where I teach CPAs/EAs/accountants, attorneys, financial planners, insurance agents, mortgage brokers, etc., how to provide the best advice possible to their clients. I cover asset protection planning, income, capital gains and estate tax planning, long-term care insurance, life insurance, annuities, and on and on. I have over 1,200 pages of text that cover three certification courses that are offered through The Wealth Preservation Institute.

Out of all the hours of pure education at the seminars, there is one story I tell over and over at my seminars. That story is the one of the **Scorpion and the Frog**. I tell the story in my seminars every time and then refer to scorpions in the seminar several times throughout the seminar. If you will allow me, I will tell that story here also because it is entertaining and because I think it will drive home the point that we are all scorpions in many ways; and this is NOT something that is helpful when advisors give advice to clients and when clients make decisions about how to build wealth.

And so the story goes.....A frog and a scorpion are sitting on the side of the river.

The scorpion says to the frog, "Would you let me get on your back and give me a ride to the other side of the river?"

The frog looks at the scorpion and says, "I can't do that. You'll sting me half way across. I'll die from the sting, and you'll drown."

The scorpion says, "That makes no sense. Why would I sting you when that would mean I'd also be killing myself?"

The frog agreed that it made no sense, and so he allowed the scorpion to hop on his back and they started across the river.

Half way across, guess what happened? That's right, the scorpion stung the frog.

As the frog was dying and about ready to go under for the last time, he looked up at the scorpion and said, "Why did you sting me? Now we are both going to die."

The scorpion looked at the frog and said, "I did it because I'm a scorpion and that's what I do" (meaning scorpions sting no matter what).

DO YOU KNOW ANY SCORPIONS?

Let me name a few, and see if you agree with me.

-<u>New or Used Car salesperson</u>. Have you ever heard a car salesperson tell you that you would be better off fixing your car instead of buying a new or new used car?

-<u>Personal Injury (PI) attorney</u>. Even if you have never had a need for a PI attorney, can you imagine visiting one after being in a car accident in which you were injured (where the injuries were caused from the negligence of others) and having the attorney tell you that you should not sue the person who hit you? Rarely does this happen because PI attorneys only get paid when they help clients sue and collect damages.

-<u>Stockbrokers</u>. If you go to a stockbroker and ask them what is the best way to grow your wealth, what do you think their answer is going to be? Invest in real estate? No, they are scorpions and they will typically recommend that you invest your money in stocks and mutual funds.

-<u>Life insurance salesperson</u>. Have you ever talked to a life insurance agent before? If you have, you know that their answer to every one of your problems can be solved by buying a life insurance policy from him/her.

-<u>Annuity Salesperson</u>. If you seek out financial/estate planning advice from someone who sells annuities, what are they going to recommend? Stocks and mutual funds? No. Annuities.

I'm being bit facetious with all of my previous examples, and I'm doing so to help illustrate my point and to help readers **think more critically** when getting advice from an advisor who is not client focused and/or not well rounded with their knowledge.

Also, for the record, I used to be a PI attorney; and I am also licensed to sell life insurance and annuities.

-<u>Certified Wealth Preservation Planner</u> (CWPP™). CWPP™ advisors have been trained by The Wealth Preservation Institute (my company) and have access to course material authored by some of the best advisors from around the country. The CWPP™ course is the only advanced education course in the country, and the goal of those who complete the course is to provide the best advice no matter how it affects the ability of an advisor to "sell" their core service.

CWPP™ advisors also have unique knowledge on asset protection and estate planning and reducing income, estate, and capital gains taxes.

I know this is a shameless plug for those advisors who have taken my courses and are also listed as "Rated" advisors on www.assetprotectionsociety.org; but since I believe readers of this book can be well served by such advisors, I felt compelled to state as such.

-Equity Harvesting "expert?" When I say Equity Harvesting expert, I am talking about those who have been trained as "salespeople" at seminars based on OTHER books in the marketplace which cover the Equity Harvesting topic. You see a "?" after the title of this paragraph because in my opinion they are not really experts in the subject matter (at least not from what they learned in the books) but instead are expert marketers.

From my own personal experience and knowledge, advisors who follow the teaching of the "sales" books have been given an incomplete education in the subject matter. It is impossible to give the best and most client-centered advice if you do not understand the real world math behind Equity Harvesting and the laws that govern the proper implementation of an Equity Harvesting plan.

The reason I put in a section in this book about "The Scorpion and the Frog" is so I can discuss a troubling trend that is evolving in the financial and insurance fields. That trend is that, as advisors learn how easy it is to manipulate the math with the Equity Harvesting concept, it has become the industry favorite for selling large life insurance policies to a public that does not fully understand what they are buying into.

What's worse is that the vast majority of advisors selling Equity Harvesting don't really understand it.

In keeping with "The Scorpion and the Frog" theme, generally speaking, when you go to someone who thinks they are an expert in the concept of Equity Harvesting, guess what advice you will receive to build your wealth? That you should borrow money from your home and reposition it into cash value life insurance.

As you will read in this book, Equity Harvesting can be a terrific tool to build wealth. Having said that, like any other topic, it is not for everyone; and it is not a topic without some element of risk (no matter what you hear from others).

As a consumer, you should be told the pros and cons of the topic so you can make an informed decision as to whether the concept is a good way for you to build wealth.

DO NOTHING

The reason I started talking about "The Scorpion and the Frog" was to get readers ready for the admission that we all must make some time in our lives; that admission being that we do nothing most of the time instead of the something we know we should be doing.

When most people are trying to decide about doing something out of the ordinary or something that is difficult, they lean towards DOING NOTHING. I know I've done the same many times throughout my life. It is so easy to do nothing instead of doing something—even if we know in our heart that doing something is the "right" thing to do.

Let me give you some examples that may seem silly, but I think you'll agree that they prove my point.

I'm going to ask you some questions, and you say to yourself whether you would do nothing or do something.

-Cut the grass/lawn, which has not been cut in over a week, or continue to sit on the couch and watch the ballgame or other favorite TV show.

<u>Answer</u>: Do nothing and watch the game.

-Clean the house now or do whatever else you happen to be doing at any given time.

<u>Answer</u>: Do nothing or in this case anything else besides what you should be doing (cleaning the house).

-Plan out your estate plan (which usually includes going to visit an estate planning attorney) or do nothing.

Answer: The vast majority of readers know they need to start, complete, or update their estate plans, but instead do nothing.

-Be proactive in building your wealth starting now.

Answer: Most readers do not know how or the best ways to grow their wealth. Because of that lack of knowledge and fear of doing the wrong thing, most readers usually do nothing.

My goal with this book is to educate readers in a manner so that they really understand the pros and cons of Home Equity Management, the use of cash value life insurance (specifically indexed life), the real benefits of IRAs and qualified retirement plans, and the real costs associated with having money in mutual funds (inside or outside of an IRA or qualified retirement plan).

As much as you may think this subject matter is difficult, it really isn't. However, to date, most readers have not had a chance to educate themselves so that they can make informed decisions about the best way to grow their wealth.

You should not come away from reading this book with one solution on how to build wealth in a tax-favorable and secure manner. Instead, you should walk away knowing several different options for growing your wealth (using real world math) and will be empowered to make decisions that are best for you based on your individual circumstances.

Chapter 4
Proper Retirement Planning

The American public is interesting in many ways. American employees work more hours per week, per month, and per year than any other industrialized country in the world.

France, for example, has committed to a 35-hour work week; Sweden just increased its paid parental leave allowance so that parents now get a combined 480 workdays off per year at 80% pay for each child. Today, the average German worker puts in about 1,400 hours per year, compared to about 1,800 hours for both American and Japanese workers. The average annual vacation allowance across Europe is about six weeks.

Why do Americans work so hard? You probably have your own opinion of why. My opinion is because Americans like to play hard, live in large houses, and really like their toys. Plus we seem to have the "keep up with Joneses" mentality which drives us to work even harder.

As I think back to my childhood, I lived in a 2,000 square foot ranch with a finished basement. I loved that house and have many fond memories as a child living there. Today, as I drive by that house, it looks so small compared to the huge houses Americans seem to be building these days.

We are a consumption society. We seem to live for the now, and we admittedly (see the various statistics) do not do a very good job of putting money away for retirement. It used to be that we thought the Government would take care of us through Social Security benefits, and that is simply not the case.

The following statistics are incredible (and depressing). They come from a very comprehensive report, which you can find at www.ebri.org (The Employee Benefit Retirement Institute).

EMPLOYER-PROVIDED RETIRMENT PLANS

Over the past few years, a number of changes have been made to the employer pension system. These changes have caused nearly half of workers to feel **less confident** about the amount of money they can expect to receive from an employer-provided traditional pension plan: Almost 2 in 10 report they are ***much less*** confident than they were five years ago (18 percent), while more than one-quarter are a *little less* confident (27 percent). Twenty-eight percent say their confidence is unchanged and 16 percent indicate their confidence has increased (Figure 1).

Change in Worker Confidence Regarding Benefits From Traditional Pension by Expectation of Receiving Benefits From Traditional Pension

		Expect Benefits From Traditional Pension?	
All Workers Yes No	All Workers	Yes	No
Much less confident	18%	12%	29%
A little less confident	27%	31%	22%
Just as confident	28%	34%	18%
A little more confident	10%	13%	5%
Much more confident	5%	7%	3%
Never expected benefits	6%	1%	16%
Don't know	5%	3%	7%

Source: Employee Benefit Research Institute and Mathew Greenwald & Associates, Inc., 2007 Retirement Confidence Survey.

Workers who do not expect to receive retirement income from a defined benefit pension plan (compared with those who do) and those not saving for retirement (compared with savers) are more likely to report they have ***much less*** confidence in the amount of benefits they will receive.

Lower-income workers are more likely than those with higher income to say they are *less* confident, while higher-income workers are more apt to say their confidence is unchanged.

Some workers appear to be expecting to rely on employer-provided benefits they are unlikely to receive. Workers are as likely to expect that they will receive retirement income from a defined benefit pension plan (62 percent) as current retirees are to receive it (63 percent). At the same time, only 4 in 10 workers report they and/or their spouse currently have this type of plan (41 percent). This means that up to 20 percent of workers are counting on receiving this benefit from a <u>future</u> employer—a scenario that is becoming increasingly unlikely as companies cut back on their defined benefit offerings.

A minority of workers have personally experienced a reduction in the retirement benefits offered by their (or their spouse's) employer within the past two years (17 percent). Of these, few say they have taken significant steps to improve their retirement security in the face of these reductions.

One-third report they are saving more, either on their own (24 percent) or in an employer's plan (8 percent). More than 1 in 10 say they are trying to stay healthy (12 percent). Other actions reported include planning on working in retirement (5 percent), making greater use of financial planning or investment information (5 percent), planning to postpone retirement (4 percent), and seeking advice from a financial professional (4 percent). Almost 4 in 10 indicate they have **done nothing** in response to the reduction in benefits. Workers age 55 and older are more likely than younger workers to report a reduction in benefits.

WHO IS SAVING FOR RETIREMENT?

It's amazing but one-quarter of workers and retirees indicate they have **no savings at all**. Among both groups, the likelihood of having no savings decreases as household income increases, education increases, or health status improves.

	Workers	Retirees
Retirement savings only	21%	27%
Other savings only	9%	8%
Both	45%	41%
No savings	25%	24%

Many Americans have little money put away in savings or investments (See the following chart).

**Reported Total Savings and Investments Among Those
Providing Response, by Age**
(<u>not</u> including value of primary residence or defined benefit plans)

	All Workers	Worker Ages 25–34	Age Ages 35–44	Groups Ages 45–54	Ages 55+	All Retirees
Less than $10k	35%	50%	36%	24%	26%	32%
$10k–$24,999	13%	18%	16%	10%	5%	13%
$25k–$49,999	10%	9%	10%	11%	9%	10%
$50k–$99,999	13%	10%	14%	15%	11%	12%
$100k–$149,999	8%	7%	7%	9%	11%	8%
$150k–$249,999	7%	1%	9%	10%	9%	12%
$250k–$499,999	7%	1%	4%	12%	11%	5%
$500k	7%	4%	4%	9%	17%	9%

I'm not sure what is most startling from the previous chart? I think the statistic that jumps out at me is the fact that less than 10% of all retirees have at least $500,000 saved for retirement.

How much do you have saved currently for retirement? How much do you think you will need to retire comfortably?

The following chart is somewhat comical after looking at the previous chart.

**Amount of Savings American Workers <u>Think</u>
<u>They Need</u> for Retirement, by Household Income**

	Total	Household <$35k	Income $35k–$74k	$75k+
Less than $250k	26%	43%	28%	13%
$250k–$499,999	18%	14%	24%	14%
$500k–$999,999	20%	31%	23%	26%
$1 mil.–$1.49 mil.	7%	5%	8%	10%
$1.5 mil.–$1.9 mil.	3%	2%	2%	7%
$2 mil. or more	8%	6%	3%	16%
Don't know/Don't remember	18%	16%	13%	13%

The earlier states that 58% of American workers have less than $50,000 saved for retirement. Unfortunately, the second chart on the previous page indicates that 38% of Americans believe they need over $500,000 to retire comfortably and 56% believe they need in excess of $250,000. Finally, 18% of workers don't know what they need to retire in a manner they deem appropriate.

While you are reading over these statistics and charts, think about your own personal situation and how much you have saved for retirement and how much you think you'll need for retirement (and where that money is going to come from).

WHEN DO YOU THINK YOU WILL RETIRE?

The following charts are also important as they illustrate that many Americans retire younger than they think (and by virtue of the rest of these charts most do so without anywhere near enough money to live comfortably until they die).

Planned and Actual Retirement Age

Retirement Age	Workers (Planned)	Retirees (Actual)
Before age 55	7%	14%
55-59	10%	21%
60-61	10%	7%
62-64	11%	25%
65	27%	13%
66 and older	24%	15%
Never Retire/never worked	6%	3%
Don't Know	5%	0%

Calculated Life Expectancy for Workers, by Gender

	Men	Women
75% expect to live until age:	78	80
50% expect to live until age:	83	85
25% expect to live until age:	90	90
10% expect to live until age:	95	95

According to the 2006 OASDI Trustees Report, a 65-year-old man today can expect to live until age 81, while a 65-year-old woman can expect to live until age 84.

Calculate How Much Money Workers Need to Save for a Comfortable Retirement

Of all the statistics I found, the following are the most comical. We can't help but laugh at ourselves and as an American public when looking at the following chart which illustrates how we go about calculating our needs for retirement.

		Did Retirement Needs Calculation	
	Total	Yes	No
Guess	44%	8%	73%
Ask a Financial Planner	19%	35%	5%
Do your own estimate	17%	33%	4%
Read or hear how much needed	11%	9%	13%
Fill out a worksheet or form	5%	10%	<0.5
Use an online Calculator	3%	8%	0%
Base on cost of living/ desired retirement lifestyle	3%	1%	4%
Other	4%	4%	4%

While the statistics seemed to show that we are confident in what we need for retirement and that we will actually amass that much, generally speaking we are wrong. It's no wonder why. 44% of those from this survey indicated they **guessed** when coming up with a dollar figure they need to retire comfortably and no surprise of those 44%, 74% did no formal calculations.

Only 19% sought out the help of a financial planner. While the vast majority of financial planners do not know how to build wealth through Home Equity Management, using a financial planner is certainly better than doing nothing (although I would prefer it if you would seek out an advisor who has been educated by the Wealth Preservation Institute (www.thewpi.org) and Rated by the Asset Protection Society www.assetprotectionsociety.org)).

Do you expect to <u>spend</u> more or less in retirement?

The following is what the American worker thinks.

	Workers (Expected)	Retirees (Actual)
Much lower than before you retired	20%	20%
A little lower	34%	24%
About the same	34%	42%
A little higher	8%	7%
Much higher than before you retired	2%	6%

I found the above chart to be very interesting. 44% of workers expected to spend as much or more in retirement whereas 55% of actual retirees ended up spending the same or more.

That tells us a few things. 1) our expenses are higher in retirement than we expect (see the next chart for statistics on health care spending) and 2) many workers are not putting enough money away for retirement because they do not believe they will spend as much or more than they do with their pre-retirement spending (in other words many workers will retire without sufficient money to live on comfortably until death).

HEALTH CARE EXPENSES

As access to employer-provided retiree health insurance declines and potential Medicare benefits decrease (given the program's projected funding shortfall), new retirees are likely to find themselves increasingly responsible for the cost of their own health care, nursing care, prescription drugs, and health insurance in retirement.

What's really interesting about the following chart is that 23% of those surveyed have <u>NO idea how much money they will need in retirement to cover their health care costs</u>. How can they possibly plan correctly for retirement if they have no idea? The answer is they can't.

Savings Needed to Cover the Cost of Health Care by Total Accumulation Needs

	All Workers	<$250k	Worker Total Accumulation Needs		
			$250k–$999,999	$1 mil. + Retirees	Retirees
Less than $50k	12%	23%	9%	7%	31%
$50k–$99,999	20%	27%	22%	12%	19%
$100k–$249,999	20%	22%	27%	21%	14%
$250k–$499,999	11%	6%	17%	12%	2%
$500k–$999,999	8%	4%	9%	16%	1%
$1 million +	5%	2%	2%	19%	1%
No idea	23%	17%	13%	12%	31%

Some of the other interesting numbers from the chart are that workers who make between $100,000-$249,999 think they will need at least $250,000-$999,999 of accumulated wealth just to pay for their health care costs in retirement.

In an early chart, 26% of workers earning more than $75,000 a year indicated that they only need $500,000-$999,999 accumulated to retire comfortably. From the health care chart, some of those same workers said they needed $250,000-$999,999 just to pay for their health expenses in retirement.

Obviously something is amiss with these numbers and the sad truth is that the American public has no idea how much they need to accumulate for retirement or how they will in fact build that retirement nest egg.

I'd like to list a few more charts before we begin discussing how to actually build your wealth in an accelerated manner for retirement planning.

Confidence That <u>Social Security</u> Will Continue to Provide Benefits of at Least Equal Value to Benefits Received by Retirees Today

Year	Very Confident	Somewhat Confident	Not Too Confident	Not at All Confident
2007	7%	24%	34%	34%
2000	7%	21%	39%	33%
1997	5%	17%	36%	39%

Confidence That <u>Medicare</u> Will Continue to Provide Benefits of at Least Equal Value to Benefits Received by Retirees Today

Currently Working	Very Confident	Somewhat Confident	Not Too Confident	Not at All Confident
2007	6%	30%	33%	28%
2002	5%	28%	40%	26%
1997	3%	21%	37%	34%
Retirees				
2007	15%	44%	22%	13%
2002	18%	38%	26%	16%
1997	10%	31%	34%	28%

SUMMARY ON PROPER RETIREMENT PLANNING

Based on the previous pages and multiple charts illustrating what the American worker thinks about and is doing to plan for retirement, it is easy to come to the conclusion that the vast majority of workers in this country are not properly preparing for retirement.

Since 95%+ of the people reading this book are interested in retiring in a quicker and more secure manner, I am basically stating that the vast majority are not properly preparing for retirement.

I'm actually being nice in the above paragraph. To be honest, not only are most Americans not prepared for retirement, but most have no idea how much money they need to accumulate to retire in the manner they'd like and most do no or little planning for retirement.

Is it too obvious to state that, if you don't know how much money you need to retire and you do no or little planning for retirement, the chances are significant you will not be prepared when retirement arrives and that you will have a significant shortfall in income in retirement?

The purpose of this chapter is two fold. First, when I read these statistics, I laughed out loud and knew I had to put them in the book for entertainment value. Second, and the main purpose the chapter is in the book is to help readers start **critically thinking** about their retirement and examine what they are doing now to plan for retirement (and determine if they have planned correctly or need additional help and tools to grow enough wealth for retirement).

Hopefully after reading this chapter I have your attention and now can move on to the various ways you can be proactive to build wealth so you accumulate enough money in retirement to live the lifestyle you desire.

Chapter 5
Understanding Life Insurance

Several places in this book I allude to "cash value" life insurance as an alternative place to reposition cash for wealth building. You've also read in several places in this book that one of the unique aspects of cash value life insurance is the ability to fund the policy with cash where once in the policy it is allowed to **grow without tax** consequences and can be removed "**tax free**" in retirement.

You have also read that I am not a big fan of other books in the marketplace which supposedly teach readers how to manage the equity in their homes.

The posturing of an entire cottage consulting industry around Home Equity Harvesting books with fuzzy math was so troublesome to me that I decided to write this book.

If it sounds like I am leading up to the conclusion that the other books in the marketplace were wrong with their conclusion that funding cash value life insurance to build wealth especially in conjunction with Equity Harvesting is a bad idea, that's not my conclusion.

My point with all the cautionary language in this book is to point out the flaws in the other books so you can **think critically** about these issues. I also want to arm you with the knowledge to make informed decisions about the best ways to grow your wealth for use in retirement.

INTRODUCTION

There are many types of life insurance policies available in the marketplace today. I will cover them in this material and break them down into two categories — the "originals" and the "hybrids." In addition to the types of products, I will also be pointing out pitfalls to policies and tricks insurance agents use to make the purchase of a policy much more advantageous.

Notwithstanding the cautionary language in the previous paragraphs, life insurance can be one of the best and simplest estate and financial planning tools you have at your disposal. What other planning tool do you have at your disposal where in day one you can contribute a monthly premium of $500 and have an immediate payout to a beneficiary of $1,000,000 dollars? What other product can you use in a supplemental retirement plan that is self-completing?

What does self-completing mean? Three things can happen to you after you buy a life insurance policy. You can live, die, or become disabled. A properly structured life plan can provide or complete itself no matter which of the three happens. Either you or your beneficiaries will receive monies from the policy.

In the following pages I will discuss the types of life products available so you will see why the words "Life Insurance" should not be taboo.

THE BASICS

The material to follow goes into detail on the various types of life insurance policies, how they work, and who is a candidate for each type of policy. Before getting into the more detailed information, the basic concept of how a death benefit is paid needs to be dealt with. The following applies to every type of individual life insurance policy.

Proceeds Payable at Insured's Death

One of the unique and beneficial aspects of life insurance is that the death benefit when paid to the beneficiary is generally done so income tax free (IRC Section 101(a)(1)). This favorable tax treatment applies even if the proceeds are paid to the insured's estate or to a corporation or partnership, trust, LLC, or other entity rather than to one or more individuals. The proceeds are income tax free regardless of whether paid in a lump sum or in installments, although any interest earned is taxable.

There are some exceptions to the general rule that life insurance death benefits are paid income tax free. These include life insurance purchased in a corporate setting where the premium is deducted or that purchased by an employee in a qualified retirement plan (not discussed in this book).

While death benefits generally pay income tax free to the beneficiary, they will **not** pass **estate tax** free through the estate to the heirs/beneficiaries (unless the benefit is being passed to a surviving spouse who then will have the estate tax problem).

The classic way to avoid estate taxes on the death benefit of your life insurance policy is to have it owned by an Irrevocable Life Insurance Trust (ILIT). If a policy is properly owned by an ILIT, the death benefit will pass income and estate tax free to the beneficiaries.

If you do not have an estate tax problem when you die (and the death benefit is includable as a counted asset in your estate), then obviously there is no estate tax due on the death benefit.

TYPES OF LIFE INSURANCE POLICIES

The two original types of insurance are term insurance (insurance for a specified period of time) and permanent/whole life insurance (insurance coverage guaranteed for the duration of your life). Both products are used in planning; and depending you're your situation, one may work better than the other.

TERM LIFE INSURANCE

Term life insurance is thought of as a simple product. It obviously has to be if people are purchasing it by droves on the Internet and from television commercials, right? While most clients and non-insurance advisors think of term life as simple, it is not as simple as it seems due to some important factors that many times should not be overlooked.

A simple explanation of term is that you pay a set insurance premium for a certain period of time (the term); if you pass away during that term, the beneficiaries receive the death benefit. If you do not die during the term, there is no refund of premium unless the policy is the new kind of term life called ROP (return of premium) term (which is not discussed in this book due to space issues). With term, you simply paid the cost of insurance during that period and received no financial benefit unless you die (except for the peace of mind). For information on ROP term life, please e-mail info@thewpi.org for a free multi-page summary.

Guaranteed Level Term (GLT)

This is the most commonly used term life insurance today. Guaranteed Level Term has a scheduled (set) **premium** for the complete term, which is set at the beginning of the contract. Generally the terms are 5, 10, 15, 20, or 30 years. Different carriers sometimes do not offer all these options. At the end of the term, you do not receive a return or refund of any premiums paid and are left with no insurance coverage (unless you have a conversion rider which would allow you to convert the term to a "permanent" policy (the price of which will be very high)).

Annually Renewable Term (ART)

Annually Renewable Term is not commonly used anymore despite its extremely low cost. ART is the **least expensive** type of new life insurance policy you can purchase in any given year.

The problem with ART is that the policy renews (re-prices) itself every year. While you do not have to go through underwriting to keep the policy for the period purchased, from an economic standpoint, it is like you are buying a new policy every year. The older you get, the more the policy costs. At some point an ART policy will cross over and cost more each year than a Guaranteed Level Premium policy. The crossover point will vary depending on your age.

For example, let's say you are 30 years old and the cost of 20-year regular Guaranteed Level Term costs $600 for $1,000,000 in death benefit. That means, if you pay $600 dollars a year for 20 years, you will have $1,000,000 in coverage in force for the full 20 years.

If you purchase 20-year ART, the first year's premium would be much lower, let's say $250. That premium would increase each year and eventually would begin to cost more than the GLT. This is the crossover point. After the crossover point, ART will always cost more than GLT.

As a general statement, GLT is always a better option for those who believe they will keep the life policy for the contract term. ART is usually purchased by people who have very little money and need insurance. They also usually hope that in the near future they will have more money so they can buy a GLT policy so they can afford to keep it for the entire term.

What about future coverage if you do not die by the end of the term of the life policy?

You better have the ability to "**convert**" your policy.

The conversion privilege is exactly what it sounds like — a right to convert the life policy into another policy. It is the right of an insured to convert a term policy into a permanent insurance product (Universal Life, Variable Life, or Whole Life) that the same carrier has to offer. The conversion is guaranteed **regardless of health at time of conversion and is the most important element of a term life policy**.

A conversion right is vitally important in case the insured nears the end of the term and then is diagnosed with a disease, such as cancer or other deadly disease, which would preclude the purchase of a new policy.

An insured may convert to a permanent product at the underwriting class of the term product, priced at the client's current age. Conversion privileges differ with each carrier, but, generally, they offer conversion privileges up to year five after contract issue. Some contracts will offer longer periods, but five years is the rule of thumb.

CONCLUSION ON TERM LIFE

Statistics show that over 95% of the term life policies sold do NOT pay a death benefit. What does that mean? It means that 95% of the people who purchased term life insurance will feel like they wasted the premium due to the fact that they didn't die (although they are usually happy they didn't die).

Generally speaking, most people who have wealth or want to or expect to have wealth do have a need for permanent insurance. If that is the case, then buying term life insurance is NOT a good idea.

You will read in this book how to use Equity Harvesting as a financial planning tool to build wealth for retirement. A nice byproduct of Equity Harvesting is that you buy a permanent life insurance policy which if properly funded will stay in place until death. Keep this in mind when weighing the pros and cons of implementing an Equity Harvesting strategy

THINGS YOU NEED TO KNOW BEFORE LEARNING/ DISCUSSING CASH VALUE LIFE INSURANCE POLICIES

A "cash value" policy is a <u>whole life</u>, <u>universal life</u>, or <u>variable life</u> insurance policy. In short, an insured pays a planned premium; and some portion of the premium will go towards the "cash value." The premium allocated to the cash account value of the policy earns interest either at an annually declared rate or a rate that fluctuates due to stock market returns such as those in variable life policies or in indexed universal life policies.

1) **Cash Surrender Value** (CSV)

The CSV of a policy is the amount of cash you would receive if you decided to give up or terminate the life policy. The CSV in the early years of a life policy (typically years 1-10 and sometimes up to year 15) is always less than the cash account value (CAV). **A good rule of thumb is that the CSV will equal the cash account value (CAV) in year 10. ***

*This is the rule of thumb. There are new policies in the marketplace which have high cash value in the early years. I will discuss this type of policy later in the book.

The CSV is lower in the early years to make sure the insurance company stays profitable in case an insured chooses to surrender the policy. The difference between the CSV and cash account value (CAV) comes from the fact that the insurance company has underwriting expenses, has to pay commissions to insurance agents, and has taxes to pay.

2) **Cash Account Value** (CAV)

The CAV in a life policy is the amount of money the company actually allocates to an insured's growth account. The cash account value is always higher than the cash surrender value in the early years of the policy. The insured **does not** have access to the entire cash account value until the "surrender" charges in the policy are gone (which is usually at the end of year 10 in most policies).

The CAV is really what grows inside a non-term life policy. If there are investment returns inside the policy, they are credited to the CAV. Then the insurance company applies its scheduled penalty (surrender charge) to the CAV to calculate the client's CSV. If an insured plans to keep the policy in place for more than 10 years, typically the surrender charge is not an issue.

3) **Policy Withdrawals**

A "withdrawal" of money from a cash value life insurance policy is the partial surrender of the policy. A policy owner will not have taxable income until withdrawals (including previous withdrawals and other tax-free distributions from the policy such as dividends) made from the cash reserves of a "flexible premium" policy (i.e., universal or adjustable life) exceed the policy owner's cost (accumulated premiums). Until the policy owner has recovered his/her aggregate premium cost, he/she will generally be allowed to receive withdrawals tax free under what is known as the "cost-recovery first" rule.

Side note: An insured's income tax liability is accelerated if a cash withdrawal/distribution occurs within 15 years of the policy's issue and the distribution is coupled with a reduction in the policy's contractual death benefits. In other words, a withdrawal within 15 years of policy issuance coupled with a drop in death benefits triggers taxable income.

4) **Modified Endowment Contract (MEC)**

To better understand the following discussion of the MEC rules, consider this question: What is the best investment in the world? The answer is one where money can grow tax free and be taken out tax free.

Assume you are a 45-year old male looking to reposition $100,000 of cash somewhere. You could invest in the stock market or in mutual funds. If you do that, you will have to deal with capital gains taxes, dividend taxes, money management fees and/or mutual fund expenses which will significantly hinder the ability of the money to grow annually.

What about repositioning money into a cash value life insurance policy? What if you could pay a $100,000 life insurance premium, receive a $105,000 death benefit and have $99,000 cash growing in the life policy totally tax free?

What if after ten years the amount of cash in the life policy had grown to $250,000, and you could access that cash income tax free? Would that be a good tool to grow wealth? The answer is absolutely yes, and in the "old days" that's just about what was happening in the insurance industry.

To counteract what was perceived as an abusive use of single-premium, limited-pay, and universal life policies as short-term, tax-sheltered cash accumulation or savings vehicles, Congress passed legislation modifying Code **section 7702**. This Code section provides the tax law definition of a life insurance contract; and the modification created Code section 7702A, which defines a new class of insurance contracts called modified endowment contracts (MECs).

The basic difference between MECs and other life insurance contracts is the Federal income tax treatment of amounts of cash received from the policy during the insured's life.

Certain "distributions under the contract" that are not generally subject to tax when received from other life insurance contracts **are subject to income tax** and, in some cases, a 10-percent penalty when received from policies deemed a MEC.

I am not going to go over the code section chapter and verse on MECs. Instead, I'll explain in layman's terms how the MEC rules affect the use of cash value life insurance to build wealth.

In essence, what the MEC law did was to create what in the industry is called the "**7-pay test**."

What is the 7-pay test?

Based on tables and formulas that I don't profess to understand, in order to avoid having a life insurance policy become a MEC, a specific death benefit MUST be purchased from day one of purchasing a life insurance policy.

The premiums paid, what amount, and in what years drive the amount of death benefit the client is **forced to purchase** in order to avoid being classified as a MEC. The variable in the test is the premiums paid over a 7-year period.

The goal of Congress was to make it more painful to purchase life insurance as a tax-free cash accumulator. To accomplish this goal through the 7-pay test, insureds after the law passed were and are still required to purchase much more death benefit than they want.

If you think about it, insureds do not typically care that much about the death benefit when a cash value policy is used to build wealth. It is a nice benefit for the heirs to have the death benefit; but if we are honest with ourselves, wouldn't we rather have a policy where the death benefit is minimized so the cash growth can be maximized?

If you don't understand what I'm getting at with the 7-pay MEC test, the following illustration should crystallize it.

Assume you could budget $10,000 a year into a cash building policy over a 10-year period. You also have the money to fund it today with a lump sum of $100,000. Knowing that once cash is repositioned into a life insurance policy, it will grow tax free and can be removed tax free, would you rather fund it in a lump sum or over 10 years?

The answer is that you should want to fund it now so the entire $100,000 can start growing in the most tax favorable environment you can find.

The problem you'll have to deal with in this example is the MEC test.

If you funded the policy with $100,000 in year one, to avoid the policy becoming a MEC, you would be **forced** to purchase $2,190,157 in death benefit coverage.

If, however, you pay a premium of $10,000 a year for 10 years, the minimum death benefit you would be **forced** to purchase would only be $561,194.

The expenses for both the actual cost of insurance coverage as well as the other costs inside the policy are much higher with a $2,190,157 death benefit vs. a $561,194 death benefit.

While it is true you would have more money growing tax favorably in the policy if you poured the $100,000 in all at once, the additional cost in the policy due to the higher death benefit would significantly hinder the growth of that cash value.

Therefore, what advisors usually counsel their clients to do when funding the MEC minimum death benefit cash building policy is to fund it over a 5-7 year period (7 being ideal as it is right at the 7-pay window).

If you have already purchased a cash building life insurance policy, one question you'll want to ask the insurance agent who sold it to you is whether the policy was funded at the MEC minimum death benefit. I'm sure it won't surprise you that the higher the death benefit the larger the commission for the insurance agent. I routinely see policies sold to clients for wealth building/cash accumulation and they were NOT MEC minimum policies. The agent only makes a few more dollars in commission with the higher death benefit, but the negative affect of having a higher than needed death benefit can significantly harm the life policy's ability to grow its cash value.

All of the life insurance illustrations in this book are run at the MEC minimum death benefit. Also for your information, others call MEC minimum funded policies as **"over funded"** policies. In other words you are intentionally over funding the life insurance with cash where the policy is not designed for a specific death benefit or a high death benefit.

5) Policy Loans

When an insured is sold a non-MEC cash building life policy, the sale, in large part, usually revolves around "loans" that can be taken from the policy "income-tax free." There are two types of loans available in most cash building policies: 1) wash loans and 2) variable loans.

You will **pay <u>NO income tax</u> if you borrow cash value from your life insurance policy** (this assumes the policy stays in place until death).

This is sometimes confusing for the insured. Often you will hear advisors (including myself) talk about receiving tax-free income from a life insurance policy. That's not technically accurate as you now know. You do not receive "income" from your life insurance policy; instead you access the cash via loans.

Generally, loans are treated as debts, not taxable distributions. This can give you virtually unlimited access to your cash value on a tax-advantaged basis. Also, these loans need **not be repaid** (the loan is repaid at death through a reduction in death benefit).

After a sizable amount of cash value has built up in a policy, it can be borrowed systematically to help supplement your retirement income. In most cases, you will never pay one cent of income tax on the gain.

The main circumstance you will need to guard against is taking too much cash out of your policy through loans. If you do that, you will run the risk of the policy not having enough cash left in it to pay the premiums for you until death.

Typically cash value policies are funded over a specific period of time, 5-7-10-20 years. If the policy is "over funded" at the MEC minimum death benefit, significant cash should grow in your policy. After your premium payment period, there is still an annual cost of insurance that is owed in the life policy. This cost is paid for out of the cash value of the policy.

When an insured borrows cash from a life insurance policy, the policy must stay in place until death (otherwise the insured runs the risk of the loan becoming taxable). Greedy clients or owners who do not budget well can get into a situation where there is not enough cash in the policy in the later years (and after loans) to continue to pay the internal costs of the policy. If the policy does not stay in force until death, the insured will have to pay taxes on the loans received from the policy that exceed the premiums paid.

To guard against the policy lapsing and having a client risk their loans being taxable, newer life insurance policies in the marketplace have added a free policy rider that kicks in when you borrow money over the age of 65. The rider once activated guarantees that your policy will **never lapse**; and, therefore, you will avoid any potential that the policy will lapse due to a lack of cash to pay annual expenses in the policy.

MORE ON LIFE INSURANCE POLICY LOANS

Many companies have created what are called "**wash loans**" to make borrowing from a life insurance policy more saleable. An example is really the best way to explain wash loans. The following is a non-wash loan example:

If an insured has $200,000 worth of cash surrender value (CSV) in a life insurance policy, the insured could call the insurance company and request a "tax-free" loan from the policy. Let's say that loan is $10,000.

The insurance company has to charge interest in the policy on the borrowed money. If loan rate is 8% on the borrowed funds, then the insured's policy is charged 8% interest on the loan and that must be paid every year.

The insured's cash in the policy is still growing but at what rate? If the crediting rate on the cash in the life policy is only 6%, then there will be a shortfall on the interest owed and the cash value in the policy will start to go backwards.

If the cash in the policy goes backwards for too long, the policy could eventually lapse (which could trigger a taxable event on the money previously borrowed from the policy). Also, to avoid a policy from lapsing, a policy holder can make new premium payments (which is something most insureds do not want to be forced to do in retirement when they planned on removing money from the policy tax free via loans).

What if the insured had a wash-loan option in the policy? If the insured had a wash loan, the interest charged on the loan would equal the growth rate on the cash in the policy. With a wash loan, the cash in the policy will not have to be used to pay the interest on the loan. Instead, the returns on the cash value will pay the interest.

If the interest on the loan is 8%, the insurance company will credit 8% on the same amount of cash in the life policy so it is a neutral transaction from the insured's point of view. The life policy was charged 8% on the $10,000 loan, but the life policy also earned 8% on $10,000 in the policy to create the neutral position.

Some of the newer policies have what are called "variable" loans. I will discuss these powerful and much abused loans later in this chapter where I discuss equity indexed life insurance.

CASH VALUE LIFE INSURANCE
-WHOLE LIFE INSURANCE

Whole Life (WL) insurance has almost become the forgotten child in the insurance industry. Many companies do not offer the product any longer due to the ever increasing demand for lower cost Universal Life policies (UL).

WL is a form of cash value life. In the old days, a WL policy was considered the only "guaranteed" death benefit policy. By guaranteed, I mean that, if an insured paid the budgeted premium, the insurance company promised to pay the death benefit.

Explaining how cash values grow in a whole life insurance policy is somewhat difficult. Technically speaking, whole life insurance companies pay "dividends" to policyholders when the insurer's investments perform well. Unlike a dividend you would receive on a stock or mutual fund, a dividend paid on a life insurance policy is essentially a **return of premium** that an insured previously paid. The dividend is based on the profitability of the insurance company. So if the insurance company which issued the WL policy did well with its investments and had a profitable year, the dividend would be high.

Dividends from the insurance company are payable into the policy which can either increase cash values or purchase Paid-Up Additions (additional insurance/death benefit coverage).

Part of the profitability of the company comes from charging clients for the premiums paid. Therefore, when your policy issues a dividend to grow the cash value account of a life insurance policy, it really is returning to you an overpayment on your annual premium.

WL policies generally speaking are the most expensive type of permanent insurance you can buy in the early years of the policy. Without getting too technical, WL polices have a more "levelized" cost structure.

For example, if you are 45 and buy a WL policy with a million dollar death benefit, the actual costs of insurance would be X. When you reach age 55, the actual cost would be let's say X times 3; and when you are 70 years old the costs are X times 10.

In a WL policy, the costs are not the annually renewable term costs (which rise each year) but again are more of an average over your life expectancy. That means in the early years the costs are higher but in the later years (especially when you get over the age of 70), the costs are lower than Universal Life or Variable Life. Because costs are higher in the early years, early cash accumulation is hindered in WL insurance policies.

Whole life is the **most stable** type of cash value life insurance you can purchase (assuming the company you are buying it from is stable).

As I go around the country giving my educational courses to advisors, I always have someone in the audience who is what I call a 'Whole Lifer." I use this term because they grew up selling WL and believe that clients who want to purchase a cash value life insurance policy should ONLY buy WL.

My view on WL is very simple. If you want a stable policy with fairly high minimum guarantees on the growth of the cash in your policy AND you understand that the returns are not going to come anywhere close to equity markets over the long term, then you should look at a WL policy.

With the advent of new universal policies which have lower expense guaranteed death benefit riders, the need to buy a WL policy to guarantee a death benefit no longer exists.

If you were to ask me if I would use a WL policy to build wealth for retirement planning, the answer would be no. Why? Because I think the equity markets will outperform what a WL policy will return. If that is my belief, I should be in the newer indexed universal life policies which have lower expenses and have other favorable features to them which make them much more attractive policies for wealth building.

THE HYBRIDS

The insurance industry, in order to stay on top with current trends, invented new product classes from the 1980's to present day. Since the products essentially combine features from term and whole life insurance, I will call them hybrids

Let's review some of the hybrid products and determine which might be the best fit for certain circumstances. The hybrids are: Fixed Universal Life Insurance, Variable Universal Life Insurance, and Equity Indexed Universal Life Insurance.

FIXED UNIVERSAL LIFE

Developed originally in the early 1980s, Universal Life (UL insurance) combines the low-cost protection of term insurance with a savings component invested in a tax-deferred account, the cash value of which may be available for a loan to the policyholder. Universal life was created to provide more flexibility than whole life by allowing the holder to shift money between the insurance and savings components of the policy.

Additionally, the inner workings of the investment process are openly displayed to the holder, whereas details of whole life investments tend to be obscure and difficult for the policy holder to understand.

The premiums, which may be variable, are divided into insurance and savings. Therefore, the holder can adjust the proportions of the policy based on external conditions. If the savings are earning good returns, they can be invaded to pay the premiums instead of injecting more money into the policy through premiums. If the holder remains insurable, more of the premium can be applied to the insurance to increase the death benefit.

Unlike whole life, the cash value investments grow at a rate which varies monthly. There is usually a minimum rate of return with UL policies, which sometimes can be 3% or more depending on the bond environment, which is locked in upon policy issue date.

Usually, policies issued during long periods of high interest rates will carry a higher guaranteed rate than those issued during or after a protracted period of low interest rates. Changes to interest rates allow the holder to take advantage of rising interest rates. The danger is that falling interest rates may cause premiums to increase or even cause the policy to lapse if interest income in the policy can no longer pay a major portion of the insurance costs (this is not likely to happen in an over-funded, non-MEC policy which has much more cash than is needed to pay the costs of insurance).

For many years, fixed UL products did not have a "guaranteed" death benefit option. Basically, a UL's death benefit stayed in place as long as the premium was paid and the crediting amount on the cash was reasonable. In recent years, UL products have been updated to allow riders that can guarantee a death benefit in a "paid-up" manner similar to the 10 and 20 pay policies of a whole life policy. In fact, some UL policies will allow a client to buy a guaranteed lifetime benefit with a single premium.

Unlike whole life policies, the investment returns of UL policies do not issue "dividends" as a way of crediting cash growth in the life policy. Depending on the company used, the dividends in a whole life policy might be higher than the investment returns in a UL policy and they might not. Both fixed UL and whole life are fairly conservative from an investment return standpoint (although those advisors who like whole life policies believe over the long term a quality whole life policy will out perform a fixed UL policy over the same period of time). Universal life insurance policies are generally restricted to safe, low-yielding investments; and the most common investments are purchased in the bond markets.

One of the major benefits of a fixed UL life policy is the lower cost of insurance. As stated earlier, whole life is more expensive early in the life of the policy (which limits the amount of cash available to grow in early years). On the other hand, if the dividends in a whole life policy grow to the point that there is the same amount of cash in the life policy as there would be in a UL policy when a client is older, the whole life policy should ultimately out perform the UL policy as a cash accumulator due to the fact that a WL policy has lower costs of insurance in the later years.

The question then becomes, should you use a traditional UL policy for wealth building and, more specifically, should you use one when implementing an Equity Harvesting strategy?

My answer is no, I would not use a traditional UL policy for wealth building. If I wanted a stable policy, I would use a good Whole Life policy with a company that has a good track record of dividends that have out performed the bond market returns.

For me, I would not use either a WL or traditional UL for wealth building. Instead, I would use an Equity Indexed Universal policy which I will discuss shortly.

VARIABLE UNIVERSAL LIFE

Variable Universal Life (VUL) is a combination of insurance products and mutual funds. Like its cousin, UL, VUL is very flexible, accumulates cash, and some newer products even offer riders that offer death benefit guarantees.

VUL was popular when the stock market was averaging returns in excess of 10% a year. I like to explain VUL policies by stating that a VUL is like investing money in a mutual fund except the mutual fund is housed inside a tax-free wrapper. Insureds who own VUL policies can avoid annual dividend and capital gains taxes associated with actively managed money in a typical brokerage account.

Honestly, everyone loved VUL policies until the stock market tanked in 2001. One of the major drawbacks with VUL is that there is typically no guarantee on the cash in your policy. Remember, the money is literally invested in mutual funds inside the policy. If those mutual funds lose nearly 50% of their value like many did from 2000-2002, the cash in your policy will decrease by that amount and more.

Why more? Because in a life insurance policy you have additional loads which you do not have in a brokerage account. I call this the double whammy. Not only do you lose money in the market which decreases your cash value in the policy, but with a VUL, the costs of insurance increase every year.

It is important to understand that in a VUL the costs of insurance are similar to annually renewable term (ART) in that they are very low early on when you are younger; but when you get older (especially over the age of 70), the internal costs for the death benefit coverage are very high. This helps grow cash early and have a high cash value early and really hurts the amount you can borrow later in the policy years and sets you up to have a call for more premiums if the policy does not perform well (especially after you borrow from the policy in retirement and if there are negative years in the stock market).

Owning a VUL in an up market is great and in a down market is a disaster.

One of the other major problems with VUL policies is the fact that many agents sell them, make their commission, and then do not annually monitor the investments in the VUL. If the investments in the VUL are not managed like a brokerage account, then the likelihood of long-term financial success decreases significantly. While properly managed VULs may significantly outperform WL or traditional UL, the success is, in good part, dependent on an insurance/security advisor who monitors the policy.

Again, the question becomes, would I recommend using a VUL to build wealth and especially to build wealth when using an Equity Harvesting concept? Absolutely not.

Why? First of all, I am not security licensed and cannot give advice on variable products. If I were security licensed, it would be against the rules set forth by the National Association of Security Dealers (NASD) to recommend that someone borrow money and reposition that money into a variable environment (including VULs).

Additionally, with the advent of Equity Indexed Life Insurance, there is virtually no need to use a VUL policy any longer.

Readers looking to earn 8-10% returns in their life insurance policy with **no investment downside risk** should look at the new Equity Indexed Universal Life policies.

EQUITY INDEXED UNIVERSAL LIFE (EIUL)

As many owners of variable life policies have found out, cash values in a variable policy not only go up with the market but they fall with the market as well (see 2000-2002 returns). This prompted proliferation of a "new" universal life policy, the Equity Indexed Life Policy (EIUL). An EIUL is a UL policy that has an annual minimum return guarantee every year but still allows the cash value in the policy to grow at **market rates** every year if the stock market performs well.

The policies also **LOCK IN THE GAINS** which is very helpful in a volatile equity market.

How are investment returns calculated in an EIUL policy?

The vast majority of EIUL products peg the cash value growth in the policies to the Standard & Poor's 500 stock Index (the best performing stock index). When I first looked at indexed life products, I actually thought the insurance companies took an insured's money, applied X amount to the costs of the policy, and invested the remainder into the S&P 500. I thought that was a bit risky, but I figured insurance companies own half the world so they could afford it if they had a few bad years.

In fact, the insurance companies DO NOT invest premium dollars inside an insured's policy into the S&P 500. After X amount of the premium dollars are allocated to pay the costs in the policy, the remaining amount of money is used to purchase income producing Bonds. The insurance company then takes the income from the Bonds and buys the most favorable "**options**" it can on the S&P 500 index.

Explaining "options" is not easy, but I'll do the best I can without boring you to tears. The best way to explain options is with an example.

Assume we are dealing with $100,000 investment. Assume you allocate $90,000 to an S&P 500 index mutual fund (also known as a spider fund).

Assume you allocate $10,000 to purchase "options" on the S&P 500. With that $10,000 you would be able to buy a "$100,000 option" in the S&P 500 index.

If the S&P 500 is 1,000 when you invested and purchased the "option" and the S&P increased 10% in the first year, what would be your returns?

The $90,000 you invested into an S&P 500 indexed fund would increase by $9,000 to a value of $99,000.

On your "option" you would earn a 10% return on the $100,000 position you purchased. This would return to you your option cost of $10,000, plus $10,000 which is the 10% return on the $100,000 position.

Total assets at the beginning of the following year:

$99,000 + $20,000 = $119,000.

In the real world, when you buy "options," there are costs to the options; and I do not want to get into the exact structure in my discussion in this book. What I will tell you is that, because of the costs and the structure of the options purchased by life insurance companies, the option returns in an EIUL policy are **capped**. By capped, I mean that, if the S&P 500 returns 25% in one year, you will not be earning 25% in your EIUL policy.

Caps on EIUL policies vary per company. Some companies have caps of 16% and some as low at 10%. Usually with the 10% cap products, the company will credit more than what the S&P 500 returns up to the cap.

My favorite EIUL product (**Revolutionary Life**) has the option of receiving a return of 140% of what the S&P 500 returns in any given year (with a cap of 10%). Therefore, if the S&P 500 returns 5%, the life policy would credit 7% growth on the cash value. That's pretty neat and is a policy for readers who think like many that the equity markets are going to be flat over the next 10 years.

It should also be noted that the returns in EIUL policies do not include the dividend income that would normally be paid to an indexed mutual fund.

Don't Forget the Guarantees

Talking about upside growth that is pegged to the best measuring stock index is great. However, what is equally as great is the fact that the policies have guarantees in them so your money does **NOT GO BACKWARDS** when the S&P 500 declines. Every year there is a positive investment return inside the EIUL, the policy locks in the gains.

When you couple the locking/guarantee feature of EIUL policies with the potential to earn returns that closely mirror the S&P 500 stock index, you really have in my opinion the "best" type of life insurance policy to grow cash for retirement planning.

I know the whole life policy advocates take issue with my stance and that's okay. Everyone is entitled to their opinion. We won't know which policy works the best for 10-20-30 years after one is purchased. At this point, all we can do is look at the numbers of past performance and make an informed opinion as to which life insurance policy will work best to grow wealth.

Here's an example to illustrate how switching to the "new" EIUL policy can save a client significant money. I intentionally used 1999 as a starting point to show you how well an EIUL policy works when the market goes negative.

Doctor Smith in January of 1999 had a variable life insurance policy with a $2,000,000 death benefit and a cash value of $250,000. Because he had his cash value invested in an XYZ aggressive growth fund (which we will assume averaged negative eighteen percent (–18%) from 2000-2001), today his cash value in his variable life policy is $168,100. Needless to say, Dr. Smith is not happy.

If Dr. Smith had the "new" EIUL policy, he would have had plus 2% credited towards growth in his policy in down years; and, therefore, his cash value would be $260,100. (The annual guarantees in EIUL policies differ with how they are credited and no example works for every policy. This example is a generic one

I created to give you round numbers which should illustrate the power of an annual guarantee/locking feature).

For those clients using a <u>traditional whole life</u> policy, an example works as well to illustrate how much money could be lost by not using the "new" indexed life insurance policy.

If Dr. Smith bought a whole life policy, the investment return inside the whole life policy could be less than 5% a year (depending on the dividends in the life policy). If he has $250,000 in cash value inside a whole life policy today making 5% in growth every year, he will have $319,070 in five years (these are approximate numbers for illustration purposes). If Dr. Smith used the "new" indexed life insurance policy and the S&P 500 Index had returns of 8%, he would have $367,332 or about $48,262 more in cash value just over that five-year period by using the "new" EIUL policy.

Pros and Cons of the "new" EIUL policy:

<u>Cons</u> –

1) If the stock market averages much more than the cap rates for the time the insured has the EIUL policy, the insured would be better off with a variable policy (not very likely).

2) If the market averages less than 5-6% in annual returns over the time, the insured would be better off with a conservative whole life policy (not very likely).

<u>Pros</u> –

1) There is a minimum guaranteed return every year (1-2% depending on the company)

2) The policy does let the owner partake in the upswings in the market, up to 16% with some companies at the time of this writing (**therefore the policy has better upside potential than a traditional universal life or whole life policy**).

3) Mortality costs (costs of insurance) are much lower in the later years than a variable life insurance policy.

4) Flexibility. Unlike typical whole life policies, the "new" EIUL policy is very flexible so the owner can choose when and how much premium is to be paid each year.

A closer look at the S&P 500

Without specific numbers, it is difficult for many to grasp how well they would have done in an EIUL policy to grow wealth.

I just so happen to have a really neat Excel spreadsheet that has the past returns of the S&P 500 (minus dividends) that will allow me to illustrate for you what kind of returns you would have received on the cash in your EIUL policy had you owned one over the last X amount of years.

I am going to go back and use the returns starting in 1984 and go until 2006. There is no specific reason to use this time frame except that's when the spreadsheet starts and ends.

Before moving forward, I should point out how EIUL polices actually credit the growth. Most of them use an **annual point-to-point** method. That means the money in your cash value life insurance policy is valued when the cash account is started and is valued again 12 months later. If the account was funded on January 1 in your policy, the S&P 500 will be valued on that date. Then 12 months later the account will be valued again; and the gains, if any, are locked in.

Actual Returns of the S&P 500

The initial value of the S&P 500 in 1984 was 166.21.

Sweep Date	End Date	Initial Value	Ending Value	Index Growth
1/21/1984	1/21/1985	166.21	175.23	5.43%
1/21/1985	1/21/1986	175.23	205.79	17.44%
1/21/1986	1/21/1987	205.79	267.84	30.15%
1/21/1987	1/21/1988	267.84	243.14	-9.22%
1/21/1988	1/21/1989	243.14	286.63	17.89%
1/21/1989	1/21/1990	286.63	339.15	18.32%
1/21/1990	1/21/1991	339.15	331.06	-2.39%
1/21/1991	1/21/1992	331.06	412.64	24.64%
1/21/1992	1/21/1993	412.64	435.49	5.54%
1/21/1993	1/21/1994	435.49	474.72	9.01%
1/21/1994	1/21/1995	474.72	464.78	-2.09%
1/21/1995	1/21/1996	464.78	611.83	31.64%
1/21/1996	1/21/1997	611.83	782.72	27.93%
1/21/1997	1/21/1998	782.72	970.81	24.03%
1/21/1998	1/21/1999	970.81	1235.16	27.23%

1/21/1999	1/21/2000	1235.16	1441.36	16.69%
1/21/2000	1/21/2001	1441.36	1342.54	**-6.86%**
1/21/2001	1/21/2002	1342.54	1127.58	**-16.01%**
1/21/2002	1/21/2003	1127.58	887.62	**-21.28%**
1/21/2003	1/21/2004	887.62	1147.62	29.29%
1/21/2004	1/21/2005	1147.62	1167.87	1.76%
1/21/2005	1/21/2006	1167.87	1261.49	8.02%

The question then becomes, what would you have earned in your EIUL policy over this period of time and how would that change based on the caps on the returns in the life policy (also remember the policy returns in negative years is not negative due to the guarantees/locking features in the EIUL policy).

What would have been your returns if the "cap" on the growth in the EIUL policy is set annually at 16%? You would have earned **9.69%** as an average rate of return in the policy over the 22 year period.

What about a cap of 15%? You would have earned **9.3%**.

What about a cap of 14%? You would have earned **8.9%**.

What if the cap on the product is 10% but the policy credited 140% of the S&P 500 returns every year? You would have earned **7.47%** as an average (remember what I said about the 140% product. It's great for clients who think the S&P 500 will be flat over a 10-year period (which was not the case from 1984-2006)).

The power of using EIUL for wealth building

What do you think of the previous numbers? My guess is that most of you will think they are pretty strong. I do.

One good thing about using an EIUL policy is that it protects you from yourself. How? If you'll recall from the chapter on Traditional Wealth Building, from 1984-2001 the average mutual fund returned nearly 10%. The S&P 500 over 12%. **The average mutual fund investor earned only 2.7%**.

The American public is professional in buying high and selling low. When you use any life insurance policy with guarantees, you have put yourself in a position not to go backwards. Those who use EIUL receive the following benefits:

1) Your growth is locked in every year (you do not partake in the downside of the market).

2) Your growth is pegged to the best measuring stock index (S&P 500) which over time has averaged well over 10% a year.

3) Your cash is allowed to grow inside the life insurance policy without capital gains or dividend taxes.

4) Your cash is allowed to grow without mutual fund expenses.

5) Your cash is allowed to grow without money management fees.

6) And, finally, when you have your money growing in an EIUL, you take out of your hands the ability to buy high and sell low and; therefore, you are positioning yourself in the best possible tax-favorable tool to build wealth for the future in a conservative and protective vehicle.

I've built up EIUL insurance policies to look like a terrific place to reposition some of your wealth. Keep in mind that with life insurance it helps to be healthy (or have a spouse who's healthy). Also keep in mind that there are annual loads in the policies for the costs of insurance and other internal expenses of the insurance company. These expenses are difficult to quantify, but I will crystallize the benefits of EIUL with several real world examples which will be compared to other places you could allow your money to grow.

Variable Loan Option in Life Insurance Policies

As I discussed previously in this chapter, after you build wealth/cash in a life insurance policy, the preferred way to remove the cash for use in retirement is through a policy loan (also referred to as tax-free retirement income).

While everyone in the industry thought "wash" loans were revolutionary as a way to allow clients to more conservatively pull larger amounts of cash out of their policies, when the new variable loans feature came out, that really excited those in the insurance industry.

As you'll recall, if you borrow money from the insurance company from your policy, the insurance company will charge you interest on the loan which is due every year. If the policy has a wash loan feature, the crediting rate on the cash in your policy will mirror the interest rate on the money borrowed from the life insurance company; and it's a wash/neutral transaction for the insured.

A variable loan option allows the insured to play the market a little by allowing the cash in their policy to grow with the equity markets and borrower money from the insurance company at whatever the fixed interest rates happen to be at the time of borrowing. If the cash in your policy grows at a higher rate than the lending rate, you actually **make money on the money you borrowed** from your policy.

Let's say the lending rate today in your policy is 6%. Unlike a wash loan where the cash in the policy would be credited with a return of 6%, with a Variable Loan, in any given year, the insured has no idea what the investment return will be in the policy.

If you purchased an EIUL policy, the growth in the policy is pegged to the S&P 500. If S&P 500 returns 10% in a year when there is a loan on the policy with an interest rate of 6%, the insured has a <u>positive arbitrage</u> (meaning the cash in the policy had a 4% positive return on the borrowed funds).

Conversely — if the S&P 500 goes negative (which in most EIUL policies will earn a return of zero-two percent in that particular year), your policy is still charged with a loan where the rate is 6%. What that means is that in the year when the S&P 500 underperforms the interest rate on the loan, the principal cash in the policy will have to be invaded to pay that interest.

Better Potential for Growth

The reason you should consider using a life insurance policy with the option of using a variable loan is because IF borrowing rates and the S&P 500 perform as they have over the last many years, you should actually make money on the money borrowed from your life insurance policy.

How? As stated in the previous example, if the borrowing rate on a loan from your policy is 6% and the life policy which pegs the growth of the S&P 500 earns 10%, you have a 4% positive arbitrage on the cash in your policy.

Historically, the S&P 500 has returned in excess of <u>2% more per year</u> than the borrowing rates used for loans. Will that trend continue? Most likely it will over the long term although as you know: "past performance is no guarantee of future performance."

It's tough to really get a feel for how a positive arbitrage on a loan can benefit you when you start borrowing from your policy. To help crystallize the benefit, I created a life insurance illustration with wash loans and variable loans to show you the difference.

Example:

Assume in my example that the client is male, 45 years old, and in good health. Assume he will fund $10,000 a year into an EIUL policy for each year until he turns 65 and then will borrow "tax free" from his policy from ages 66-85. Assume the average S&P 500 returns over the life of the policy are slightly less than 8%. How much could he remove from his policy with wash loans and how much from a variable loan where the interest rate spread is a positive 2%?

If the policy used wash loans where the interest rate is 4.25% and the crediting rate on the cash at the time of the loan is also 4.25%, the client could borrow **$38,724** "tax free" from the policy every year from ages 66-85.

If the policy credited on average slightly less than 8% a year as a credited amount on the cash value AND the interest rate is 6%, the client could borrow **$57,421** from the same policy from ages 66-85.

I'm not so sure that it is wise to assume there will be a 2% spread on average between what the S&P 500 returns and lending rates at the time loans are accessed from a life policy. I also do not believe that the S&P 500 over time will return less than what lending rates are when an insured borrows from his/her policy.

Typically when I run illustrations like the majority you'll see in this book, I manually changed the interest rate on the loan to equal whatever the assumed crediting rate is. In this example, the assumed crediting rate is slightly less than 8% annually. Therefore, if I used a 7.9% loan interest rate, how much could this same client borrow from his life insurance policy? **$46,561** every year from ages 66-85.

I personally have no idea what the S&P 500 will do or what lending rates will be like in 10-20-30 years. What I simply want to do with my illustrations is come up with something that is not over-the-top aggressive and not pathetically conservative.

I also want to make sure readers understand how life insurance agents can manipulate illustrations to make them look very good based on the best of all worlds. I'll do more of this in an upcoming section when I show you an illustration at what many in the life insurance community think the S&P will return in an indexed life policy.

Further Protection

I alluded to an EIUL policy which credits 140% of what the S&P 500 returns every year. I like this policy when discussing the Variable Loan issue, and I think with an illustration you'll see why.

Assume the interest rate on a loan from a life insurance policy is 6%. In most policies, if the S&P 500 returns say 4.5%, the insured is going to go backwards by 1.5% in the policy due to the fact that the return is less than the interest rate (the client would have been better with a wash loan). If the insured had a policy that credited 140% of what the S&P 500 returns, the insured would have been credited with 6.3% in the policy and would have done slightly better than a wash loan.

Carrying that forward, what if the S&P 500 returned only 3%? The client would be upside down 3% if the interest rate on the loan were 6% in a normal policy but would only be upside down by 1.8% in a policy that credits 140% of what the S&P 500 returns.

My point is simply that the 140% crediting policy <u>allows for more security</u> for the client and better growth for clients who think the S&P 500 is going to be flat for a period of time.

Summary on variable loans

Variable loans are a good option to have in a policy. When buying a policy with a variable loan option, you can choose each year that you borrow from the policy whether to use the variable option or the fixed wash-loan option. The more options the better. Also, if you want to protect yourself when purchasing cash value policies, it is recommended that you consider using an EILI policy that allows you to move your money when in the borrowing phase to the 140% crediting method.

Conclusion on EIUL insurance policies

If you like the possibility of earning upwards of 10-16% return on the cash value in your life insurance policy in any given year, would like to allow your cash to grow tax free and be removed tax free, and would like to avoid the stock market's negative years with a 1-3% minimum guarantee, then you are a candidate to use EIUL for wealth building.

AVOID THE DANGERS OF LIFE INSURANCE WHEN "REAL LIFE" HAPPENS

What you are about to read in this section of the book is not only critical to you from a protection standpoint, but after you read the next few pages, I guarantee you will know more about the problem I will be discussing than 95% of the life insurance agents in their industry.

I created this section of the book because I had a personal experience with an advisor's client I was asked to work with. What I learned nearly got me sued (thanks to the misinformation from the insurance company I was working with at the time); and as I do with <u>The Wealth Preservation Institute</u> certification courses, I always try to translate what I've learned (even if painful) to others so they can avoid the same problems I've encountered.

Let me just ask you a simple question that I know you will not know the answer to. **What happens to the expenses in a life insurance policy when you lower the death benefit?**

Great question, right? What's the answer? It will surprise you.

Expenses in life insurance policies

When I discuss costs in a life insurance policy, I want to discuss the "**costs of insurance**" and the "**per 1000**" charges.

The costs of insurance are based on your age and amount of death benefit coverage. If you purchased a policy with a $2,000,000 death benefit, the insurance costs are based off the costs for $2,000,000 of insurance. If you had to reduce the death benefit to say $1,000,000 of coverage for whatever reasons (like not having the money to pay the premium), the costs allocated to the actual death benefit coverage would be lowered accordingly (which makes sense).

I like to define the "per 1000" charges as the "other" costs that an insurance company charges the client annually in the policy. Other costs are internal administration costs, DAC taxes, and more. These costs are not insignificant.

The dirty little secret

Did you know that most life policies in the marketplace have a quirk which you won't believe and which can have catastrophic consequences when things don't go as planned?

What quirk? When an insured needs to or is forced to reduce the premiums paid into a cash building life insurance policy and, in turn, lowers the death benefit to reduce costs in an attempt to build the most cash in the policy, the insurance companies **DO NOT** lower their per 1000 charges.

It sounds harmless, but it's not.

Let's look at an example and see how this policy "quirk" can hurt or destroy the cash value in a life insurance policy.

I want you to assume you purchased a cash building life insurance policy to grow your wealth. Assume that you budgeted paying into the policy $10,000 a year for ten years. If you purchased an over-funded/minimum non-MEC death benefit policy to minimize your expenses and maximize your cash growth, assume the death benefit purchased is $500,000.

Also assume that in year 3 you lost your job, got divorced, or became disabled. Why do I want you to assume one of these three things happened? Because I want you to assume you can no longer afford to pay your life insurance premium. Since 50% or more of Americans get divorced, I do not think this example is anything but real world.

Finally, assume that, when you can't pay the premium any longer, you call the insurance company and tell them to <u>drop the death benefit</u> down to the lowest possible non-MEC death benefit.

When you reduce the death benefit to the new non-MEC death benefit, you assume that you will pay no further premiums into the policy. By doing so, the policy has a chance to continue for some years to come without lapsing due to lack of premium payments (the premiums will be paid from the cash value which hopefully is growing in the policy).

Is it fair to say that one of the first expenses you'll not want to pay when you have a cash crunch is your life insurance premium?

When you tell your life insurance agent that you have decided not to pay the premiums because of financial problems, what will a typical advisor say to you? Sorry, your policy will explode in the next few years; and the $30,000 in premiums will evaporate?

Probably not. An advisor will probably advise you to lower the death benefit down to the lowest point possible (the new non-MEC minimum death benefit assuming no or little future premiums). The theory being that, if the death benefit is lowered, the expenses will be lowered; and the policy will still build cash and certainly won't lapse.

Right? Wrong.

What's the problem with this thinking? The "costs of insurance" will be lowered when the death benefit is lowered, but the <u>per 1000 charges WILL NOT</u>. If, in the above example, the insured started with a $500,000 death benefit and lowered it down to say a $100,000, the "costs of insurance" would be lowered to the costs for $100,000 of coverage; but the "per 1000" charges will be charged as if the insured still had $500,000 coverage.

The end result will be that in a few years after an insured lowers the death benefit and reduces or stops paying premiums, he/she will likely receive a letter from the insurance company telling him/her that the policy is going to **lapse** unless more premiums are paid.

Why do companies NOT lower the "per 1000" charges?

I've been told by actuaries at several companies that the reasons have to do with the costs incurred by the insurance company in the early years after issuing a policy which must be recouped regardless of whether a client lowers the death benefit or not.

What costs? Little costs like insurance agent commissions (which are usually paid up front) and taxes the insurance company pays which are based on the initial death benefit at issue.

Usually the insurance companies spread these costs over the first 10-15 years; and if an insured lowers the death benefit after that time frame, then the "per 1000" charges will be lowered.

Do all life insurance policies have this problem?

No. When I learned of this "per 1000" charge problem several years ago, I looked high and low for a policy that was more client friendly. There are a few in the marketplace, and one in particular that I prefer is called Revolutionary Life. I'm proud to say that the policy has a rider (with little cost) where you can choose to have the "per 1000" charges lowered in the event the death benefit is lowered in the first 10 years.

Why am I discussing this narrow topic in a general public book?

First and foremost, I wanted to put everyone (advisors and general public readers) on notice of the problem and the fact that there are client-friendly policies in the marketplace you might want to look into.

Also, as you know, I've been discussing what's wrong with the other books in the marketplace when discussing Equity Harvesting. One significant problem with these books that they seem to indicate to readers that cash value life insurance is a "safe" place to reposition cash. If you didn't know any better after reading the other books in the marketplace, you'd think an indexed equity life insurance policy acts more like a tax free money market account with no surrender charges and no insurance costs than a life insurance policy.

For those who are financially stable or have a decent amount of liquid wealth in various accounts, there is not much of a need to have a high cash value life insurance policy with the rider that lowers the "per 1000" charges. Why? Remember there is a slight cost to the riders; and if the rider is not necessary, then you can choose not to use it and build more wealth in your policy.

Let's look at another real world <u>example</u>.

What if you remove $100,000 of equity from your home and reposition it in an indexed equity life insurance policy that does not lower its "per 1000" charges in the event you need to lower the death benefit in the first 10 years?

What if you were sold a policy by someone who read one of the other books in the marketplace on Equity Harvesting which told you that you could access your life insurance policy's cash in a time of need including during the early years of the policy?

If you were unfortunate enough to get such advice by an advisor and needed the cash in your policy the first 1-3-5-7 years, you are in for a shock as to how much cash you'll have access to and how the "per 1000" charges in the policy will significantly hinder the ability of the policy to remain solvent.

This scenario will make you very upset and could potentially be a lawsuit waiting to happen for the life insurance agent.

This situation could be avoided if the insurance advisor simply offered you a policy where the "per 1000" charges will be lowered in the event you are forced to stop paying premiums into the policy for financial or other reasons.

SUMMARY ON THE DANGERS IN LIFE INSURANCE POLICIES

It's important for the general public to be armed with the appropriate knowledge as to how life insurance policies work. Everyone will want to tell you how an over-funded, non-MEC cash building life insurance policy can be a terrific wealth builder due to tax-free growth and tax-fee loans.

When working with advisors, however, you not only want to know the good about products, you want to know the bad or downside and the options to mitigate that risk if you so choose. Unfortunately, there are few advisors who really understand the "per 1000" charge issue and few who are familiar with high cash value policies.

CONCLUSTION ON LIFE INSURANCE

To say that life insurance is a misunderstood tool when it comes to wealth building would be a dramatic understatement. When insureds do not understand how and why a wealth-building tool works, how can they be expected to embrace its use as part of a main tool in their overall financial/retirement plan?

While this one chapter will not make you a life insurance expert, I hope you have learned a few things you didn't know before you read this chapter. I hope now you know the differences between term, whole, universal, variable and indexed universal life insurance.

I hope you understand the tax-free aspects of building wealth in life insurance policies which are designed as over-funded, non-MEC policies.

Since I believe EIUL is the best type of cash building policy, I spent quite a bit of time explaining how the policy works to protect your cash from downturns in the stock market while providing you good upside potential in the equity market (the S&P 500).

If you understand how variable loans work with EIUL, I can guarantee you that you know more about the product than half of the agents selling it.

While many readers think that anyone can get a life insurance license and, therefore, anyone can give good advice about life insurance policies, you now know that there are many variables and nuances to life insurance policies that must be known in order to give the best advice to clients.

Most non-insurance advisors do not try to give advice to clients on the issue of life insurance except to tell the client to purchase a policy with the lowest possible costs with a highly rated carrier. With the information learned in this book, you should be able to have a meaningful discussion with a life insurance agent about the best type of life insurance that is best for you to grow your wealth.

I also suspect that many readers learned that the last life insurance agent they purchased a policy from did not fully disclose the pros and cons of the product or simply did not come to the table with the best product. If you are one of those people, do not hesitate to contact The Wealth Preservation Institute for a referral to a CWPP™, CAPP™ or MMB™ advisor who can help you review your current policy to determine if there is a way fix it or 1035 exchange it to a newer better policy.

Now that you should have a good working knowledge about life insurance, I will move on to discuss how cash value life insurance compares as a wealth building tool to funding stocks, mutual funds after tax in a broker account or building wealth through tax deferred IRAs/401(k) plans and Roth IRAs/401(k) plans.

I think you will find my conclusions and illustrations with real math very interesting, and I guarantee you it will surprise you (I know it did me when I initially ran the numbers).

Chapter 6
Funding Qualified Retirement Plans and/or Post-Tax Brokerage Accounts vs. Cash Value Life Insurance

To date there has been no "authoritative" writing with **real detail** on two questions which are raised over and over in the life insurance and financial planning communities.

<u>Question 1</u>: Is it better for you to fund a qualified retirement plan such as a 401(k) plan or Roth 401(k) plan; or, is it better to take your income home, pay tax on it, and fund cash value life insurance as a retirement vehicle?

In this chapter, I will show you with real-world math using different variables how much you can anticipate receiving after tax in retirement from Roth or traditional 401(k) plans vs. after tax from a cash value life insurance policy.

<u>Question 2</u>: Is it better to fund a post-tax brokerage account to grow your wealth or use cash value life insurance? Again, I will show you with real-world math how much you can anticipate receiving after-tax in retirement from a brokerage account vs. after-tax from a cash value life insurance policy.

In my opinion, other books in the marketplace dealing with Equity Harvesting do not give real-world math that you can verify for yourself. Fuzzy math without details and relying on an author's word for things is not what I would like if I really wanted to learn the best way to protect and grow my wealth. Therefore, I have gone out of my way to give you the needed details so you can determine for yourself which course of action is best for you.

LAYOUT OF THIS CHAPTER

This is not going to be the easiest chapter of a book you've ever read. I usually have a good knack for breaking down complex topics into English for people, and this chapter will challenge that ability. Actually, the subject matter of this chapter is not too bad; but because of the multiple comparisons and charts and graphs, it will probably be a bit confusing for some readers.

The good news is that the details that support the conclusions are in this chapter, but I also have summaries with just the conclusions. Therefore, you can read as much as you want and read it over a few times to get all the details; or you can take the conclusions as they are. I recommend learning the details that support the numbers; but, the bottom line is that I want you to know the outcome of the math, which will be very interesting and eye opening for most readers.

The chapter will be laid out as follows when dealing with a particular client (Mr. Smith) who is looking to build wealth for retirement.

The material:

1) Illustrates how much after-tax retirement income Mr. Smith will have available using a **Roth 401(k) plan**.

2) Illustrates how much after-tax retirement income Mr. Smith will have available using a **traditional/deductible 401(k) plan**.

3) Compares what Mr. Smith has available from a **Roth and traditional 401(k)** plan to what he could receive if he funded a **cash value life insurance policy**.

4) Illustrates how much after-tax retirement income Mr. Smith will have available when funding a typical **after-tax brokerage account**.

5) Compares what Mr. Smith has available from the **post-tax brokerage account** to what he could receive if he funded a **cash value life insurance policy**.

Why Roth plans first?

Because as the numbers indicated in the chapter on Traditional Wealth Building, Roth plans, for the vast majority of clients, are a better way to build wealth than traditional tax-deferred IRAs or 401(k) plans.

The maximum contribution amount to a Roth 401(k) plan as a salary deduction in 2007 is $15,500. For easier math, I will use $15,000 as the annual contribution as the baseline for all the examples in this chapter.

The material to follow will illustrate the economics of a Roth 401(k) plan for a client who is in the 40%, 30%, and 15% income tax brackets, both when contributing to a Roth 401(k) plan, and when removing money from a Roth, income-tax free in retirement.

For the examples in this chapter, assume the client, Mr. Smith, who is age 45, contributes $15,000 to a Roth 401(k) plan each year for 20 years and takes distributions from the plan from ages 66-85.

Because the contribution is <u>non-deductible</u> to the Roth 401(k) plan, he will have to pay the following taxes on his contribution to a Roth. The amount of tax depends on his income tax bracket. As stated, I will show you numbers for each tax bracket so you can look at the one that most closely fits your situation:

- 40% tax bracket = $6,000 tax

- 30% tax bracket = $4,500 tax

- 15% tax bracket = $2,250 tax

The examples in this chapter all assume a fairly conservative <u>7%</u> investment return over the life of plan.

For a comparison example using a traditional 401(k) plan, Mr. Smith will invest an amount of money equal to the taxes he <u>would have saved</u> had a "regular" non-Roth 401(k) plan been implemented (a <u>side account</u>).

In other words, if Mr. Smith funded a traditional tax deductible 401(k) plan, he would NOT have had to pay the additional taxes listed above when funding a non-deductible Roth 401(k) plan.

Therefore, when comparing numbers for Mr. Smith to fund a Roth 401(k) plan, he would have to fund into the side fund $6,000 in the 40% tax bracket, $4,500 in the 30% tax bracket, and $2,250 in the 15% tax bracket.

When most advisors discuss a side fund, they are talking about a typical investment account. When clients actively invest money in the stock market (after-tax), in order to have a "real-world" example, the numbers must reflect <u>capital gains/dividend</u> <u>taxes</u> on the post-tax brokerage account. The following are the assumed annual taxes on the growth in the side account:

- 25% for a client in the 40% tax bracket

- 20% for a client in the 30% tax bracket

- 15% for a client in the 15% tax bracket

Alright, now that you have an understanding of some of the variables (and if you don't, don't' worry, I'll give you the charts which show you the answers), let's see how Mr. Smith does with retirement planning using these various plans.

1) How much can Mr. Smith receive in retirement from his <u>Roth</u> 401(k) plan?

Clients who contribute to a Roth or any 401(k) plan typically use mutual funds as the investing tool. The average annual mutual fund expense is approximately 1.2%. To make this a conservative example, I am only going to assume a .6% annual mutual fund expense for Mr. Smith.

Remember, Mr. Smith is funding <u>$15,000 a year into his</u> <u>Roth 401(k) plan from ages 45-65</u>.

The answer is: Mr. Smith could remove **$56,541** from the Roth 401(k) plan income-tax free every year for 20 years starting at age 66 and withdrawing the money until age 85.

Age	Year	Start of Year Balance	Annual Contrib.	Withdrawal From Roth	Growth 6.40%	Year end Balance
45	1	$0	$15,000	$0	$960	$15,960
50	6	$90,689	$15,000	$0	$6,764	$112,453
60	16	$383,004	$15,000	$0	$25,472	$423,476
65	21	$612,979	$15,000	$0	$40,191	$668,169
66	22	$668,169	$0	$56,541	$39,144	$650,772
70	26	$591,611	$0	$56,541	$34,244	$569,315
75	31	$464,915	$0	$56,541	$26,136	$434,510
80	36	$292,144	$0	$56,541	$15,079	$250,681
85	41	$56,541	$0	$56,541	$0	$0

Again, remember the examples in this chapter all assume a gross rate of return on investments of 7%. The previous chart shows a net investment return annually of 6.4% due to the assumed annual mutual fund expense of .6%.

2) How much can Mr. Smith receive in retirement from his traditional <u>tax-deferred</u> 401(k) plan?

If Mr. Smith instead funded a regular income-tax-deferred 401(k) plan, the following is how much he could receive from ages 66-85 after-tax. Remember that money, when withdrawn from a traditional 401(k) plan, is fully income taxable in the year received.

Mr. Smith could remove annually from ages 66-85 the following, depending on his income tax bracket in retirement:

- **$33,925** in the 40% tax bracket
- **$39,579** in the 30% tax bracket
- **$48,060** in the 15% tax bracket

As I like to do, I'd like you to be able to see how money grows for yourself. However, for the sake of brevity, I'll only include a chart with the actual math for how money grows and is withdrawn from a traditional 401(k) plan for Mr. Smith, assuming he is in the 30% income tax bracket (see below).

Age	Start of Year Balance	Annual Contrib.	Withdrawal 401(k)	Growth 6.40%	Year end Balance	Available After-tax
45	$0	$15,000	$0	$960	$15,960	$0
50	$90,689	$15,000	$0	$6,764	$112,453	$0
60	$383,004	$15,000	$0	$25,472	$423,476	$0
65	$612,979	$15,000	$0	$40,191	$668,169	$0
66	$668,169	$0	$56,541	$39,144	$650,772	**$39,579**
70	$591,611	$0	$56,541	$34,244	$569,315	**$39,579**
75	$464,915	$0	$56,541	$26,136	$434,510	**$39,579**
80	$292,144	$0	$56,541	$15,079	$250,681	**$39,579**
85	$56,541	$0	$56,541	$0	$0	**$39,579**

The $39,579 after-tax withdrawal from the traditional 401(k) plan **must be added** to the **side account** Mr. Smith would have funded with the extra dollars he would have had from funding an income-tax-deductible 401(k) plan (remember, we are comparing a contribution to a non-deductible Roth 401(k) plan). From the side account, Mr. Smith could receive the following amounts <u>after-tax</u> each year from ages 66-85:

- $16,533 in the 40% tax bracket

- $13,206 in the 30% tax bracket

- $7,031 in the 15% tax bracket

Totaling the numbers:

To compare numbers for the various wealth building options for Mr. Smith, you really just need the total amount he can withdraw after-tax from the traditional 401(k) plan and the after-tax side fund. From a regular 401(k) plan **plus** side account, Mr. Smith would receive, after-tax, the following from ages 66-85:

- **$50,458** in the 40% tax bracket

- **$52,785** in the 30% tax bracket

- **$55,091** in the 15% tax bracket

Which one wins?

As you found out in the chapter on Traditional Wealth Building, you should have already guessed prior to looking at the numbers that a Roth would beat out a traditional, tax-deferred 401(k) plan.

Since Mr. Smith would receive **$56,541** from a Roth each year, he would be much better off with a Roth if he were in the 40% bracket, better off if he were in the 30% bracket, and slightly better off if he were in the 15% income tax bracket.

Therefore, if you are currently participating in a traditional 401(k) plan at work, you might copy this section of the book and give it to your employer to help the employer understand the benefits of a Roth 401(k) plan over a traditional plan.

3) 401(k) plan funding vs. life insurance and Roth 401(k) plan funding vs. life insurance

Now that we have some baseline numbers to work with, we can now compare them to repositioning money in a cash value life insurance policy instead of a traditional or Roth 401(k) plan.

When Mr. Smith positions wealth in a life insurance policy, he will do so <u>after-tax</u> just like a Roth 401(k) plan.

Therefore, in this life insurance example, Mr. Smith needs to pay a life insurance premium of $15,000 a year from ages 45-65, and then borrow money "tax-free" from his policy from ages 66-85. For illustration purposes, I will actually assume a little less than a 7% rate of return on the cash in the life insurance policy.

If Mr. Smith did in fact over-fund a low-expenses, non-MEC equity indexed life insurance policy in the amount of $15,000 each year from ages 45-65, how much could Mr. Smith borrow from his life insurance policy income tax-free from ages 66-85?

<u>**$56,568**</u> a year!

Skeptical? How can that be? How can a cash value life insurance policy funded with after-tax dollars possibly outperform a traditional 401(k) plan or the new and better Roth 401(k) plan?

While the vast majority of the people who read this book will not know me personally, I imagine by the tone and way this book is written you can tell that I do not have tolerance for people who do not give full disclosure and for people who use fuzzy math when illustrating such examples.

No one is more of a skeptic than I am. Having said that, skepticism can easily be overcome when you look at the numbers for yourself. That's why I went out of my way to give you real-world math and the actual charts that go with the math.

The following spreadsheet comes right from an insurance company's software. It "is what it is" based on the assumptions (the main one being a 7% rate of return based on the S&P 500 index).

Age	Annual Premium	Cash Account Value	Death Benefit	"Tax-Free" Loans
45	$15,000	$0	$759,503	$0
50	$15,000	$65,289	$759,503	$0
55	$15,000	$169,098	$759,503	$0
60	$15,000	$321,249	$759,503	$0
65	$15,000	$546,163	$759,503	$0
70	$0	$446,393	$565,564	**$56,568**
75	$0	$328,067	$386,284	**$56,568**
80	$0	$191,117	$276,723	**$56,568**
85	$0	$30,145	$155,720	**$56,568**
90	$0	$183,162	$366,332	$0
95	$0	$506,151	$560,025	$0
100	$0	$1,118,146	$1,197,789	$0

Let me summarize the past few pages so I can bring this all together for those who are not quite following me.

Mr. Smith could invest in a Roth 401(k) plan, traditional 401(k) plan, or he could reposition some of his money into a cash building life insurance policy to build his retirement nest egg.

I assumed he could position $15,000 into a Roth 401(k) plan or cash value life insurance after-tax.

To make a comparison to a traditional 401(k) plan, I had Mr. Smith tax-deduct $15,000 into such a plan AND, depending on his income tax bracket, fund money into a side fund so he has the same out-of-pocket costs when funding all the various options.

I then created three charts so you could review the outcome for yourself.

I created one chart for Mr. Smith in the 15% income tax bracket, one chart for the 30% income tax bracket, and one chart for the 40% income tax bracket. Remember that Mr. Smith's tax bracket doesn't matter when taking money out of a Roth 401(k) plan or from a life insurance policy as there are no income taxes due on either, but it does matter when taking money out of a taxable/traditional 401(k) plan.

The following chart summarizes the outcome.

	"After-Tax"
	Retirement income
	Ages 66-85
Regular 401(k) (15% tax bracket)	$55,091
Regular 401(k) (30% tax bracket)	$52,785
Regular 401(k) (40% tax bracket)	$50,458
Roth 401(k)	$56,541
Life Insurance Policy	**$56,568**

I don't know about you, but I find this above chart and supporting math to be fascinating. Who knew that funding a cash value life insurance policy as an after-tax investment could possibly work out better than investing at the same pre-tax rate as a 401(k) plan or even a Roth 401(k) plan?

Also keep in mind that Mr. Smith, in my example, also had a sizable initial death benefit ($759,000), which would pay income-tax free upon death. The death benefit far exceeds the cash values in the 401(k) plans.

Also, keep in mind that Mr. Smith will have to pay a 10% penalty to remove money from his 401(k) plans before the age of 59 ½ (with the exception of the annuitization option which most people will not want to use). There is no such penalty with a life insurance policy loan at any age.

Also, keep in mind that Mr. Smith did not have to worry about the cash in his life insurance policy going backwards in a down market because of the annual locking feature in the life insurance policy (something that cannot be said of money in a traditional or Roth 401(k) plan).

MORE REAL-WORLD MATH

Let's make the numbers a bit more real world. My previous numbers were very conservative and really made a best-case scenario with the expenses in a 401(k) plan.

Now let's assume that Mr. Smith's money in his traditional and regular 401(k) plan have the typical 1.2% mutual fund expense and a .6% money management or "wrap" fee on the plans. How does that affect the numbers?

	"After-Tax" Retirement income Ages 66-85
Regular 401(k) (15% tax bracket)	$43,761
Regular 401(k) (30% tax bracket)	$41,157
Regular 401(k) (40% tax bracket)	$38,676
Roth 401(k)	$44,717
Life Insurance Policy	**$56,568**

What's interesting is that the amount Mr. Smith can remove from his life insurance policy does not change and the amount which can be withdrawn every year from either a Roth or traditional 401(k) plan are reduced quite a bit.

Why? Because I added on typical mutual fund annual expenses and the wrap fee typically associated with a company's 401(k) plan. Such expenses are not a variable in a cash value equity indexed life insurance policy.

I think this set of numbers is the most "real" world, but I did want to give you a few different looks at the numbers based on conservative expenses and typical expenses.

Actually, the previous numbers have nothing to do with the real world. If you remember in the chapter on Traditional Wealth Building, the American public proved that when the average mutual fund returned nearly 10% a year and while the S&P 500 returned in excess of 12% a year, the average investor returned less than 3% annually.

Let me throw one more little real-world twist in the equation. Do you remember me discussing the variable loan option with indexed equity life policies? You can read about it in the chapter on Understanding Life Insurance.

Most "experts" in the industry think that over time there will be a 2% positive spread between what the policies return every year (pegged to the S&P 500) and what the lending rates will be for loans on money borrowed from life insurance policies. If I use just a 1% positive spread on the lending rate vs. the crediting rate in the life policy example, how much more cash could Mr. Smith borrow?

Mr. Smith would be able to borrow **$63,258** instead of **$56,568** from his policy from ages 66-85. Wow!

Just because I know your curiosity is getting the better of you, I figured I would give you the numbers for the 2% spread that "experts" think will happen. If the borrowing rate inside the life policy is 2% less than the assumed crediting rate for Mr. Smith, he could borrow **$70,373** out of his policy from ages 66-75 instead of **$56,568**.

Very interesting isn't it? What's interesting to me is that there are "what if" variables with an equity indexed cash value life insurance policy, which can really increase the amount borrowed. These variables are not available in a 401(k) plan.

Also, do NOT forget that the indexed life insurance policy has an annual locking feature for the gains; and the investment returns can never go negative due to down years in the stock market.

4) Comparing post-tax investing in a brokerage account to funding cash value life insurance

In the previous material, I've shed some light on the real numbers that can be accumulated in a tax-deferred 401(k) plan and an after-tax Roth 401(k) plan. My guess is that most readers, before reading this book, were of the mind set that it is a very good idea to fund as much money as possible into a 401(k) plan or Roth 401(k) plan.

If you are one such person, after reading this book, you will have something to think about as an alternative (funding cash value life insurance after-tax).

If you were/are of the opinion that funding a 401(k) plan is a good or the best way to build wealth in a tax-favorable manner, what are your thoughts about funding an **after-tax brokerage account** to build wealth?

Most people have some sort of brokerage account, whether the account is with a professional money manager or whether they day trade their own money online at places like E-Trade.

Obviously, you have to pay income taxes on your take-home income before you can invest your money in a brokerage account. Then when you invest in the stock market, you have to deal with mutual fund expenses, money management fees, and dividend and capital gains taxes.

In Chapter 3 on Traditional Wealth Building, I discussed, to my own amusement, how money grows in the stock market and how poorly the average investor did over the last 20+ years. If you didn't read that chapter yet, please read it over. I think you'll find it fascinating reading.

Assuming that you've read how money grows in the real world in a brokerage account, let's get back to our Mr. Smith example and see how investing money in the stock market compares to positioning money for growth in a cash value life insurance policy.

Remember that I assumed Mr. Smith could find $15,000 to fund a Roth 401(k) plan or cash value life insurance policy, which are after-tax investments.

On the next page is a condensed chart I created to show you how much money Mr. Smith could remove from his brokerage account from ages 66-85.

Remember he is 45 years old when he started funding his brokerage account and funded it in the amount of $15,000 a year from ages 45-65. You'll also notice that I have different numbers depending on the assumed blended tax rate annually on the investments.

Blended annual tax rate	A	B	C	D	E
15%	$51,793	$46,874	$42,405	$38,346	
20%	$48,367	$44,020	$39,970	$36,442	
25%	$45,159	$41,333	$37,818	$34,592	
Average Investor Returns					$34,592

The following are the variables used for A-E in the above chart, which as you can see, changes the amount of money that can be taken out of Mr. Smith's brokerage account from ages 66-85:

A- NO mutual fund or money management fee

B- A .6% annual mutual fund expense (the industry average is 1.2%)

C-1.2% annual mutual fund expense

D-1.2% annual mutual fund expense AND .6% money management fee

E- NO mutual fund expense or money management fees. E is what the typical mutual fund investor earned with his/her investments invested from 1985-2005 <u>without</u> throwing in mutual fund expenses, money management fees, and taxes.

What should first jump out at you is that the amount of money that can be removed from a post-tax brokerage account in any of the columns is **<u>less</u>** than what could be removed from almost all of the Roth or traditional 401(k) examples.

Therefore, if you are one of the many who believed that funding a Roth or traditional 401(k) plan is a better idea than paying tax on your money and investing post-tax in the stock market, you were right.

What should really jump out at you is that none of the columns have an annual withdrawal amount that are anywhere close to what Mr. Smith could remove from his life insurance policy via tax-free policy loans (**<u>$56,568</u>**) using conservative assumptions.

For many, this material will be counter-intuitive. Why? Because the vast majority of readers do not understand how financially viable an over-funded, low-expense, non-MEC cash-value life insurance policy can be when trying to grow wealth for retirement.

I could spend a lot more time explaining why specifically cash value life insurance outperforms Roth and traditional retirement plans and a post-tax brokerage account, but I believe for this type of book (which is not a technical certification course), simply showing you the charts so you can see it with your own eyes should be sufficient.

QUESTIONS TO PONDER

Question:

If you die before retirement, are you better off with a 401(k) plan, Roth 401(k) plan, or cash value life insurance?

Answer: Cash value life insurance - due to the fact that a large death benefit will be paid out income-tax free to the beneficiary and maybe estate-tax free.

Question: When do you have access to the money in either kind of 401(k) plan or a cash value life insurance policy?

Answer: You have access to the cash in all three; but with the Roth and the regular 401(k) plans, there are negative tax consequences if the money is removed before age 59.5 (although there is an exception for systematic payment paid prior to age 59.5).

With a cash value life insurance policy, you have access to the cash immediately in two usable ways:

1) You can "surrender" the policy for the cash surrender value ("CSV"). This can work okay for readers if you use a high early cash value indexed universal life insurance policy.

2) You can access the cash through tax-free loans. Again, this can work okay if you use a high cash value policy.

For either 1) or 2), if you do not use a high cash value life insurance policy, the amount of cash you'll have access to will be limited in the first 10 years.

Having said that, it works okay if you need access to the cash in your policy in the early years; it is always best to wait at least 10 years to access cash in a life insurance policy. As you read in the chapter where I explained how life insurance works, the surrender charges in most policies will be gone after 10 years; and the ability to remove cash from the policy greatly increases.

Therefore, our Mr. Smith, who is age 45, could feel comfortable borrowing from the policy at age 55 (although waiting until age 65 would be preferable).

WHAT HAPPENS IF YOU ARE NOT HEALTHLY OR HAVE MARGINAL HEALTH?

If you or your spouse (if you have one), are not healthy, using life insurance as a wealth-building tool becomes much more problematic. The costs of insurance annually inside the policy will significantly affect how much cash you will build and be able to borrow from in retirement from the policy.

As I try to do with all parts of this book, I like to put real-world numbers with every discussion.

Let's go back to our Mr. Smith. He was 45 years old and in good health. He funded a life insurance policy with $15,000 in annual premiums from 45-65. Then he could borrow **$56,568** a year from his life insurance policy income-tax free for 20 years (using the conservative assumptions). The assumed annual return was based on the S&P 500 index returning slightly less than 7%.

Let's now assume Mr. Smith has <u>average</u> (which in the insurance industry means below average) <u>health</u>. How will that affect the amount he can borrow from his policy?

He would only be able to borrow out **$52,861** a year for 20 years instead of **$56,586**. That's still quite a bit higher than what he would receive after-tax from his traditional 401(k) plan and much more than funding an after-tax brokerage account in our previous example.

Let's now assume Mr. Smith is in <u>really bad health</u>. How does that affect the amount he can borrow from his life insurance policy?

If Mr. Smith was "table rated" E, he could expect to be able to borrow **$39,141** from his policy each year tax-free from ages 66-85.

The table rating system at many insurance companies uses the alphabet. A is slightly rated, E is much worse, and P is just plain awful.

It is interesting to note that, even if Mr. Smith is table E rated, the amount he can borrow from his policy is still higher than a few of the post-tax brokerage account outcomes.

Getting back to the real world, most people who read this book will be rated standard or better. Those who do not receive the top or close to the top table rating can use a spouse's life to help with the process and can even use a 2nd-to-die policy, which can also help lower the expenses.

WHAT IF A DIFFERENT COMPANY'S LIFE INSURANCE POLICY IS USED FOR THE ILLUSTRATION?

Great question.

For this book, I chose to use illustrations from the life insurance company I prefer to use with my favorite policy at that company (Revolutionary Life). There are many insurance companies that offer cash value life insurance policies.

As I indicated in the chapter in the book where I explained life insurance, my preference is to use equity indexed life insurance products because I believe over the long term they have the best chance for growth.

I also like the protective features which guard against losing money in the policy due to market forces.

If I used a different insurance company's indexed life policy, I could actually increase or decrease the numbers you'll read in this book. That's probably why most readers do not trust most life insurance agents. Life insurance is not the easiest wealth-building tool to understand; and at some point, you have to trust the advisor you are working with to put forth the best life insurance policy that will benefit you.

It means it is very important that readers find an advisor who knows "all" the useful cash-building policies and helps you choose one that is in your best interest, not that of the advisor.

CHAPTER SUMMARY

I know that there are a lot of numbers and assumptions and tax brackets that are dealt with in this chapter. For many, you will have a bit of a headache after reading this chapter; and I certainly understand why.

What you need to take from this chapter is that putting your blinders on and funding a traditional 401(k) plan at work is not always in your best interest. There are other options that you'll want to look at when deciding which way is the best to grow your wealth.

If you are going to fund a 401(k) plan or IRA, you should fund a Roth. The numbers are unmistakably clear.

For those who understand how a low-expense, over-funded, non-MEC life insurance policy works as a retirement vehicle, many will prefer to fund such a policy instead of funding a 401(k) plan. It sounds counter-intuitive, I know; but again, the numbers are what they are.

I think what is fairly clear is that funding a low-cost, over-funded, non-MEC cash value life insurance policy is a better idea for many than simply handing money over to a stockbroker or money manager. The caveat to my previous statement is that the equity indexed life insurance policies are never going to average returns in excess of 10%. I used examples in this book which are fairly conservative (investment returns of 7% (gross)).

If you are able to have your money actively managed and earn in excess of 12% a year (gross), you will be better off after-tax than funding a cash value life policy. The caveat to that is when your money is actively traded in the stock market there are no guarantees; and if your money is in the market in a time span like what happened from 2000-2002, you will wish you never had a dollar actively traded in the stock market.

The bottom line is that there is no "right" answer or one perfect tool when it comes to building wealth. You've heard the saying, "different strokes for different folks." It's that way with how you choose to build your wealth.

For those who don't mind risk, they will not mind their money in the stock market, a 401(k) plan, or an after-tax brokerage account.

For those who are adverse to risk, they will prefer the safety of the *appropriate* cash value life insurance policies, which have minimum guarantees and a low death benefit.

For those readers who want to have their cake and eat it too, they will gravitate specifically to an equity indexed life insurance policy, which has tax-free accumulation, no money management fees, tax-free withdrawals, good growth pegged to the best measuring index, and principal protection from downturns in the market with a lock feature that never lets the money go backwards due to market declines.

Which option should you use to build your wealth? I could not say for certain unless I looked at your individual situation; but hopefully after reading this book, you'll be armed with more information and knowledge to be better prepared to make decisions about which way is the best way to grow your wealth.

Finally, I must say that this chapter, while interesting, is not why I decided to write this book. I decided to write this book so I could shed light on the correct way to grow your wealth using the concept of Equity Harvesting.

Equity Harvesting for most readers will be an additional wealth building tool you can use in addition to a 401(k) or other means by which you decide to grow wealth.

So, let's move onto the very interesting and useful topic of Equity Harvesting.

Chapter 7
Mortgages

While I promised at the end of the last chapter to move on to building wealth through Equity Harvesting, I need to slip in this chapter on mortgages. Why? Because Equity Harvesting revolves around the concept of removing equity from a home, and that will be accomplished through the use of a new mortgage, refinanced mortgage, or home equity loan.

Also, like life insurance, most readers do not fully understand how mortgages work, what their best options are, and which one is best in each particular situation.

Finally, many readers who are good candidates to build wealth through Equity Harvesting are also good candidates for the 1% Cash Flow Arm (CFA) mortgage. The 1% CFA mortgage is a powerful mortgage but one that is very misunderstood by clients who use it and advisors who sell it.

Most readers, at one time or another, have researched the various options for a traditional home mortgage. Isn't it true that most people know the basics about 30-year and 15-year amortization mortgages sold by local banks or mortgage brokers?

Isn't it true that most people have heard of 1-, 3-, and 5-year adjustable rate mortgage (ARM) programs?

Isn't it true that most people have heard of interest-only loans?

While not everyone is familiar with loans that have the interest pegged to the London Inter Bank Offering Rates (LIBOR), many are.

Won't most readers know how to pay off their mortgage in X years instead of 30 years on a 30-year amortization mortgage? Sure—simply make an extra payment each year, and you turn a 30-year mortgage into a 24 year (more or less) mortgage.

If the above is true, why do I need to educate readers on mortgages? Because there is so much more you are not familiar with that you need to be familiar with in order to purchase the correct type of loan to use with your Equity Harvesting plan.

The initial part of this chapter is the ABC's of mortgages. I will state, in a matter-of-fact manner, the basic elements of various loans and loan programs. In the later part of the chapter, I will discuss specifically which loans I believe are best for Equity Harvesting and why.

CONVENTIONAL LOANS

Conventional mortgages are the typical 30- and 15-year amortization mortgages as well as the 1-, 3-, and 5-year adjustable rate mortgages (ARMs).

*Side Note: Unless specifically stated, the material in this chapter explains mortgages in the context of home/residential mortgages (not commercial).

AMORTIZATOIN SCHEDULES

It is absolutely amazing how the American public views amortization schedules when it comes to a home loan.

See if the following sounds like a typical conversation you might have with a mortgage broker.

Advisor: "Jim, I understand you just re-financed your home?"

Jim: "Yes, I did."

Advisor: "What kind of loan did you end up going with?"

Jim: "I went with a 15-year amortization mortgage."

Advisor: "Really? Why? Doesn't that increase your mortgage payments?"

Jim: "Well, the 15-year mortgage had a slightly lower interest rate (6% instead of 6.5%), and I can pay off my house in 15 years instead of 30."

Advisor: "Ok, I guess that makes sense."

Does that make sense to you?

Do you see a protection problem for Jim?

What happens if Jim becomes disabled? What if he was an executive at GM or Ford during a period of downsizing and lost his job? The answer is that Jim would have a significant drop in income (maybe to zero). If this happens to Jim, what would he think about his 15-year amortization loan?

Jim will curse the banker or mortgage broker who suggested a 15-year loan instead of a 30-year loan.

However, Jim really wanted a loan where he could pay off the home in 15 years instead of 30 years; and we all know the odds are that Jim is not going to get laid off or become disabled. What's the big deal?

The big deal is that Jim should have been counseled as follows:

Advisor: "Jim, I want to explain to you how mortgages work. If you obtain a 30-year mortgage and want to pay off your home in 15 years, you simply have to make monthly payments just as if you had a 15-year mortgage."

"For example, Jim, if you have a mortgage of $400,000, the payments for a 30-year amortization would be $2,528 a month if the interest rate was locked at 6.5%".

"If you had a 15-year amortization loan, your monthly payments would be $3,375 a month if the interest rate was locked at 6%."

"Jim, I also want to let you know that there are loans that can be amortized over 40 years. I thought you might want to look at the numbers. If you had a 40-year amortization loan, your monthly payments would be $2,200 a month."

"So Jim, can you confirm that you understand that, if you go with a 30- or even a 40-year amortization schedule, you can still make a $3,375 monthly payment, which will pay off your house in 15 years?"

Jim's response should be a simple, "Yes, I do understand and thank you for helping me purchase a mortgage that also protects me should I run into financial troubles."

TYPES OF MORTGAGES

As stated earlier, most readers know certain types of mortgages typically sold by their local bank or mortgage broker. Most simply, think of 15- and 30-year conventional mortgages. Because this book is supposed to help you understand mortgages so that you can make the best decisions possible when obtaining a loan, I will be somewhat detailed in my explanation of certain mortgages that are best used with an Equity Harvesting plan.

All mortgage plans can be divided into categories in two different ways. First: conventional and government loans. Second: all the various mortgage programs may be classified as fixed-rate loans, adjustable-rate loans, and their combinations.

CONVENTIONAL AND GOVERNMENTAL LOANS

Generally speaking, any mortgage loan other than an FHA or VA loan is a **conventional** loan.

FHA LOANS

The Federal Housing Administration (FHA), which is part of the U.S. Department of Housing and Urban Development (HUD), administers various mortgage loan programs. FHA loans cannot exceed the statutory limit (which varies per state and is capped at $261,609).

The FHA loan program was created to help increase home ownership. The FHA program makes buying a home easier and less expensive than other types of real estate mortgage home loan programs. Some highlights of the FHA loan program are:

Minimal Down Payment and Closing Costs.

a) Down payment less than 3% of Sales Price

b) 100% financing options available*

c) Gift for down payment and closing costs allowed

d) No reserves are required

e) FHA-regulated closing costs

f) Seller can credit up to 6% of sales price towards buyers costs

Easier Credit Qualifying Guidelines such as:

g)   No minimum FICO score or credit score requirements

h)   FHA will allow a home purchase **two** years after a **Bankruptcy**

i)   FHA will allow a home purchase **three** years after a **Foreclosure**

Easier Debt Ratio & Job Requirement Guidelines such as:

j)   Higher Debt Ratio's than other home loan programs

k)   Less than two years on the job is allowed

l)   Self-Employed individuals O.K.

* Except Alaska, Hawaii, Guam, and the Virgin Islands, where the limit is adjusted 150% to $555,147

These advantages of the FHA loan program have made it one of the best options for most first-time home buyers, as well as move-up home buyers.

The greatest disadvantage of FHA home loans is the upfront mortgage insurance premium. On a 30- or 15-year FHA home loan, it is 1.50% of the loan amount and in addition the 0.5% annual renewal premium that a borrower will pay for the life of the loan. In addition, the FHA limits the amount a borrower can borrow.

Generally speaking, if you are a candidate for an FHA loan, you are probably not a good candidate for an Equity Harvesting plan.

VA LOANS

VA loans are guarantied by U.S. Department of Veterans Affairs. The guaranty allows veterans and service persons to obtain home loans with favorable loan terms, usually without a down payment. In addition, it is easier to qualify for a VA loan than a conventional loan. Lenders generally limit the maximum VA loan to $203,000. The U.S. Department of Veterans Affairs does not make loans—it guaranties loans made by lenders. VA determines your eligibility; and, if you are qualified, VA will issue you a certificate of eligibility for applying for a VA loan. VA-guarantied loans are obtained by making application to private lending institutions.

CONFORMING LOANS

Conventional loans may be <u>conforming</u> and <u>non-conforming</u>. Conforming loans have terms and conditions that follow the guidelines set forth by Fannie Mae and Freddie Mac. These two stockholder-owned corporations purchase conforming mortgage loans from mortgage lending institutions, package the mortgages into securities, and sell the securities to investors. By doing so, Fannie Mae and Freddie Mac, like Ginnie Mae, provide a continuous flow of funds for home financing that result in the availability of affordable mortgage credit for Americans.

Fannie Mae and Freddie Mac guidelines establish the maximum loan amount, the borrower's credit and income requirements, the down payment requirements, and the suitability requirements of the properties. Fannie Mae and Freddie Mac announce new loan limits every year.

Conforming loan limits may adjust annually. The conforming loan limits adjustments are based on the October-to-October changes in the mean (average) home price as published by the Federal Housing Finance Board (FHFB).

The current loan limit for a loan to be qualified as a conventional mortgage is $417,000.

JUMBO LOANS

Loans above the maximum loan amount established by Fannie Mae and Freddie Mac are known as "jumbo" loans. Because jumbo loans are bought and sold on a much smaller scale, they often have a <u>slightly higher interest rate</u> than conforming loans; however, the spread between the two varies with the economy.

B/C LOANS

Loans that do not meet the borrower credit requirements of Fannie Mae and Freddie Mac are called "B," "C," or "D" paper loans, whereas "A" paper loans refer to conforming loans. B/C loans are offered to borrowers who may have recently filed for bankruptcy or foreclosure or who may have had late payments on their credit reports. Their purpose is to offer temporary financing to these applicants until they can qualify for conforming "A" financing. The interest rates and programs vary based upon many factors of the borrower's financial situation and credit history.

FIXED-RATE MORTGAGES

With fixed-rate mortgage (FRM) loans, the interest rate and the mortgage monthly payments remain fixed for the period of the loan. Fixed-rate mortgages are available in terms of 30, 25, 20, 15, or 10 years. Generally, the shorter the term of a loan, the lower the interest rate you can obtain. Some lenders will go out 40 years on the amortization, which is important to many clients (and not known to many advisors).

As discussed earlier, the most popular mortgage terms are 30 and 15 years. With the traditional 30-year fixed rate mortgage, your monthly payments are lower than they would be on a shorter term loan. However, if you can afford higher monthly payments, a 15-year, fixed-rate mortgage allows you to repay your loan twice as quickly and save more than half the total interest costs of a 30-year loan. I do not recommend shorter term loans because they make it more difficult to protect your assets in the event of financial hardship.

The payments on fixed-rate, fully amortizing loans are calculated so that, at the end of the term, the mortgage loan is paid in full. During the early part of the amortization period, a large percentage of the monthly payment goes towards paying the interest on the loan. As the loan is paid down over the years, more of the monthly payment is applied towards the principal.

With a bi-weekly mortgage payment plan, you pay half of the monthly mortgage payment every 2 weeks. It allows you to repay a loan much more quickly. For example, a 30-year loan can be paid off within 24.7 years if the loan has a 6% interest rate. This topic is covered in full detail, along with the Home Equity Acceleration Plan (H.E.A.P.), in Chapter 11.

BALLOON LOANS

Balloon Loans are short-term, fixed-rate loans that have fixed monthly payments based usually upon a 30-year fully amortizing schedule and a lump sum payment at the end of its term. Usually, they have terms of 3, 5, or 7 years.

The advantage of this type of loan is that the interest rate on Balloon Loans is generally lower than 30- and 15-year mortgages, resulting in lower monthly payments. The disadvantage is that, at the end of the term, you will have to come up with a lump sum to pay off your lender. Usually, the lump sum comes from a refinancing of the loan or from your own savings.

Balloon Loans with a refinancing option allow borrowers to convert the mortgage at the end of the balloon period to a fixed-rate loan based on the outstanding principal balance if certain conditions are met. If you refinance the loan at maturity, you need **not** be re-qualified; nor does the property need to be re-approved. The interest rate on the new loan will be the current rate at the time of conversion. There may be a minimal processing fee to obtain the new loan. The most popular terms are 5/25 Balloon and 7/23 Balloon.

ADJUSTABLE RATE MORTGAGES (ARMs)

A variable or adjustable loan is a loan whose interest rate, and, accordingly, monthly payments, fluctuate over the period of the loan. With this type of mortgage, periodic adjustments to the interest rate are made based on changes in a defined index. The **index** used for this particular loan is established at the time of application.

Well-known indexes include:

- Constant Maturity Treasury (CMT)
- Treasury Bill (T-Bill)
- 12-Month Treasury Average (MTA)
- 11th District Cost of Funds Index (COFI)
- London Inter Bank Offering Rates (LIBOR)
- Certificates of Deposit (CD) Indexes

- Prime Rate

"MARGIN"

It is vitally important for readers to understand what a margin is and how it is used in ARM loans. The margin is where the lender is typically making its money. The lender will procure funds pegged to an index (like LIBOR). Then, the lender will add to that a "margin," which is really code for "profit margin."

The margin is a fixed amount of percentage points that are added to the index to compute the actual interest rate. The result will then be rounded to the nearest one-eighth of a percent.

An example is really the best way to understand how a margin affects your loan.

Example:

If the index on a loan is 5.3% and the margin is 2.5%, then the new actual interest rate = 5.3% + 2.5% = 7.8%.

The nearest to 0.8% is 0.75% = 6/8%. The result will be 7.75%.

The margin remains fixed for the term of the loan and is not impacted by the financial markets or the movement of interest rates. Lenders use a variety of margins depending on the loan program and adjustment periods.

Most ARMs have **interest rate caps** to protect clients from enormous increases in monthly payments. A lifetime cap limits the interest rate increase over the life of the loan. A periodic or adjustment cap limits how much the interest rate can rise at one time.

Examples:

1. The initial interest rate pegged to an index is 4.5%, the new adjusted rate is 7%, and the margin is 3%. Therefore, the new fully indexed rate is 7% + 3% = 10%. If the lifetime cap is 5%, then the client's actual new interest rate will be limited to 4.5% + 5% = 9.5%.

2. The initial interest rate is 6%, the new adjusted rate is 5%, and the margin is 3%. Therefore, the new fully indexed rate is 5% + 3% = 8%. If the periodic cap is 1%, then the actual new interest rate will be 6% + 1% = 7%.

NEGATIVELY AMORTIZING LOANS

Some types of ARMs offer payment caps rather than interest rate caps, which limit the amount the monthly payment can increase. If a loan has a payment cap but no periodic interest rate cap, then the loan may become negatively amortized.

If the interest rates rise to the point that the monthly mortgage payment does not cover the interest due, any unpaid interest will get added to the loan balance so the loan balance increases. **However, you always have the option to pay the minimum monthly payment or the fully amortized amount due**.

Example:

Your loan has a payment cap of 7.5%. If your payment is $1,000 per month and interest rates rise, your new payment would normally be $1,200/mo (for example) but your capped payment is only $1,075. The other $125 gets added to your loan balance to be paid off over time unless, of course, you decide to pay that additional amount now.

The advantage of negatively amortizing loans is that you can control cash flow (relatively stable payment), take advantage of low interest rates relative to the market at any given time, and pay back the money borrowed today at a depreciated value years from now (because of natural inflation). This makes such loans a great tool for homeowners as long as you understand the mechanics of what's going on.

This is the type of loan I many times recommend for financially stable clients who are interested in Equity Harvesting.

With most ARMs, the interest rate can adjust every six months, once a year, every three years, or every five years. The interest rate on negatively amortized loans can adjust monthly. A loan with an adjustment period of 6 months is called a 6-month

ARM, while one with an adjustment period of 1 year is called a 1-year ARM, and so on.

Most ARMs offer a lower interest rate than the fully indexed rate (index plus margin) during the initial period of the loan. This initial period could last a month, a year, or even longer. These rates are sometimes called teaser rates.

There are also new ARM products that have been introduced that will fix the fully indexed rate for five years while allowing clients to make monthly payments based on a lower start rate (usually a 1% start rate).

All ARMs are available with 30-year terms, and some are available with 15-year terms.

Adjustable Rate Mortgages generally have a lower initial interest rate than fixed rate loans.

INDEXES

There are a number of different indexes you can use when obtaining a loan. I will only discuss a few of the ones that are most commonly used.

Constant Maturity Treasury (CMT) Indexes

These indexes are the weekly or monthly average yields on U.S. Treasury securities adjusted to constant maturities*. Yields on Treasury securities at "constant maturity" are interpolated by the U.S. Treasury from the daily yield curve, which is based on the closing market bid yields on actively traded Treasury securities in the over-the-counter market.

* Constant Maturity Treasuries is a set of "theoretical" securities based on the most recently auctioned "real" securities: 1-, 3-, and 6-month bills; 2-, 3-, 5-, 10-year notes, and also the 'off-the-runs' in the 7- to 20-year maturity range. The Constant Maturity Treasury rates are also known as "Treasury Yield Curve Rates".

The CMT indexes are volatile and move with the market. They reflect the state of the economy and respond quickly to economic changes. These indexes react more slowly than the CD index but more quickly than the COF index and the MTA index.

1-Year Constant Maturity Treasury index (1 Yr CMT)

This is the most widely used index. Roughly half of all ARMs are based on this index. It's used on ARMs with annual rate adjustments. It is also referred to as the 1-Year Treasury Bill (1 Yr T-Bill), the 1-Year Treasury Security (1 Yr T-Sec), or the 1-Year Treasury Spot index.

3-Year Constant Maturity Treasury index (3 Yr CMT)

This index is less popular than the 1-Year CMT. ARMs based on the 3-Year CMT will adjust every three years (3-Yr ARMs).

5-Year Constant Maturity Treasury index (5 Yr CMT)

ARM loans indexed to the 5-Year CMT will adjust once every five years (the ARM's adjustment period is usually the same as the security's constant maturity).

12-Month Treasury Average (MTA)

The Monthly Treasury Average, also known as 12-Month Moving Average Treasury index (MAT) is a relatively new ARM index. This index is the 12-month average of the monthly average yields of U.S. Treasury Security adjusted to a constant maturity of one year. It is calculated by averaging the previous 12 monthly values of the 1-Year CMT. Because this index is an annual average, it is steadier than the 1-Year CMT index. The MTA and CODI indexes generally fluctuate slightly more than the 11th District COFI, although its movements track each other very closely.

London Inter Bank Offering Rates (LIBOR)

London Inter Bank Offering Rate (LIBOR) is an average of the interest rates on dollar-denominated deposits, also known as Eurodollars, traded between banks in London. The Eurodollar market is a major component of the international financial market. London is the center of the Eurodollars market in terms of volume.

The LIBOR is an international index that follows world economic conditions. It allows international investors to match their cost of lending to their cost of funds. The LIBOR compares most closely to the 1-Year CMT index and is more prone to quick and wide fluctuations than the COFI rate is.

There are several different LIBOR rates widely used as ARM indexes: 1-, 3-, 6-Month and the 1-Year LIBOR. The 6-Month LIBOR is the most common.

LIBOR-indexed ARMs offer borrowers aggressive initial rates (lower than many other ARMs) and have proven to be competitive with such popular ARM indexes as the 11th District Cost of Funds Index, the 6-Month Treasury Bill, and the 6-Month Certificate of Deposit. With the LIBOR, ARMs borrowers are generally protected from wide fluctuations in interest rates by periodic and lifetime interest rate caps. LIBOR ARMs usually do not have negative amortization.

Prime Rate

The Prime Rate is the interest rate charged by banks for short-term loans to their most credit-worthy customers whose credit standing is so high that little risk to the lender is involved. Only a small percentage of customers qualify for the prime rate, which tends to be the lowest going interest rate and thus serves as a base for other, higher risk loans.

The Prime Rate is almost always the same among major banks. Adjustments to the Prime Rate are made by banks at the same time; although, the Prime Rate does not adjust on any regular interval. The Prime Rate is not a very volatile index; however, it generally rises quickly but declines very slowly.

Many home-equity loans and lines of credit are tied to the Prime Rate as published in the Wall Street Journal. The Journal number is derived from the rate posted by at least 75 percent of the 30 largest U.S. banks.

The "Cash Flow Arm" Mortgage

There are a number of "option ARM" mortgages in the marketplace.

This section of the chapter is meant to deal with what we call the "Cash Flow" ARM mortgage, also known as the 1% CFA mortgage program.

It should be noted that while the mortgage is sometimes called the "1%" CFA, the 1% number varies per lender and can go up periodically depending on a number of variables in the mortgage marketplace. For purposes of this material, it will be called the 1% CFA mortgage.

1% Cash Flow ARM Mortgage

The 1% CFA mortgage program is designed for borrowers who would like to **minimize their current monthly home mortgage payments** while, at the same time, **reposition the saved money for future retirement savings**.

This program is **not** designed for homeowners who are looking to reduce their monthly mortgage payments with an eye on paying off their home mortgage in the standard time frame of 15-30 years.

This cannot be stressed enough. Advisors are not supposed to use this powerful loan to help clients buy houses they really can't afford because the initial mortgage payments are low. This is a recipe for disaster and will subject advisors to potential lawsuits.

The whole point of the 1% ARM is to minimize current costs, which frees up money for use in building wealth for retirement.

The 1% CFA is typically a five-year <u>ARM</u> where the **payments** of the ARM can (but don't have to) increase at the rate of 7.5% a year (see the following chart for an example).

At the end of the 5th year, you can re-finance the loan back into a 1% ARM (or you can keep the going interest rate on the loan or completely re-finance with any other loan program). Technically speaking, you can re-finance anytime, although some loans have pre-payment penalties during the first three years.

Mechanics of the 1% CFA Mortgage

As stated earlier, the 1% option ARM is a five-year ARM where the **payments** of the ARM can, but do not have to, increase at the rate of 7.5% a year.

The main question everyone asks is whether the loan is really a 1% loan? The answer is that the **payments** a borrower pays over a five-year period are based on a 1% introductory rate.

The ultimate rate charged to the borrower is, however, **linked to a measuring index** such as LIBOR or MTA. In addition to that linked interest rate, there is a "**margin**" charged to the borrower. This creates a situation where there can be a "deferred interest payment" due at the end of the 5th year.

Let's look at an example using the following numbers:

Loan amount = $250,000; Margin = 2.45%; LIBOR Index = 5.25%

"Fully Indexed" is the margin + index, i.e., 7.70%.

1% "Minimum Payment" ARM: A starting minimum payment is calculated by using the loan amount amortized over 30 years at the start rate. This gives the first year minimum payment of $804.10.

This is a "plug in number" used just to determine the starting minimum payment and is not intended to provide amortization.

The "Minimum Payment" for the following year is calculated each year based on the "fully indexed" rate on the anniversary date. However, the payment amount cannot change by more than 7.5% each year. This limitation applies to the payment only and not to the interest rate. In the above example, the second year minimum payment could not be higher than $804.10 (+/-) 7.5% = $864.40 or lower than $743.79

Side note: Like with any mortgage, the borrower can choose each month what payment to make towards the loan. The borrower could make an interest-only payment, which would guarantee that there would be no deferred interest. The borrower could also choose to pay it as if it were a 15-year loan. Obviously, the reason the borrower chose this loan was so money could be repositioned somewhere else; but it is important to know that the borrower can make payments above the minimum.

Additionally, if continued payment of the "minimum payment" results in "deferred interest," as in this case ($1,604.17 - $804.10 = $800.07/mo), the mortgage is "recast" when it hits a "cap" on the loan amount or at the end of the fifth year, whichever happens sooner.

Most of the 1% CFA mortgage programs will have a cap of 110%-125%. For example, if the initial loan is $100,000 and the loan negatively amortizes and reaches a debt level of $110,000-$125,000, the loan will automatically recast itself to pay off in the initial amortization period (30 years for example).

When the loan recasts itself, the payments will be higher than what they would be for a traditional 30-year (assuming the amortization period is 30 years) conventional loan. Why? Because for some amount of time, a payment lower than the 30-year amortization payment was made, and now the payments need to be higher so that the loan will be paid off in that initial 30-year window.

Many readers will be a bit fearful of this type of loan. Believe me, though, when you understand the concept of Equity Harvesting, you will understand why this is the loan of choice for many people who implement such plans.

If you did not have a 1% CFA mortgage, what would you normally have done? You would have a traditional 7%, 30-year mortgage.

You would have very high mortgage payments, thereby not freeing up extra money for wealth building. With a traditional mortgage, you are maximizing what you must pay the bank every month.

Let's assume you had a $250,000 mortgage. How much would the 1% CFA mortgage reduce your out-of-pocket expenses?

Option Arm Cash Flow Analysis	30 Year @ 7.000%	Option Arm @ 1.000%	Option Arm Savings
Year 1	$19,959	$9,649	$10,310
Year 2	$19,959	$10,373	$9,586
Year 3	$19,959	$11,151	$8,808
Year 4	$19,959	$11,987	$7,972
Year 5	$19,959	$12,886	$7,073
5 Year Totals	$99,795	$56,046	$43,749

As stated earlier, if you only make the "minimum" payment each year in a 1% CFA, you would be adding debt to your loan balance (negative amortization).

The following is what the deferred interest would look like if the rates stayed the same throughout the five-year window.

Minimum Monthly Payment	Interest only payment (loan balance x fully indexed rate)	Deferred interest per month	Deferred interest each year
$804.10	$1,604	$800.07	$9,600.81
$864.41	$1,604	$739.76	$8,877.13
$929.24	$1,604	$674.93	$8,099.16
$998.93	$1,604	$605.24	$7,262.85
$1,073.85	$1,604	$530.32	$6,363.81
		$3,350.31	$40,203.76

To calculate the potential deferred interest, you simply take the **minimum payment** ($804.10 in year 1 in the example) and subtract that from the **interest only** payment ($1,604 (a rounded number) in year 1, which is calculated by taking the fully indexed rate (which is 7.7% in our example) and multiplying it by the loan balance)).

As you can see by the above numbers, there was deferred interest all five years. It is interesting to note that the deferred interest decreases every year. That's because the minimum payment increased every year and, in turn, reduces the amount of deferred interest each subsequent year.

The average reader will look at the above chart and wonder why in the world anyone would use such a loan. The client with the above loan is doing just the opposite of what the American public has been told by their ancestors for years, which is that the American dream is to own your own home free and clear of debt.

While there is nothing wrong per se with paying down debt on your home (and if you want to learn how to do so years quicker, turn to Chapter 11 where you can read about the Home Equity Acceleration Plan), the majority of this book is about building wealth using the equity in your home rather than paying off debt.

What you will learn from this book is that you can build more wealth by never paying off the debt on your home and using the money you would have used to pay down that debt to grow more wealth in a tax-favorable manner in other vehicles.

With a 1% ARM, the client frees up significant money to reposition NOW. That's what Equity Harvesting is all about: maximizing dollars now to build wealth in the most tax-favorable and efficient manner possible. That cannot be accomplished by allocating dollars to pay down debt on a personal residence.

You may believe this is complicated, and it kind of is. What is sort of comical and pathetic at the same time is that many of the mortgage brokers selling the 1% CFA mortgage don't really understand it. If you go over the explanation of how the 1% CFA mortgage works in this book, you'll understand how it works as well or better than the majority of mortgage professionals out there.

Floating interest rate

The 1% CFA mortgage is typically set up with a floating interest rate. The "margin" stays the same, but the index (usually LIBOR or MTA) typically floats. This is vitally important to understand when determining if this loan is best for your situation. On a typical 1% CFA mortgage, the index is fixed for 12 months; and then it simply floats up or down based on market forces.

For example, if you obtained the 1% CFA mortgage where LIBOR is 5%, that rate is locked for 12 months. If in month 13, LIBOR is 5.5%, your "fully indexed" rate will increase by .5%. A floating index will not affect your minimum payments but can increase or decrease the amount of deferred interest you will have at the end of the term.

As of the time this book is being published, there is a newer 1% CFA mortgage on the market that will fix the index for the entire five-year period. If you are of the opinion that lending rates are going to stay at the same rate or move higher, you will want to opt for this five-year fixed version.

If you are of the opinion that interest rates will start to slide lower, then having a 1% CFA that floats monthly will be the one you want.

Real World Planning with the 1% CFA

In the real world, when you use this loan, you traditionally will refinance back into the 1% CFA every 3-5 years. This keeps your payments to a minimum and allows the maximum amount of money to be used to grow wealth in more tax-efficient and profitable vehicles.

While you could use the money saved and/or repositioned money to pay the deferred interest, most clients, when they refinance, will refinance the deferred interest (if any) into the new 1% ARM. This allows the repositioned money to grow and to be used for retirement when the time comes.

Remember that your home should be appreciating at a minimum of 3.5% a year (in most parts of the country), and in many parts of the country, it is actually growing at 10%+ a year. The national average for home appreciation is above 5% annually. So while your home debt could increase when refinancing the home and using the 1% CFA, the increase in home equity should more than offset this debt.

If you live in a part of the country where property is decreasing in value, that needs to be taken into consideration when deciding if the 1% CFA is the proper loan for you.

Interest-only loans

When you hear others talk about Equity Harvesting or read about it in other books, you'll mainly hear why you should have an interest-only loan, with their theory being somewhat similar to that of the 1% CFA in that you are trying to have lower monthly payments, NOT pay down the debt on your home. You are trying to have the maximum amount of cash on hand every month to reposition into a tax-favorable, wealth-building vehicle.

I wish there was something exciting I could tell you about an interest-only loan. There really isn't.

The mechanics of the loan are fairly simple. When obtaining the loan, you will pick an amortization period of 15-30 years. Most clients will opt for 30 years. Then, the way the loan is structured, you will have an interest only period, after which the loan payments will be recalculated to pay off the loan in the fully amortized period.

The typical maximum period you can lock in the interest-only payment is 10 years. Therefore, if you had a 30-year amortized loan with a 10-year, interest-only period, in year 11, the payments would dramatically increase so that the entire loan is paid off in the remaining 20 years.

If you would like to continue with an interest-only payment, you will simply go refinance the loan elsewhere anytime before the end of the 10th year or negotiate with your current lender at the end of the 10th year to refinance the loan using a new 30-year amortization period with the first 10 years being interest only.

The interest rate on the loan is fixed for the entire life of the loan, which is different than what you are able to obtain with a 1% CFA, which presently will only fix the interest rate for five years as a maximum.

It is also important to remember that the interest-only lending rate will be slightly higher than the same loan for a traditional 30-year conventional.

Just to give you a peek at why someone would use an interest-only loan, let's look at a **quick example**.

Say you were going to buy a new home worth $400,000 where you were going to put down 20%. That would leave you with a home mortgage of $320,000. If you went with a 30-year conventional at 6.75%, your monthly payments would be $2,075.50 a month (without taxes and insurance).

If you went with an interest-only loan, the interest rate will probably be about a quarter-point higher. Therefore, the interest rate would be 7% and your interest-only payment would be $1,867 a month.

Therefore, with an interest-only loan, you would be saving $208.50 a month or $2,502 a year. If you wanted to build wealth through Equity Harvesting, you would reposition that $208.50 a month into a low-expense, over-funded, non-MEC cash value life insurance policy.

It is my belief that those pitching Equity Harvesting around the country counsel clients to use interest-only loans for a few reasons:

1) Most are not aware of the 1% CFA mortgage.

2) Those who are aware of the 1% CFA mortgage do not understand it.

3) Most advisors want easy and quick closes, and it's much easier to explain an interest-only loan than the 1% CFA mortgage

4) Most clients, frankly, will not understand and/or will be fearful of the 1% CFA; and, so again, advisors looking for quick closes on sales will not want to muddy the waters, so they typically pitch interest-only loans.

I prefer the 1% CFA mortgage for many clients because, if the goal is to have the maximum amount of money on hand on a monthly basis to build wealth, the 1% CFA is the best way to accomplish this goal.

For those who care what type of mortgage I have (and I get the question all the time), I have the 1% CFA, which has the interest rate locked for the first five years.

LITTLE SECRET

I really do not have much more to add that I think you need to know when it comes to understanding mortgages.

I did, however, want to talk about how mortgages are used in the life insurance industry.

The subtitle above is "Little Secret." It's not so much that what I'm going to tell you is a secret; it's just that I want you to be aware of certain sales pitches when it comes to selling life insurance. Also, because I call it a secret doesn't mean there is something wrong with it.

You should know that life insurance agents believe that it is difficult to motivate clients to buy what the agent thinks is in their best interest, e.g., cash value life insurance.

Most readers of this book have probably seen the movie Groundhog's Day. If you have seen it, you'll remember Bill Murray reliving Groundhog's Day over and over in what seems to be an endless loop.

Each day, when he wakes and relives Groundhog's Day, he runs into the same people. One person in particular I found funny. Everyday, Bill Murray would run into an old classmate who is now a life insurance salesman.

Everyday, Bill would run into the same friend, and every day, the friend would try to sell him life insurance. Of course, the friend was what you would consider a pushy and obnoxious life insurance salesman.

I tell this story because, in general, clients do not like life insurance. They don't usually like life insurance salespeople because they are tired of always being hit on to buy life insurance.

As I explained in the chapter of the book on understanding life insurance and in the chapter of the book where I compared building wealth in 401(k) plans, brokerage accounts, and cash value life insurance policies, cash value life insurance can be a terrific and, many times, the best way to build a tax-favorable retirement nest egg.

For the most part, life insurance is very misunderstood and was one of the reasons I wrote this book (to explain how cash value life insurance works and how it can benefit readers).

What about the "little secret?" The little secret has to do with how some life insurance agents will "**find**" money to reposition into cash value life insurance.

The sales pitch is somewhat powerful.

186

What if I could come to you and "find" $2,500 a year you to position into a vehicle for wealth building so you would NOT have to alter your current spending habits?

Sounds interesting, and it certainly should play well to the instant gratification society we live in where we seem to need every available dollar all the time so that we can buy what we want when we want it.

How can an insurance advisor "find" money so that you can use that found money to pay a premium into a cash value life insurance? I'm sure you already know the answer. The answer is by taking your 15- or 30-year conventional mortgage and refinancing that mortgage into an interest-only loan.

From my previous example, I found, for the client with a $320,000 mortgage, $208.50 a month by changing the client from a 30-year conventional mortgage to an interest-only loan. Assuming the client has the discipline to reposition that money into a cash value life insurance policy, he/she will fund the policy with nearly $2,500 a year. Doing so will help the client build wealth quicker and certainly in a better manner than doing nothing and slowly paying down the debt on a home, which will appreciate regardless of whether there is debt on it.

BANKS VS. BROKERS

I did want to briefly touch on the different types of professionals you can obtain mortgages from. Depending on who you go to, you'll potentially be offered different programs.

Generally speaking, there are mortgage brokers, mortgage bankers, and banks.

Mortgage brokers help clients by finding lending institutions that will allow them to broker out their funds/programs to clients. The mortgage is closed in the name of the lender, not the broker. Broker are sort of free agents, who can work with a few lending institutions to upwards of several hundred.

Mortgage bankers (as used in the individual vs. corporate sense) use their own funds (typically through a line of credit from a warehouse lender) to fund mortgages. Mortgage bankers usually turn around and sell their mortgages to investors and do not retain the risk and debt as their own.

Many times a mortgage banker sells clients the same kinds of loans as a mortgage broker but is able to close the loans quicker because he/she does not have to get permission from a lender to close the loan. This is a riskier way to sell mortgages, but it is also a way to make more money and sometimes provide better service.

Banks are also thought of as mortgage bankers; but when I use the term, I'm talking about the bricks and mortar bank on the corner in your hometown. Whether large or small, banks in your community can sometimes offer better loans than a mortgage broker or banker can offer you and sometimes not.

Many local banks will not offer the 1% CFA mortgage, which is disappointing for clients who want to use it.

On the other hand, if the client is seen as an important client, many banks can choose to take the loan "in house" and not posture the loan to be sold on the open market. When doing so, the terms of the loan can be better than what a mortgage banker or broker can offer a client.

The bottom line with whom you will use to obtain your next mortgage is that the most important thing is to work with an advisor who knows all the various types of loans and will work to provide you with the loan that is in your best interest and not in the best interest of the broker or bank.

SUMMARY ON MORTGAGES

While mortgages, in general, are not a difficult topic, when dealing with Home Equity Management and Equity Harvesting, you have to have a working knowledge of your mortgage options.

Knowledge is power; and even more important, by having a working knowledge of mortgages, you will not have to blindly take advice from advisors who may or may not have your best interest at heart.

When I later explain various Equity Harvesting strategies, I will show you in more detail how an interest-only and 1% CFA mortgage affects your ability to grow wealth.

FUNDAMENTALLY EQUITY HARVESTING IS SIMPLE

There is nothing overly complicated about Equity Harvesting.

Explaining Equity Harvesting is very simple and does not need to be dragged out with 200 pages of marketing content. In this book, I'll get to the point fairly quickly and will use the space in this chapter to give you "real world math" and examples so you can see for yourself how beneficial Equity Harvesting can be when trying to build the maximum amount of wealth for retirement.

To implement an Equity Harvesting plan to build your wealth is to 1) borrow equity from your home and 2) reposition that money into a low-expense, over-funded, cash-building, non-MEC life insurance policy.

The cash in the life insurance policy grows without tax and can be removed tax free in retirement.

That's it. Wasn't that simple?

If that was really all you needed to do, this book would only be a few pages long. As you've noticed so far, I have not spent much time discussing Equity Harvesting. So far, I've spent pages explaining:

-the deductibility of home equity debt and home acquisition debt.

-how cash value life insurance works to grow wealth in a tax-favorable manner;

-tips so you could avoid getting scammed by a life agent or mortgage broker who is looking out for his/her interest instead of yours.

-I've spent pages discussing the real math when comparing using cash value life insurance to build wealth vs. using a qualified retirement plan or IRA or a post-tax brokerage account.

As I continue with this chapter, I will try hard not to "sell" you on the concept of Equity Harvesting; but instead I will give you the real math and give you my opinion as to whom is a candidate for Equity Harvesting and why Equity Harvesting is

NOT for everyone (not withstanding what any salesperson will tell you or book will tell you).

WHO IS A GOOD CANDIDATE FOR EQUITY HARVESTING?

First, in order to be a candidate for Equity Harvesting you need to have equity in your home. Obviously, the more equity you have in your home, the more you can take advantage of the concept.

Second, it helps if you have decent credit. Why? Because most readers will implement an equity harvesting plan by removing equity from their current house and that will require a new loan. In order to obtain that new mortgage, you will have to have adequate credit.

Third, you or your spouse need to be healthy. Why? Because when you implement Equity Harvesting correctly you will reposition the borrowed funds into a cash value life insurance policy. If you are not healthy, buying cash value life insurance to build wealth will be cost prohibitive.

The above three requirements are really the main ones you'll absolutely have to have in order to use Equity Harvesting to build your wealth in a tax favorable manner.

Most salespeople who pitch clients the concept of Equity Harvesting will only qualify you with the above three requirements. Why? Because the more requirements you add, the fewer clients you'll qualify and sell.

My goal is not to have everyone read this book, think it's terrific, and then go out and borrow equity from their homes to build wealth. My goal is to be as honest with readers as possible, and I can't be honest unless I caution certain readers **NOT to implement** an Equity Harvesting plan.

Therefore, before you run out and implement an Equity Harvesting plan, think about the following qualifying questions.

1) Do you have a stable income?

2) Do you have a stable marriage?

3) Do you have other wealth besides the equity in your home?

4) Are you in a profession where disability is possibility?

5) Are you over the age of 60?

It's important for you to make sure you are a candidate for Equity Harvesting before jumping in with two feet to build wealth through such a plan. Notwithstanding the fact that pure marketers of this topic will tell you there is "no risk" and that you are an ignorant fool for not using this powerful tool to build your wealth, Equity Harvesting is NOT for everyone.

1) Do you have a stable income?

Why does this matter? Let's just look at an example.

Say you make $75,000 a year (gross), have a $300,000 house with $100,000 of equity. If you remove only $50,000 of equity to reposition into a life insurance with an interest-only loan at 7.5%, you'll have an additional interest payment of $3,750 a year (which equates to 5% of your annual pre-tax income).

Allocating 5% of your annual income to a wealth-building tool is not a decision you'll make lightly.

Assume you are like many people in that you are married (stay-at-home spouse), have two children, two cars and car payments, etc...my point is that your take-home income is allocated to a lot of different places; and while you can find an extra $3,750 a year to pay the interest on your new $50,000 of home equity debt, there is not a lot of wiggle room.

Now let's say you implement an Equity Harvesting plan and reposition $50,000 into a cash building life insurance policy— except in year five of the plan you lose your job.

Now what do you do? The pure marketers of Equity Harvesting will tell you it's no problem; it's a good thing that you funded a cash building life policy because you have control of and access to your money instead of having it locked up in a house.

However, as you know, unless you were one of the lucky few who used an advisor who sold you a high cash value life insurance policy, you don't have anywhere near $50,000 of cash surrender value in your policy and borrowing from the policy "tax free" is not really a viable option due to the early surrender charges of the policy.

Again, what do you do? The first thing you're going to want to do is NOT pay the interest on the additional $50,000 of debt you took out on your home so you could build wealth through Equity Harvesting.

You're probably going to be living on credit cards for awhile as well until such time as you can find a new job. That could happen soon or not.

Do you see where I'm going with this example? Yes, Equity Harvesting as you'll see can be a great tool to build wealth in a tax-favorable manner. However, it is not without risk no matter what salespeople tell you.

You have to commit to an Equity Harvesting plan. If you want wiggle room when something goes wrong in your life financially, you should use a high cash value life insurance policy. This will significantly mitigate your risks and increase the amount of cash you have in the policy that you'll need to surrender early to pay bills.

2) Do you have a stable marriage?

Over 50% of American marriages end in divorce. If that is the case, then the stability of your marriage needs to be taken into consideration when looking at implementing an Equity Harvesting plan.

Imagine that you borrow more debt, fund a cash value life policy to build tax-favorable wealth, and then get divorced 3, 5, 7 years later. How's that going to affect your plan? It's going to destroy it. Why? Because one spouse will move out of the house (which now has more debt on it because of the Equity Harvesting plan) and into a rental.

This immediately increases your family expenses; and, therefore, if implementing an Equity Harvesting plan used up your "extra" funds each year to pay the interest expense, you are in big trouble.

You will either not have the money to pay the interest or will not have the money to pay the rent on your new temporary rental (which also has utility, cable, Internet and other expenses).

Oh yea, both spouses will spend $5,000-$10,000 each on divorce attorneys and more if there is a custody battle over the children.

Once the divorce is final or even before, the current marital residence with the new Equity Harvesting debt will be sold and whatever's left will be divided.

You'll most likely surrender the life insurance policy for whatever the cash is while you are going through this process (even though that amount will be less than the loan balance if you do so in the first five-seven years of funding the policy). If you don't surrender the policy, one of the battles you'll pay attorneys to deal with is who should get the Equity Harvesting life insurance policy in the divorce?

As you know from reading this book, I try to live in the real world; and in the real world 50% of Americans will get divorced. If you have had problems in your marriage or are having them now, while Equity Harvesting is a great way to build wealth, I'd rather see you err on the side of caution and wait until you are confident the marriage will last for awhile before implementing an Equity Harvesting plan.

3) Do you have other wealth besides the equity in your home?

As a general statement, the more "other" wealth you have, the better candidate you are to use Equity Harvesting. Does that mean Equity Harvesting is one of those rich-get-richer topics? Sort of. Someone with moderate wealth and/or income and equity in a home can implement an Equity Harvesting wealth building plan, but those who already have some wealth or have a higher income have more wiggle room should something go wrong in their lives.

In 1) and 2) that I just previously discussed, what if the family had $100,000 in stocks, bonds, CDs, or a money market account? Would that help the family deal with the loss of a job or a divorce? Would that give them more wiggle room so they wouldn't have to cash in a life insurance policy that has surrender charges?

Would that allow them to get back on their feet and potentially keep the Equity Harvesting policy as a long-term financial tool? (Or in the divorced couple situation, one of the spouses will end up with the life policy that should stay in force and have available cash which can be used in retirement).

The more money you have and the more money you make, the more you are a candidate for Equity Harvesting. Beside the "what could go wrong" issues just discussed, as you read in the chapter on funding cash value life insurance vs. a qualified retirement plan or IRA, using a tax favorable life insurance policy works better the higher your personal income taxes are now and will be when you retire.

4) Are you in a profession where disability is possibility?

Similar to the discussion about losing your job, if you implement an Equity Harvesting plan and then become disabled and can't work in the early years after implementing such a plan, you will probably wish you never heard the term Equity Harvesting.

When marketers of plans try to sell you this concept, it is not in their best interest to talk about what could go wrong. Most peddlers of this topic simply want to show you a life insurance policy illustration where the cash grows tax free at a high rate and comes out in retirement tax free. If nothing ever goes wrong in your life and the policy returns are good, you'll look back and think the best thing you ever did financially is implement an Equity Harvesting plan.

Unfortunately, people do become disabled and depending on when you become disabled will determine how fondly you think of your Equity Harvesting plan.

As a general rule, if you can fund your life policy and have nothing go wrong in you life for ten years, the plan will work out very well even if you need the money from the policy before retirement.

If you use a high cash value policy, you can move the number down from ten years to less than five years.

My point being that you just need to look at your personal situation and think about real life when deciding to implement an Equity Harvesting plan. When some readers do that, some who otherwise would implement a plan after talking to a good salesperson, will not.

5) Are you over the age of 60?

As I've stated a few times in this book, Equity Harvesting is not a cure all to solve all of your problems when it comes to retirement income. Even though pure marketers of this plan say that it works for nearly everyone, I will tell you that it is difficult to make the numbers work if you are over the age of 60; very difficult to make the numbers work if your are over the age of 65, and nearly impossible for the numbers to work if you are over the age of 70.

Remember, with Equity Harvesting, you are funding a cash value life insurance policy. The insurance companies charge for the death benefit and the closer you get to death (meaning the older you are), the more expensive the policy becomes.

I know I talk about how the newer policies when structured with a MEC minimum death benefit have very low expenses. That's true, but there comes a point in time when your age makes life insurance a price prohibitive wealth building tool.

If you are over the age of 60, just be very careful when a salesperson shows you illustrations for how wonderful Equity Harvesting can work as a retirement tool. As you should have surmised by reading the chapter on life insurance, illustrations can be manipulated many different ways to make them look better or worse.

I know I could make an illustration look great for a 60-year old by manipulating the insurance company software; but in doing so, I know that the policy probably would never perform as I've manipulated it.

Have I talked you out of using Equity Harvesting before I've even really giving you the math that will show you how it can work as a very nice conservative way to build your wealth? I hope not, but like most things in life there are good and bad aspects of Equity Harvesting; and I want you to know both before deciding to move forward to implement a plan.

EQUITY HARVESTING

Simply put, Equity Harvesting for many readers will be the single best way for you to build your wealth for retirement.

Wow, that's a bold statement and one which needs to be quantified.

What do I mean by the "best" way to build wealth for retirement? When I say best, I mean that the concept has the following characteristics.

-Implementing a plan will have **little or no effect on how you currently live your lifestyle** (meaning after you implement an Equity Harvesting plan, you do not have to forego eating out for dinner, buying gifts for loved ones, or taking vacations).

-**The plan's "risk" factor is very low**. If you reposition money into the "right" cash value life insurance policy, the risk of you being hurt financially with an Equity Harvesting plan is very low. With the "right" policy, you will have a minimum guaranteed rate of return on the cash in your policy as it grows tax free, and the returns will be pegged to the best stock index, the S&P 500.

-**The wealth that can be created using the equity in your home is significant**. Those who implement an Equity Harvesting plan will significantly increase their overall wealth vs. simply paying down the debt on a home that appreciates (remember, a home appreciates whether it has debt on it or not). I will illustrate how much wealth in the next several pages.

ILLUSTRATIONS

I can pontificate for pages about how wonderful Equity Harvesting is from a financial standpoint and that would be interesting reading to some, but I'd rather just get right to the numbers so you can see for yourself how powerful the concept of Equity Harvesting can be to grow your wealth in a safe environment.

The best way to understand the benefits of Equity Harvesting is to use examples.

Example 1

This will be the every day/middle American example (Mr. Smith). My "Joe lunchbox" example will be for a married couple who have a home with a fair market value (FMV) today of $235,000.

I know there are many statistics out there which state that the "average home value" is higher, but I believe those numbers are skewed by the many mega-homes that are being built these days.

Mr. Smith is 45 years old, has 2 children, a spouse who works and, generally speaking, has no idea how to save money for retirement. The "breadwinner" earns $50,000 a year, and the other spouse earns $28,000 a year. The couple has all the normal expenses as anyone else and has a few extra dollars every year that they try and then never end up putting away for retirement.

Mr. Smith's home was purchased for $185,000 seven years ago and that the current debt on the home is $135,000 (I assumed the house has appreciated at a conservative rate of less than 4% annually). Mr. Smith put 20% down on the house when purchasing it, and over time he has also paid down some of the debt on the house.

Assume the loan on the home is currently at 6.5% with a 30-year mortgage payment of $935 a month.

For all the Equity Harvesting examples, I will assume Mr. Smith has good credit (which is a pre-qualifier to being able to use the program).

IMPLEMENTING EQUITY HARVESTING

While Mr. Smith could remove 100% of his equity, I will assume he will harvest the equity through a home equity line of credit (not a refinance) and will remove an amount that will bring his overall loan balance to 90% debt on the property. Therefore, Mr. Smith could remove **$76,500** of equity ($235,000 x 90% = $211,500; $211,500-$135,000 = $76,500).

Mr. Smith will then reposition the removed equity into an indexed equity life insurance policy (if you have not read the chapter on life insurance you should read that before reading this chapter). As you'll know from reading the chapter on life insurance, Mr. Smith should pay premiums into the cash building policy over a five-seven year period so as to minimize the death benefit and maximize the cash value.

I will assume Mr. Smith will borrow $15,300 every year from his home equity line of credit for five years and reposition that money into a cash value life insurance policy.

HOW MUCH COULD MR. SMITH REMOVE "TAX FREE" FROM THE POLICY IN RETIREMENT?

For simplicity, I will assume with all of my retirement examples that Mr. Smith will withdraw money from ages 66-90 (25-years).

I will also assume that the life insurance policy has a return of 7.5% annually as growth on the cash value in the policy (a conservative number for the equity markets).

You may ask yourself why I used age 90 as the cut-off age for retirement income?

The answer is because most of the information I've received from actuaries about the assumed age of death for Americans indicates that 90 is more realistic today than what the insurance companies use (which is between 84-85 years old). Therefore, with my real world examples, I wanted to make sure the people did not run out of money until age 90 (an age I think many readers of this book will reach).

The amount Mr. Smith could borrow **tax free** from his life insurance policy is **$23,000 each year for 25 years** for a total amount of **$575,000**.

$23,000? You probably thought I would show you some huge number for as much as I built up the concept of Equity Harvesting.

Understand that Equity Harvesting is one tool to help you build wealth. For this example, Mr. Smith only harvested $76,500 of equity; and in retirement he received tax free $575,000. That's not bad at all.

The real kicker is: what would Mr. Smith have done if he did not implement an Equity Harvesting plan? You know the answer to this question. Mr. Smith would have **done nothing**. Therefore, $23,000 a year is a significant improvement to Mr. Smith's retirement income.

What is the cost to Mr. Smith for having an interest-only loan on $76,500 of equity?

If the home equity line of credit is at 7.5%, the costs to Mr. Smith would be $478 a month or $5,736 a year.

Therefore, when trying to create an apples-to-apples comparison between Mr. Smith using an Equity Harvesting plan and doing nothing, Mr. Smith needs to invest $5,737 every year into the stock market and let it grow. Then I will compare how much money he could remove from that account from ages 66-90 to how much could be removed from this cash value life insurance policy.

Really, this is not a real world example due to the fact that Mr. Smith is probably not going to invest the $5,737 every year if he didn't implement an Equity Harvesting plan. Most Mr. Smiths of the world would figure out a way to spend/waste the money. In this book, I will give Mr. Smith the benefit of the doubt so I can run comparison examples.

Like I did in the section of the book where I discussed how money grows (in the real world), I will need to assume a blended tax rate annually on money growing in the stock market. For these examples, I'll assume a 20% blended tax rate (capital gains/dividend tax which is very conservative). I'll assume 50% of the average annual mutual fund expense (50% of 1.2% is .6%) and 50% of the average money management fee (50% of 1% = .5%).

To learn more about how these fees affect how money grows in the stock market in the real world, please read the chapter on Traditional Wealth Building.

In my opinion, the numbers I am using are very conservative. I use conservative numbers to show you that even when money grows in the stock market with fewer expenses than are typical, Equity Harvesting works better as a tool to grow your wealth.

For these examples, I assumed the money would grow at a gross rate of 7.5% annually (the same rate as the funds will grow in the life policy).

If Mr. Smith invested $5,737 ever year in the stock market, he could remove **$19,038** a year every year after tax from ages 66-90.

Remember how much Mr. Smith could remove from his cash value life insurance after tax? **$23,000** every year for from ages 66-90.

How much <u>better</u> did Mr. Smith do by using <u>Equity Harvesting</u> to build wealth vs. <u>doing nothing</u> and simply investing money after-tax in the stock market?

$3,962 a year or $99,050 over the entire withdrawal period.

Wait, you say, this is not a fair comparison because there is still $76,500 of debt on the home? That is true and can be factored into the equation a few different ways. Two of them are as follows:

1) Mr. Smith has a $114,399 death benefit that will pay income-tax free from the life insurance policy if he were to die at age 90. That will more than pay off the $76,500 debt on the home.

If Mr. Smith pays off the debt on the home from the death benefit, his after-tax retirement income **increased by more than 20%** using Equity Harvesting vs. the do-nothing scenario.

2) Mr. Smith could choose to pay down the debt on the house using just over the last three year's of loans from the policy and he still comes out on top. Option 1) is more preferable and more likely to happen.

CHANGING THE VARIABLES

My previous numbers for the equity indexed life insurance policy were very conservative. What if I made them more real world? By real world, I mean that I will assume a small spread between the lending rate on the life insurance policy loans and the crediting rate on the cash inside the policy (if you do not know what I am referring to, please turn to the chapter on Understanding Life Insurance where you can read about the variable loan features in indexed life insurance policies).

With a small spread, Mr. Smith would be able to remove tax free from his life insurance policy **$26,800** every year from 66-90. This would be **$5,691** a year better or **$149,025** better over the withdrawal period as compared to post-tax investing.

See the following numbers from the actual life insurance illustration (I've taken several years out of the chart to make the size more manageable).

Age	Premium Payment	Cash S. Value	Death Benefit	Tax-Free Loans
45	15,300	8,075	331,589	0
46	15,300	20,102	331,589	0
47	15,300	36,700	331,589	0
48	15,300	54,445	331,589	0
49	15,300	73,422	331,589	0
55	0	108,726	331,589	0
60	0	156,418	331,589	0
65	0	227,838	331,589	0
66	0	217,643	303,047	26,800
70	0	175,811	226,558	26,800
75	0	121,979	147,336	26,800
80	0	72,781	110,930	26,800
85	0	37,170	94,436	26,800
90	0	28,896	114,379	26,800
95	0	270,379	296,111	0
100	0	738,311	777,245	0

You'll notice that in these illustrations I did not use a high cash value life insurance policy. I assumed Mr. Smith is financially stable and doesn't need to use one (remember, there is a small cost to having a high cash policy; and since Mr. Smith does not need that extra protection, there was no need to use such a policy when doing the illustrations)

What if the interest rate on the life insurance policy loan is consistent with where interest rates have been and crediting rates have been over the last 20+ years?

Mr. Smith would be able to remove tax free from his life insurance policy **$30,000** every year from 66-90. This would be **$9,161** a year better or **$229,025** better over the withdrawal period as compared to post-tax investing.

See the following numbers from the actual life insurance illustration (I've taken several years out to make the chart size manageable).

Age	Premium Payment	Cash S. Value	Death Benefit	Tax-Free Loans
45	15,300	8,075	331,589	0
46	15,300	20,102	331,589	0
47	15,300	36,700	331,589	0
48	15,300	54,445	331,589	0
49	15,300	73,422	331,589	0
55	0	108,726	331,589	0
60	0	156,418	331,589	0
65	0	227,838	331,589	0
66	0	214,535	299,939	30,000
70	0	161,677	212,425	30,000
75	0	99,632	124,989	30,000
80	0	53,754	91,903	30,000
85	0	41,739	99,005	30,000
90	0	90,689	176,172	30,000
95	0	457,241	482,973	0
100	0	1,127,901	1,166,834	0

The previous numbers allow me to remind readers of the positive aspects of the proper cash value life insurance policy.

One of them is that there are annual principal guarantees inside an indexed equity life insurance policy, and the gains on the growth each year are locked in.

With money actively traded in the stock market, there is NO principal protection; and as nearly everyone found out between 2000-2002, the market not only goes backwards, it can do so in a dramatic and swift manner.

One of the others is the ability to use or not use the variable loan feature. All the much smarter actuaries believe long term the interest rate on loans in policies will lag crediting rates of the S&P 500 by more than 2%. This is an option which can significantly increase the amount of money you can borrow from a life insurance policy WITHOUT increasing the actual rate of return on the cash in the policy. This is NOT possible with a post-tax brokerage account.

What everyone wants to know from the author is what do I think will happen over the next 20-40+ years. I can't state with any certainty; but, I believe there will be a spread on the interest rates as compared to the crediting rates. I'm not sure it if will be 2% or more, but 1% is certainly conservative (this is more fully explained in the chapter on Understanding Life Insurance).

One last positive to remind readers of is the fact that, from day one of funding the life insurance policy, Mr. Smith had a $331,000 death benefit. Therefore, if Mr. Smith died early, his beneficiaries would receive much more money than if he had simply invested money into a typical brokerage account.

DO NOTHING

Let's re-examine how much better Mr. Smith did by using Equity Harvesting vs. doing nothing. In the real world, doing nothing means spending every penny you have and not saving. In this book and my examples, doing nothing means allocating the money Mr. Smith would have used to pay interest on a loan to a brokerage account to build wealth and comparing that to how much wealth he can build borrowing Equity Harvesting and funding a cash value life insurance policy.

The following is a summary chart listing the previous numbers. The numbers below <u>Loan 1</u> come from the life insurance illustration where I assumed NO spread between the interest rate on the loan and what the S&P 500 credits in the policy. <u>Loan 2</u> is with a 1% spread on the borrowing rate (meaning the lending rate on the loan is 1% less than what the S&P 500 will credit in the policy). <u>Loan 3</u> is with a 2% spread on the borrowing rate.

	After-Tax From Brokerage Account	Tax-Free Loan 1	Tax-Free Loan 2	Tax-Free Loan 3
From ages 66-90	$19,038	$23,000	$26,800	$30,000
Total for 25 years	$475,950	$575,000	$670,000	$750,000
Improvement with EH		**$95,000**	**$194,050**	**$274,050**
% Improvement with EH		**20%**	**41%**	**58%**

SUMMARY OF THE FIRST MR. SMITH EXAMPLE

The previous chart should really crystallize the benefits of Equity Harvesting. With very conservative assumptions, Equity Harvesting improved Mr. Smith's cash flow by 20% in retirement. With a 1% spread on the borrowing rate, cash flow improved by 41%; and with Loan 3 (which is what most "experts" think will happen), Mr. Smith's cash flow improved by 58%.

That's the power of Equity Harvesting.

Also remember that the equity indexed life insurance policy Mr. Smith used is a conservative wealth building tool due to the fact that the policy has an annual growth guarantee and locks in upside gains annually (something you would never be able to do with money invested in the stock market).

Mr. Smith also had a nice death benefit to protect the family; and if the past 20+ years is any indicator of the future, he should end up with over $100,000 more in tax-free dollars from his Equity Harvesting plan than simply funding a brokerage account.

DO I HAVE YOU SOLD ON EQUITY HARVESTING AS A WAY TO BUILD WEALTH?

That's not really my goal with this book. When I started writing it, I did not have an agenda. I just wanted to write a unique book which in a matter of a fact way gives readers the real math and numbers with the topics covered.

I'd say that the previous example makes a very compelling argument for why readers should use Equity Harvesting to build wealth.

WHAT ABOUT THE HOME MORTGAGE INTEREST DEDUCTION?

The interesting thing about the previous example is that it worked even though Mr. Smith did **not** write off the interest on his home equity debt (remember the 163 limit on writing off a refinance or home equity loan is limited to $100,000 of new debt).

If you read the chapter on The Laws That Govern Equity Harvesting, you can read the section of material for how to posture Equity Harvesting so that you have the best chance to write off the interest.

Let's assume that Mr. Smith **can** use one of the ways to posture his $76,500 of home equity debt as tax deductible.

How will writing off the interest on the loan affect the financial viability of Equity Harvesting (which you know from what you already read works well even if you do not write off the interest on the loan)?

You'll recall that with the Mr. Smith example I had him remove $76,500 of equity from the home with an interest rate on the loan of 7.5%. That created a new interest payment for him of $5,737.

In the previous examples, I assumed for comparison that Mr. Smith invested the entire $5,737 into the stock market earning 7.5% annually as a gross investment return.

Now I will illustrate the numbers for Mr. Smith assuming he can write off the interest on the $76,500 of home equity debt.

Because readers will be in several different tax brackets, I'm going to show you the number for the 15%, 30% and 40% tax brackets. I am also assuming that Mr. Smith itemizes his deductions on his tax return.

If Mr. Smith is in the 15% income tax bracket, he would get a $5,737 deduction on his taxes when he pays the interest expense on the $76,500 loan. The "real" cost to Mr. Smith is not $5,757 but instead is **$4,876**. Therefore, when I create the financial comparison between Equity Harvesting using life insurance and doing nothing and investing money in the stock market, I will allow $4,876 to grow instead of $5,737.

If Mr. Smith is in the 30% income tax bracket, his real cost to borrow the money annually would be **$4,015**.

If Mr. Smith is in the 40% income tax bracket, his real cost to borrow the money annually would be **$3,442**.

Let's see how much money Mr. Smith could take out of a brokerage account after tax from age 66-90 in the three different tax brackets.

In the 15% income tax bracket he could remove $16,181 from ages 66-90 for a total of $404,525.

In the 30% income tax bracket he could remove $13,324 from ages 66-90 for a total of $333,100

In the 40% income tax bracket he could remove $11,442 from ages 66-90 for a total of $286,050.

Let's see how Equity Harvesting using life insurance with the numbers from earlier examples compares to post-tax investing in the market with the money Mr. Smith would have had to allocate to the interest expense.

The following chart is eye popping. For the chart, I used the only the **most conservative** numbers when Mr. Smith accesses tax-free loans from his life insurance policy.

	Brokerage Acct. (15%)	Brokerage Acct. (30%)	Brokerage Acct. (40%)
From ages 66-90	$16,181	$13,324	$11,442
Total for 25 years	$404,525	$333,100	$286,050
Total Tax-Free from EH			
Life policy from 66-90	$575,000	$575,000	$575,000
Improvement with EH	**$170,475**	**$241,900**	**$288,950**
% Improvement with EH	**42%**	**73%**	**101%**

Because I know you are curious, I thought I would show you the difference with the other two higher amounts that Mr. Smith could borrow form his life insurance policy if there is an interest rate spread in a positive fashion when he borrows it in retirement.

With a 1% spread, Mr. Smith could borrow $26,800 each year from ages 66-90 for a total of $670,000.

	Brokerage Acct. (15%)	Brokerage Acct. (30%)	Brokerage Acct. (40%)
From ages 66-90	$16,181	$13,324	$11,442
Total for 25 years	$404,525	$333,100	$286,050
Total Tax-Free from EH			
Life policy from 66-90	$670,000	$670,000	$670,000
Improvement with EH	**$265,475**	**$336,900**	**$383,950**
% Improvement with EH	**66%**	**101%**	**134%**

With a 2% spread, Mr. Smith could borrow $30,000 each year from ages 66-90 for a total of $750,000.

	Brokerage Acct. (15%)	Brokerage Acct. (30%)	Brokerage Acct. (40%)
From ages 66-90	$16,181	$13,324	$11,442
Total for 25 years	$404,525	$333,100	$286,050
Total Tax-Free from EH			
Life policy from 66-90	$750,000	$750,000	$750,000
Improvement with EH	**$345,475**	**$416,900**	**$463,950**
% Improvement with EH	**85%**	**125%**	**162%**

To say that Equity Harvesting works better if you can write off the interest would be an understatement.

While I believe there are ways you can posture yourself to write off the interest on home equity debt, if you simply borrow money from the home and reposition it into a cash building life insurance policy with the contemplation of borrowing from it, the interest is not deductible.

As you've seen, that's not the end of the world; but I'm sure you like the last set of numbers much better where I show Mr. Smith being able to write off the interest.

When I tell clients and advisors that Equity Harvesting is nearly a no brainer from a financial standpoint if you can write off the interest, now you know why. The numbers also make a great argument for why Equity Harvesting is close to a no brainer even if you can't write off the interest.

Example 2

The previous example was my Joe lunchbox example. I know that many readers earn less annually than Mr. and Mrs. Smith in my example and many make more. But since many readers have at least $76,500 of equity in their homes that could be removed, I think the previous example will apply to many readers.

My next example is going to be a bigger/more affluent client example.

Let's assume Mr. Smith is 45 years old and has been living in his current home for 10 years. Mr. Smith and his wife bought the home when their combined income was $80,000 a year, and now their income is in excess of $125,000 a year. Additionally, since they bought the house, they've added another child to the family and generally speaking need/want a bigger house to live in.

Therefore, Mr. and Mrs. Smith are now ready to **sell the current house** and "upgrade" to a new house with four bedrooms instead of three and three-and-a-half baths instead of two.

The Smiths bought their current home for $200,000, and it is now worth $400,000 (I used 7% annual appreciation on the home which is 2% higher than the national average). The current debt on their home is $75,000 (I assumed the Smiths put $50,000 down when they purchased the house and have been aggressively paying down the debt for the last ten years with the goal of having no debt as soon as possible).

Their current equity in the home is $325,000.

Let's assume for easy math that after realtor fees the Smiths will have after selling their home **$300,000** of equity.

Assume the Smiths found a new home which they can purchase for $500,000.

The Smiths read this book on <u>The Home Equity Management,</u> and the light bulb went on. They have decided that having debt on their home is a good thing especially when they can write off the interest.

Therefore, assume the Smiths put 20% down on the purchase of the new home ($100,000) which leaves them with **$200,000** of equity left over from the sale of their current home to reposition into a low-expense, non-MEC cash building life insurance policy.

EQUITY HARVESTING

Let's see how the Smiths can grow their wealth with Equity Harvesting using the $200,000.

REMEMBER: When you sell your home, remove equity, and purchase a new home with more or significantly more debt, you **can write off the interest** on the new home's debt up to $1,000,000 of debt (with certain phase-out exclusions).

HOW MUCH COULD MR. SMITH REMOVE "TAX FREE" FROM HIS EQUITY HARVESTING LIFE INSURANCE POLICY IN RETIREMENT?

Remember that in these examples, I'm assuming a 7.5% rate of return inside Mr. Smith's over-funded, non-MEC equity indexed life insurance policy which pegs its growth to the S&P 500 index. I am also assuming that Mr. Smith will start taking tax-free retirement money from his insurance policy from ages 66-90.

I am also going to assume that the home loan on the new home is a 7% interest-only loan.

The amount Mr. Smith could borrow tax free from his life insurance policy starting at ages 66 is **$61,000 each year for 25 years** for a total amount of **$1,520,000**.

Unlike Example 1 where the Smiths could not really live on the retirement proceeds from their life insurance policy ($23,000 a year), with this example, the Smiths can live very nicely on $61,000 a year TAX FREE in retirement.

Question: What is the cost to the Smiths to create this retirement nest egg?

In this example, I assumed the Smiths used an interest-only loan instead of a 30-year amortized loan. Why? Because the Smiths "get it" and understand that the best place for their money is not in their home. They understand that it is better to control their own money vs. giving it to a bank.

Therefore, the Smiths opted for an interest-only loan where the debt on the home will remain constant (even though the home is still appreciating).

The new home loan amount will be $400,000. At a 7% interest rate, that creates an annual mortgage payment of $28,000. However, remember that the debt caused by Equity Harvesting is only $200,000, and, therefore, when I talk about the cost of Equity Harvesting for this example, the costs I will be talking about relate to $200,000 worth of debt not $400,000.

What is the cost to borrow $200,000 for the Smiths? $14,000 a year.

<u>Question</u>: If you could have an expense where the costs were $14,000 a year and where the "tax-free" retirement income is $61,000 a year for 25 years, would you incur the expense?

Your answer should be yes all day long. Remember, if the debt was non-deductible for the Smiths and the numbers were similar to the Example 1, the plan should work out 20%-58% better than "doing nothing."

With this Example, I will be showing you how well Equity Harvesting worked for the Smiths when the interest is deductible.

If you are curious, if the Smiths funded $14,000 a year into a typical brokerage account (which is what the comparison would be if the interest is not deductible) with the same conservative assumptions from Example 1 (which used a 7.5% gross rate of return on the brokerage account), the Smiths would be able to remove approximately $46,500 from the brokerage account from ages 66-90 vs. the **$61,000** after tax that could be removed from the life insurance policy (for a total of **$1,525,000** over the 25-year period).

With the most conservative life insurance illustration, the Smiths ended up doing approximately **31% better** with Equity Harvesting vs. doing nothing (if we assumed they could **NOT** write off the interest).

However, in this example, we know that the Smiths **CAN** write off the interest because the debt is home acquisition debt. Let's see how that affects the financial viability of this example.

Even though I know the Smiths are in the 25% federal income tax bracket, I will show you the numbers for the 15%, 30% and 40% tax brackets. I know those who read this book will be all over the map when it comes to their personal tax brackets. Some will be in the highest tax bracket (35%) which could also be compounded by living in a state like California that has nearly a 10% state income tax.

If the Smiths are in the 15% income tax bracket, they would receive a $14,000 deduction on their taxes when they pay the interest expense on the $200,000 worth of debt allocated to the Equity Harvesting concept.

The "real" cost to the Smiths is not $14,000 but instead is **$11,900**. Therefore, when I create the financial comparison between Equity Harvesting using life insurance and doing nothing and investing money in the stock market, I will allow $11,900 to grow instead of $14,000.

If the Smiths are in the 30% income tax bracket, their real cost to borrow the money annually would be **$9,800**.

If the Smiths are in the 40% income tax bracket, their real cost to borrow the money annually would be **$8,400**.

Let's see how much money Mr. Smith could take out of a brokerage account after tax from age 66-90 in the three different tax brackets.

In the 15% income tax bracket he could remove $39,490 from ages 66-90 for a total of $987,250.

In the 30% income tax bracket he could remove $32,521 from ages 66-90 for a total of $813,025

In the 40% income tax bracket he could remove $27,875 from ages 66-90 for a total of $696,875.

Let's see how Equity Harvesting using life insurance compares to post-tax investing in the market with the money the Smiths would have had to allocate to the interest expense. The following chart is eye popping. For the chart below, I used the **most conservative numbers** when Mr. Smith accesses tax-free loans from his life insurance policy.

	Brokerage Acct. (15%)	Brokerage Acct. (30%)	Brokerage Acct. (40%)
From ages 66-90	$39,490	$32,521	$27,875
Total for 25 years	$987,250	$813,025	$696,875
Total Tax-Free from EH			
Life policy from 66-90	$1,525,000	$1,525,000	$1,525,000
Improvement with EH	**$537,750**	**$711,975**	**$828,125**
% Improvement with EH	**54%**	**88%**	**119%**

As I indicated previously, the above numbers are with the conservative life insurance illustration where there is no spread in the interest rate when Mr. Smith borrows money from the policy (meaning no positive arbitrage on the borrowed funds).

As I indicated previously, most experts believe that the long-term lending rates on life insurance policy loans will be 2% less than the average return inside the policy with growth pegged to the S&P 500.

If there is a 1% spread between the S&P 500 crediting rate and the loan interest rate on the tax-free policy loans, Mr. Smith could remove from his life insurance policy **$69,800** each year from ages 66-90 for a total of **$1,745,000**.

	Brokerage Acct. (15%)	Brokerage Acct. (30%)	Brokerage Acct. (40%)
From ages 66-90	$39,490	$32,521	$27,875
Total for 25 years	$987,250	$813,025	$696,875
Total Tax-Free from EH			
Life policy from 66-90	$1,745,000	$1,745,000	$1,745,000
Improvement with EH	**$757,750**	**$931,975**	**$1,048,125**
% Improvement with EH	**77%**	**115%**	**150%**

If there is a 2% spread between the S&P 500 crediting rate and the loan interest rate on the tax-free policy loans, Mr. Smith could remove from his life insurance policy **$80,000** each year from ages 66-90 for a total of **$2,000,000**.

	Brokerage Acct. (15%)	Brokerage Acct. (30%)	Brokerage Acct. (40%)
From ages 66-90	$39,490	$32,521	$27,875
Total for 25 years	$987,250	$813,025	$696,875
Total Tax-Free from EH			
Life policy from 66-90	$2,000,000	$2,000,000	$2,000,000
Improvement with EH	**$1,012,750**	**$1,186,975**	**$1,303,125**
% Improvement with EH	**103%**	**146%**	**187%**

The previous numbers are truly amazing and, again, why I say with confidence that the best way for most Americans to build wealth for retirement is through Equity Harvesting.

Also remember that the equity indexed life insurance policy Mr. Smith used is a conservative wealth-building tool due to the fact that the policy has an annual growth guarantee and locks in upside gains annually (something you would never be able to do with money invested in the stock market).

Mr. Smith also had a nice death benefit ($866,789) to protect the family; and if the past 20+ years is any indicator of the future, he will end up with literally hundreds of thousands of additional income over the "do-nothing" scenario.

THE 1% CASH FLOW ARM (CFA) MORTGAGE

As I stated in the chapter of the book on mortgages, the 1% CFA mortgage is a terrific mortgage for many readers who fit the profile to take advantage of Equity Harvesting.

In Example 1 and 2, Mr. Smith could have and probably should have used the 1% CFA. Why? Because the 1% CFA mortgage substantially lowers the mortgage payments, frees up more money to reposition in a tax-favorable wealth-building vehicle and slowly removes more equity from the home (because the loan creates deferred interest).

I could create illustrations and examples until I'm blue in the face, and I think if I did that I'd create confusion rather than clarity on the issues I am discussing in this book.

Therefore, the following example will simply be for a Mr. Smith who **does not** want to remove equity from the home and instead wants to simply lower his payments and reposition the savings from the lower payments into a tax-favorable, wealth-building vehicle.

Example 3

Let's assume this time that Mr. Smith lives in a $250,000 home with traditional 30-year fixed mortgage. Assume he just refinanced the home two years ago and has $200,000 of debt on it with a 7% fully amortized loan.

His payments on the loan are $1,497 a month (not including taxes and insurance).

While Mr. Smith understands the concept of Equity Harvesting, he does not have a lot of equity to harvest but he would like to start building wealth in a tax-favorable and conservative manner.

In order to help Mr. Smith free up some cash to reposition into a low-expense, non-MEC cash building life insurance policy, Mr. Smith will use the 1% CFA mortgage.

One assumption that needs to be made with the 1% CFA mortgage in this example is that the house will appreciate at 5% a year. Why specifically for "this" example? Because the client does not have much equity in the home. Therefore, in order to have the 1% CFA work as a long-term solution, the house needs to appreciate (otherwise the debt ratio will get out of an acceptable range, and he'll have to then get out of the 1% CFA loan and back into a more conventional loan). This is not an issue for clients who have significant equity in the home when using the 1% CFA.

What is the new mortgage payment for Mr. Smith after implementing the 1% CFA mortgage? **$723**

As you'll recall from reading the mortgage chapter of this book, the 1% CFA mortgage can be set up in a number of different ways. Traditionally speaking, the mortgage is set up where the payments increase at 7.5% annually. The following chart shows the numbers for the first five years of the 1% CFA mortgage.

Option Arm Cash Flow Analysis	30 Year @ 7.000%	Option Arm @ 1.000%	Option Arm Cash Flow Over Other
Year 1	$17,963	$8,684	$9,279
Year 2	$17,963	$9,336	$8,628
Year 3	$17,963	$10,036	$7,927
Year 4	$17,963	$10,788	$7,175
Year 5	$17,963	$11,598	$6,366
5 Year Totals	**$89,816**	**$50,442**	**$39,374**

With this type of mortgage, Mr. Smith freed up **$39,374** in the first five years to be repositioned into a tax-favorable, wealth-building vehicle.

I'd like to show you an example extrapolating the 1% CFA mortgage for Mr. Smith where he keeps the loan like I did for the previous examples; but it's a nightmare from an accounting standpoint, and there are more variables which could change that would make the illustration not very useful.

Instead I decided to use an illustration of what the savings from just the first five years can grow to for Mr. Smith. It won't be a huge amount or something he can use as the only source of retirement funds, but it can be one nice piece of his retirement puzzle.

If Mr. Smith repositioned $39,374 as budgeted from the previous spreadsheet for the first five years of the loan and let only that money grow in a low-expense, non-MEC indexed equity life insurance policy that pegs its growth to the S&P 500 with a conservative 7.5% annual rate of return, he could remove **$13,686** tax free from the policy from ages 66-90.

The total amount Mr. Smith could remove tax free from the policy for the 25-year retirement period is **$342,150** (tax free). That's not too shabby.

The key with the 1% CFA mortgage when used with the Equity Harvesting concept is that it DOES NOT change your lifestyle.

Think about that for a minute. Did it cost Mr. Smith anything out of pocket to use the 1% CFA mortgage to build a nice little retirement nest egg? No. If Mr. Smith would not have used the 1% CFA, he would have been out of pocket on his interest payment for the traditional 30-year mortgage in the amount of $1,497 a month.

With the 1% CFA, Mr. Smith still had out of pocket $1,497, but he instead repositioned the savings in mortgage payments into a cash building life insurance policy.

The previous comment is not 100% accurate due to the fact that I have not assumed a current or future income tax bracket for Mr. Smith. To obtain the exact and specific numbers, you would need a much more complicated spreadsheet that could be created but didn't seem to make sense for this book since the numbers I am using for this example will drive home my point.

My point again, with the discussion about the 1% CFA mortgage was not to give you an ultra-complicated illustration/example to look at. Instead, I wanted to put forth an example with round math so you understand the concept of how the 1% CFA can be used to slowly remove equity from your home so you can reposition that equity into a better and more tax favorable, wealth-building vehicle.

INTEREST-ONLY LOANS

If you do not have equity in your home to remove or if you do and you are not comfortable removing it AND you are not comfortable with the 1% CFA mortgage, the other way to raise money without changing your lifestyle is to convert your 15-30 year fixed mortgage to an interest-only loan.

For example, if you had a $300,000, 30-year mortgage with a 6.5% interest rate, your monthly payments would be $1,996.

If you refinanced your home and obtained a new interest-only loan amortized over the same period where the interest rate is

7% (interest-only loans typically have higher interest rates), the new monthly mortgage payment would be $1,750.

The difference in the two payments is $246 a month or $2,952 a year. The savings per year would be repositioned into a low-expense, non-MEC cash value life insurance policy where the money would grow tax free and be removed tax free in retirement.

It's not a huge amount of money each year; but when you are putting together an overall financial/estate plan for yourself and are tying to use every avenue to build wealth in a tax favorable manner, every little bit helps.

Also with this example, 100% of the interest is deductible even if the repositioned money goes directly into a cash value life insurance policy.

SUMMARY ON EQUITY HARVESTING

Simply put, Equity Harvesting can be one of, if not, the best way for many readers to build a tax-favorable retirement nest egg. While Equity Harvesting is not a cure-all topic to fix the shortfall of retirement wealth that nearly every reader has, the concept has many more pros than cons.

There are several ways to raise money to reposition into cash value life insurance for tax favorable wealth building.

You can: 1) remove equity from your home with a refinance; 2) sell your home and use the profits from the sale; 3) use the 1% CFA mortgage and use money from the difference in payments; and 4) use an interest-only loan and use the money from the difference in payments.

Equity Harvesting can be postured as a low-risk concept if you choose to use a high cash value life insurance policy (which protects those who may need access to the cash in the policy in the early years after implementing an Equity Harvesting plan).

Additionally, because you can use a life insurance policy that has guarantees on your cash value and locks in the investment gains which can be pegged to the S&P 500 each year, you can have money positioned in a much safer and less expensive environment than investing money in stocks and mutual funds.

There are ways to posture Equity Harvesting so the interest on your home loan is deductible. If you use one of those methods, using an Equity Harvesting plan to grow your wealth it is as close to a no-brainer wealth-building tool as you'll ever find. Having said that and as you've seen by reading over the numbers in this chapter, Equity Harvesting can still work out much better for you than the typical "do-nothing" position we all take in life more often than we should.

Also, remember the list of questions you want to ask yourself when determining if an Equity Harvesting plan is right for you.

1) Do you have a stable income?
2) Do you have a stable marriage?
3) Do you have other wealth besides the equity in your home?
4) Are you in a profession where disability is possibility?
5) Are you over the age of 60?

While I think Equity Harvesting for many is a terrific tool to build wealth in a conservative and tax-favorable manner, it is not for everyone. If you have worries or concerns over aspects of your life which could make you financially unstable, caution is always the better course of action. It is better to wait until you feel stable enough to move forward with any kind of long-term financial planning tool. If you have concerns in your life but really want to start building wealth through an Equity Harvesting plan, just make sure you use a high cash value life insurance policy which will help you mitigate your risk.

Finally, I've done my best to give you real world numbers and examples in this chapter. In order to keep the chapter relatively short, I did not insert examples for every age and economic status for every reader. To do so would be interesting to some but boring to others.

The way to determine if Equity Harvesting is "right" for you to use as a conservative, tax-favorable, wealth-building tool is to find an advisor who can help you.

As I've stated a few times in this book, if you had an advisor who was nice enough to give you this book to read or one who simply recommended it, it is likely that the advisor is familiar with the topics covered in the book and can run illustrations for your particular situation to determine if an Equity Harvesting plan makes sense for you.

Since you have read the book, you should be armed with the knowledge to make sure whatever advisor you work with is not using fuzzy math and/or unrealistic life insurance illustrations to make the concept look better for you than it really is.

If you cannot find a local advisor you feel comfortable working with, you can also feel free to go to www.thewpi.org and find a local advisor who has taken the CWPP™ or MMB™ certification courses who should be well equipped to help you review your particular situation.

If all else fails and you want to contact me for help or need a question answered, feel free to send me an e-mail at roccy@thewpi.org or give me a call at 269-216-9978.

Chapter 9
IRA Rescue Using
Home Equity Management

IRA planning is hot right now as our public gets older and as more and more money is transferred from qualified retirement plans into IRAs when employees retire.

Like many topics covered in this book, the IRA rescue topic has been covered in its typical lack of detail manner by other books in the marketplace.

The following material was designed to give you real world math behind using Home Equity Management when trying to mitigate taxes on IRA distributions.

I'd like to preface this chapter by saying that when giving the details and math behind this subject matter, it was not easy to create it in my typical easy-reader style. If you find the end of the chapter a bit confusing but get the overall sense that you could benefit by using some of the tools described to help you mitigate income and estate taxes, please feel free to e-mail me for clarification or with your questions at info@thewpi.org.

SCARE TACTICS

Before discussing IRA rescue, I want to forewarn readers about the scare tactics you'll read about in other books or hear from advisors who have been taught Home Equity Management from those who teach it based on the other books in the marketplace.

Fear is a very motivating factor in many parts of our lives. We are afraid to get hurt when driving our cars, so we wear seat belts. We cook certain foods at high temperatures to make sure we do not expose ourselves to certain diseases. We ask our children to look both ways before they cross the street because we fear they will be injured. These are normal fears we deal with in everyday life.

What if someone were to tell you could lose your "retirement nest egg" through a fearful story?

Would you treat this as an everyday fear; or would this fear get you to sit up, take notice, and potentially take action?

Because it takes many people 10-20-30+ years to build their retirement nest egg, when they hear such a story, their fear will be elevated to a very high level; and they will listen to the advisor telling the story or pay more careful attention to the book they are reading.

As I do in several parts of this book, I'm gong to let you in on the selling secrets of the advisors who are trying to get your business. Many of them will use fear as a motivating factor in situations where fear should have no or little impact on your decisions.

Quality advisors who use the techniques described in this book will lay out for you all the pros and cons of implementing Equity Harvesting plans and will help you **make decisions that are in your best financial interest** without playing on your fear (although they may play on your greed or desire to build more wealth or save on taxes).

The fear tactics you will find in other books revolve around the money you have in your individual IRA or pension plan at work, which, for many, are one of their largest assets. You will read how you may be risking a "huge part" of your wealth by having it in "liquid investments." By liquid investments, I mean stocks and mutual funds.

It's easy to point to Enron, and say, if you work for a big company and if you have the company's stock in your pension plan that the money is at risk for loss (you'll remember Enron is the company that went bankrupt, and the employees lost their retirement plan money).

Let's be practical. While people did lose money in their retirement plans at Enron, the laws have changed dramatically since then to mitigate this risk in the future. Furthermore, the number of people who lose money like the employees of Enron is so small a percentage of the population that it can hardly be used as a motivating factor for reasonable people.

After you have the fear put into you about losing significant portions of your retirement money, you will be told to liquidate the money in your IRA or other retirement plan and reposition that money somewhere else. That somewhere else will be a "special kind" of wealth-building tool where your money will grow tax free and come out tax free (which can be accomplished without the risk of loss in the stock market).

It sounds like it makes sense when you read it in a book or are pitched the idea by an advisor, doesn't it? If your money is at risk in your IRA or retirement plan and someone can show you how to move it to this "special investment" where it will grow tax free, come out tax free, and be protected against market downturns, shouldn't you entertain such an idea?

There is one little problem with this special kind of investment: In order move your money from your IRA or retirement plan to the special wealth-building tool, you have to **pay income taxes** on it first.

Also, if you are under the age of 59 ½, you'll have to pay a **10% penalty** on top of the taxes.

Hmm. How do the taxes and penalties change your thoughts about moving lump sum money from an IRA or qualified plan and into this special investment?

If your instincts tell you that the taxes, and penalties if you are under 59 ½, hurt the financial viability of moving money into the special investment, you are right.

By the way, where can you reposition your money to allow it to grow tax free, come out tax free, and have principal protection while the money grows? If you've read the earlier chapters of this book, you'll know the answer is cash value life insurance.

You also may remember the story of the Scorpion and the Frog. Advisors advocating that clients remove money from an IRA or qualified retirement plan and pay taxes (and penalties if under the age of 59 ½) are classic Scorpions in that they simply want to use whatever motivating factors they can to entice a client to fund cash value life insurance (where the advisor can make a commission).

The vast majority of the time, it is **NOT** a good idea to remove money from an already taxed-deferred account to reposition it into cash value life insurance. Having said that, I will cover this issue in the context of IRA rescue in the coming pages and show you, with real numbers, how doing so can work to your benefit **IF** you are doing so for estate planning purposes and not for future tax-favorable income.

Finally, if you are fearful of losing money due to risky investments in an IRA or qualified plan, you should consider moving some of the money into fixed-indexed annuities (also known as equity-indexed annuities (EIAs)). EIAs work similar to the equity indexed life insurance policies you read about in Chapter 5 on Understanding Life Insurance. EIAs never allow your money to go backwards; they lock in gains annually and peg investment gains to the S&P 500 (with a cap). You may wonder why I have not talked about EIAs as a place to reposition wealth when implementing an Equity Harvesting plan, and the simple answer is that the money that comes out of an EIA is income taxed, whereas the money removed from a cash value life policy is not.

WHY DOES AN IRA NEED RESCUING?

IRA rescue is an old term that has been around for years. "Rescuing" IRA assets means that you will be pro-active to **reduce the overall taxes** levied upon your IRA assets when you die.

It should be noted that the taxes I will be discussing also apply to income-tax-deferred money you may have in a qualified plan (401(k), 403(b), profit sharing plan, defined benefit plan, 412(i) defined benefit plan, KEOGH, etc.) or money in an income-tax-deferred annuity.

What taxes am I talking about? **Income** and **estate taxes**.

As just stated, I am talking about income-tax-deferred dollars. Most Americans strive, although don't always succeed, in deferring a portion of their annual income into IRAs or qualified retirement plans.

As you read about in Chapter 6, this can be a good idea or not, depending on your tax bracket. As I indicated in Chapter 6, many readers would be better off not going out of their way to fund a qualified retirement plan due to the fact that funding a low expense, non-MEC cash value life insurance policy can generate more after-tax income in retirement.

For now, let's just use the assumption that it is a good idea to defer money now in tax-favorable plans or IRAs to grow wealth for retirement.

Because the money in IRAs and qualified retirement plans has been income-tax deferred, you will have to pay income taxes when you pull the money out at the income tax bracket you are in when the withdrawals happen.

Most readers understand that and fund income-tax-deferred retirement plans anyway so they can take advantage of the tax-deferred growth (the theory being it's better to have $1.00 growing tax-deferred than to pay 15-45% income taxes on your take-home pay, thereby leaving 55-85 cents on the dollar to invest in a tax-hostile environment (the stock market)).

What most readers do not think about are the **taxes due upon death** should there be money left in an IRA or retirement plan.

What taxes? **Estate taxes**.

IF you DO NOT have an estate tax problem when you die, you will not have the double tax discussed in this chapter.

Will you have an estate tax problem? Congress is always threatening to change the laws; but as it stands today, the following chart shows you the estate tax exemption amounts depending on the year when you die.

Exemptions and Maximum Tax Rates		
Year	Estate Tax Exemption	Highest Rate
2007	$2 million	45%
2008	$2 million	45%
2009	$3.5 million	45%
2010	N/A (taxes eliminated)	0%
2011	$1 million	55%

For this book, I will assume all readers will die after 2011. What the above chart tells you is that you have a $1,000,000 per spouse estate-tax exemption if you die after 2010.

If you are not married and your estate is less than $1,000,000, you do not have to worry about estate taxes. If you are married and your estate plan is set up properly (using living trusts to maximize your estate tax exemptions), your estate should pay NO estate taxes if it is less than $2,000,000.

You also need to understand that your estate is made up of ALL of your assets, which includes IRA/qualified retirement money and life insurance proceeds not passed through an Irrevocable Life Insurance Trust.

THE 75-85% TAX TRAP

IF you have an estate-tax problem when you die AND money in an IRA, qualified retirement plan, or an income tax-deferred annuity, that money can be taxed at between 75-85%. I say can instead of will because if you were married that money will likely pass to your spouse who then will have the tax problem.

The tax trap comes into play because not only does the IRS want **estate taxes** at your death, but the IRS also wants the **income taxes** dues on your deferred money.

Remember, the reason you use an IRA, qualified retirement plan, or tax-deferred annuity is so you can build wealth in a more tax-favorable manner due to the fact that you can invest money into such vehicles with pre-tax dollars and have tax-deferred growth (no dividend taxes or capital gains taxes are due annually in such accounts).

Therefore, when you die, your estate will be valued; and if there is an estate tax problem and assets with deferred income taxes due, **the IRS will collect both,** and the taxes will, in fact, be between 75-85% of the value of such assets.

When most people with estate tax problems and money in income-tax-deferred accounts hear about this tax dilemma, they usually get depressed and wonder why they ever deferred the money in the first place (again, you can read Chapter 6 to determine if funding a tax-deferred qualified plan or IRA makes sense for you).

Readers need to understand that this topic, in and of itself, could merit its own 100+ page book. My intent with this book is to make readers aware of the problem and then discuss a solution using a <u>Home Equity Management</u> technique.

The best way to explain the 75-85% tax trap is with an example.

Example

Dr. Smith has a $5,000,000 estate, a $1,000,000 IRA and lives in a state with a 5% income tax. Assume Dr. Smith dies after his spouse and with an estate tax problem. What taxes will be due on the IRA?

IRA	$1,000,000
Estate Tax:	($550,000)
<u>Income Taxes (State and Federal)*</u>	<u>($250,000)</u>
Total Taxes	($800,000)
<u>TOTAL IRA ASSET AFTER TAX</u>	<u>$200,000</u>

*The exact calculation of the income tax due in the above example is quite complicated and the $250,000 number used is an approximation. Also do not forget that the estate tax in 2011 will revert back to 55%.

If you have no state income tax, the taxes due will be approximately 70%. If you live in California, where the state income tax is near 10%, the taxes due will be approximately 85%.

To some, this will be counterintuitive, since many readers have always been under the assumption that it is good to defer income into IRAs/retirement accounts. Look at the following example, which illustrates the taxes due and how the problem grows as your IRA grows.

The following chart assumes the client has $500,000 in an IRA and has an estate tax problem when he/she dies and lives in a state with at 5% income tax.

Age	Start of Year Balance	6.00% Growth	Year End Balance	To Heirs After 80% Income & Estate Tax
60	$500,000	$30,000	$530,000	$106,000.00
65	$669,113	$40,147	$709,260	$141,851.90
70	$895,424	$53,725	$949,149	$189,829.90
75	$1,198,279	$71,897	$1,270,176	$254,035.20
80	$1,603,568	$96,214	$1,699,782	$339,956.40
85	$2,145,935	$128,756	$2,274,691	$454,938.30
90	$2,871,746	$172,305	$3,044,050	$608,810.10
95	$3,843,043	$230,583	$4,073,626	$814,725.20
100	$5,142,859	$308,572	$5,451,431	$1,090,286.10

This above chart is truly depressing. It took you 30+ years to amass $500,000 in your IRA at age 60. You were lucky enough to have it grow to over $2,000,000 at age 85. Now, when you die, 80% of the money will go to the government via income and estate taxes.

The above chart is not technically accurate. It has been skewed intentionally to drive home how painful the double tax can be at your death. It is skewed because I did not take out the required minimum distributions the client would have been forced to take at age 70 ½ (this is not an issue with a cash value life insurance policy that is owned individually).

In this example, the client will be forced to take a taxable distribution of $32,679.71 at age 70½ if we assume his wife is the beneficiary and is the same age as primary IRA owner. This happens annually to millions of people, and the forced distributions increase every year as people get older. When people turn 70½ and their financial planner or CPA says to them that they must start taking money out of their IRA, they usually become upset and wonder why such a stupid rule even exists. Then they will look back at their decision to aggressively fund a tax-deferred retirement plan and will wonder if that was really a decision that can cost their heirs hundreds of thousands of dollars in wasted taxes.

WHAT ARE THE SOLUTIONS TO THE DOUBLE TAX DILEMMA?

The first solution is to not have an estate tax problem at your death. Because most people with wealth do not plan properly, most have money in qualified accounts or IRAs and an estate tax problem. If you do not have an estate tax problem, you can use the following tool to defer the income taxes due on your qualified money or IRA for years after your death.

STRETCH IRAs

One solution that works OK if you do NOT have an estate tax problem is a Stretch IRA. Stretch IRAs do just what their name implies—they stretch the time until the income taxes will be due on IRA assets.

With a Stretch IRA, you can name a child as the beneficiary so that the child's life will be the measuring life for the distribution purposes of the IRA. If you die prior to reaching 70½ years old, the IRA will pass to your child/beneficiary, and he/she can allow the money to continue to grow tax deferred in the IRA.

Essentially, you are trying to avoid paying lump sum **income** taxes on the IRA by using a Stretch IRA. This can work and is a good way to mitigate **income** taxes due on an IRA at your death

However, Stretch IRAs do **NOT** eliminate the **estate** tax for someone with an estate tax problem. Therefore, if you pass an IRA to a child/beneficiary through a Stretch IRA, your estate will have to deal with the 55% estate tax (after 2011), which is due when passing that asset to the heirs.

The following **example** is why Stretch IRAs do not work for people with estate tax problems.

If your IRA balance is $1,000,000 when you die, the estate taxes due when passing the IRA to a beneficiary will be $550,000 (remember I am assuming you will die after 2011 when the estate tax will be 55%) .

Where do you think the beneficiary is going to find $550,000 to pay the estate taxes? Chances are significant that the money will come from the IRA.

The problem is that the beneficiary will have to pay income taxes upon taking the money out of the IRA to pay the estate taxes; and if the beneficiary is under the age of 59 ½, a 10% penalty will be levied upon the withdrawal from the IRA.

Where will the beneficiary find the money to pay for the income taxes and penalties upon withdrawing money from the IRA? From the IRA of course.

This creates a vicious cycle, and is why, generally speaking, Stretch IRAs **DO NOT** work for clients with **estate** tax problems, and why, many times, IRA money needs to be "rescued" before a client passes away.

IRA RESCUE

What is IRA rescue? Simply put, IRA rescue is when you take action to mitigate the double tax and creates a scenario where you will pass more wealth to the heirs after all taxes. As stated, IRA rescue is much more important if you have an estate tax problem.

There are a handful of ways to deal with the double tax of money in an IRA upon your death. The simplest way to deal with the problem is to find the money to pay for the double taxes that will be levied on the IRA assets.

The "classic" way to "find" the money to pay for the taxes due is to plan ahead and fund a life insurance policy owned by an Irrevocable Life Insurance Trust (ILIT). Estate planning 101 says to have clients with estate tax problems buy life insurance in an ILIT because, when the death benefit is paid from the ILIT, it does so **income and estate tax-free**.

Many people ask themselves why they would want to incur a large life insurance premium just so they can pass IRA assets to a child/beneficiary.

I hear several times a year from clients who put their children through college, gave them a good life, and are not interested in incurring more expenses just so a large IRA balance can pass to the children without expense (meaning without paying the double tax due upon passing the IRA to the children).

I understand the thinking, and most clients who have that mindset end up with the do-nothing estate plan. I don't agree with the do-nothing approach because the only winner is the IRS. The vast majority of clients, when they understand that they can either give their money to the IRS or, with good planning, to their children, usually opt for good planning. My goal is to help readers use their assets in such a manner that they can sock away money in a "not–so-painful" manner and in a tax-favorable manner so as to "maximize" the overall estate value after taxes at their death.

CONVERTING ASSESTS

As discussed earlier, authors of other books write them in a way to motivate readers to convert trapped IRA money into cash. This is done by taking taxable distributions from the IRA and repositioning the money into cash value life insurance. I will show you in the upcoming pages why this doesn't work well if you are trying to maximize income. In the immediately following pages, I will discuss converting IRA assets so as to maximize the overall after-tax estate for your heirs.

The viable ways to maximize your non-taxable estate requires you to convert (start liquidating) your IRA money and reposition it into other more tax-favorable and more valuable vehicles, as far as your taxable estate is concerned.

"LIQUIDATE AND LEVERAGE"

You may not have heard of the above term, but in the "industry," many are familiar with the concept of "Liquidate and Leverage".

Again, when I am going over the solutions of how to maximize your estate and mitigate the double tax trap, I am discussing how to help you with an estate tax problem at death and minimize taxes on the money in IRA accounts. If you do not have such an estate problem or don't anticipate having one, then you simply have an income tax problem at death, which could be mitigated by using a Stretch IRA (although a Stretch IRA is still not the best way to maximize the amount of money you can pass on to your heirs).

"Liquidate and Leverage" is a very simple concept. You would simply start systematically liquidating your IRA assets (usually you should be over age 59 ½ so that you do not incur a 10% penalty when withdrawing the money) and gift the money after taxes to an Irrevocable Life Insurance Trust, which will purchase a cash value life insurance policy with a large death benefit. The death benefit will be used to pay for the double tax due on the IRA balance at death.

It's really that simple. Let's look at an **example**.

Dr. Smith is age 60. He has a $5,000,000 estate, which is comprised of a $1,000,000 home, $1,000,000 in various rental properties, a $2,000,000 brokerage account, and $500,000 in his IRA. Assume he is married and has two adult children and four grandchildren. Let's also assume Dr. Smith earns enough income from the rental properties and the brokerage account that he does not need the IRA money to live on in retirement. Finally, assume Dr. Smith is in the combined 40% income tax bracket (state and federal).

Dr. Smith has identified the double tax dilemma with his IRA money and would like to pass the maximum amount of wealth to his children upon his death.

Luckily for Dr. Smith, he seeks out an advisor who has been educated by the Wealth Preservation Institute (www.thewpi.org). The advisor then illustrates, as one of the solutions to mitigate the double tax dilemma, the "Liquidate and Leverage" solution.

Let's see how the numbers turned out.

You already know the approximate numbers of the do-nothing scenario from an earlier chart. 80% of the Dr. Smith's IRA will go to the government via income and estate taxes at the second spouse's death. Assume for the following charts that the money in the IRA continues to grow at 6% annually.

What if Dr. Smith were to take systematic withdrawals of $31,500 from his IRA every year and gift that money to an Irrevocable Life Insurance Trust, which would use the money to purchase a large death benefit on his life through a life insurance policy? You'll notice that the death benefit from the policy purchased in the ILIT starts at $559,000 and increases to $2,081,000 at age 100.

Age	IRA Start of Year Balance	Year End Balance	To Heirs After 80% Tax	Death Benefit L&L	IRA After Tax Plus DB
60	$500,000	$490,780	$98,156.0	$559,000	$657,156
65	$448,026	$435,688	$87,137.5	$645,000	$732,138
70	$378,473	$361,961	$72,392.3	$762,000	$834,392
75	$285,396	$263,299	$52,659.9	$952,000	$1,004,660
80	$160,837	$131,267	$26,253.4	$1,200,000	$1,226,253
85	$0	$0	$0.1	$1,484,000	$1,484,000
90	$0	$0	$0.0	$1,705,000	$1,705,000
95	$0	$0	$0.0	$1,904,000	$1,904,000
100	$0	$0	$0.0	$2,081,000	$2,081,000

Now let's compare the **do-nothing** scenario from the earlier pages to the "Liquidate and Leverage" scenario.

Age	To Heirs After 80% Income & Estate Tax	IRA After Tax Plus DB	Improvement with Liquidate & Leverage
60	$106,000	$657,156	$551,156
65	$141,852	$732,138	$590,286
70	$189,830	$834,392	$644,562
75	$254,035	$1,004,660	$750,625
80	$339,956	$1,226,253	$886,297
85	$454,938	$1,484,000	$1,029,062
90	$608,810	$1,705,000	$1,096,190
95	$814,725	$1,904,000	$1,089,275
100	$1,090,286	$2,081,000	$990,714

How did the heirs fare with the "Liquidate and Leverage?" Much, much better. $551,156 better at age 60, $886,297 at age 80, and over a million dollars better at age 90.*

* These numbers would apply at the second spouse's death due to the fact that the IRA balance can transfer to the spouse without taxes at the first spouse's death. The chart also does not take into account the Required Minimum Distribution (RMD) that will start to come out at age 70 ½. To incorporate RMD numbers into the chart would be very confusing, and my point with this illustration is simple: by doing nothing, you are not maximizing what you can give your heirs. By using other planning measures, your heirs will be much better off financially at your death.

Is it fair to say that Dr. Smith's heirs would be much happier if Dr. Smith and his wife sat down with a qualified planner to help him deal with the double tax trap of money in his IRA?

What if it was a planner who knew how to implement the relatively simple "Liquidate and Leverage" concept?

CREATING MORTGAGE DEDUCTIONS

While you might have thought the "Liquidate and Leverage" concept was beneficial, you can improve the finances of the concept if you incorporate Home Equity Management.

This concept is also very simple on its face (although fully understanding the math can get a bit complicated). IF clients can create a deductible home mortgage payment, they can remove money from an IRA to pay for the mortgage without paying taxes on the money removed from the IRA.

Why? Because the taxable dollars removed from the IRA will be allocated to a deductible home mortgage interest expense (**IF set up correctly**).

The following example is very specific. It deals with a couple who want to **sell their home**. If the clients simply want to re-finance the home, the interest might be deductible up to the first $100,000 of debt or not at all.

Example:

Let's use our Dr. Smith again. Assume he is now retired and has a paid-off home worth $1,000,000 dollars and has $500,000 in his IRA. Let's assume he would like to downsize the current house now that the children are all grown up and that he wants a vacation home in another part of the country.

Assume Dr. Smith buys a new, smaller home or condo locally (where he lives) for $400,000 and a new home or condo in a nice vacation spot for $400,000. Assume he puts down approximately $158,000 on each property and has a deductible mortgage expense on each property with the same $242,000 mortgage at 6.5%.*

With two interest-only mortgages at 6.5% with a total amount of deductible debt of $484,000, the interest expense on the mortgage payments will be approximately $31,500 a year.

*As you can see I'm manipulating the numbers to fit a particular example. This is exactly what you will do in the real world when calculating how much money you want to draw out of the IRA every year. Some people will want to draw out X amount so that the IRA balance is zero at age 100, 90, or 85. Others will not want to draw down the IRA balance to zero for fear that they will need some of the money.

For this example, I'm assuming the money in the IRA grows annually at 6% and that Dr. Smith can take withdrawals of $31,500 from age 60 to 98 ½.

If Dr. Smith removes $31,500 per year from the IRA to pay the mortgage payments, there will be <u>no taxes due</u> on the withdrawn money because he can deduct the $31,500 of IRA income on his tax returns due to the fact he has a corresponding home <u>acquisition</u> debt payment for the same amount.

REPOSITIONING THE MONEY FOR ESTATE PLANNING

After Dr. Smith removes the money from his IRA tax free, he then needs to do something with the profit from the sale of his house (his available cash is $684,000 after putting down the two $158,000 payments on his two new houses or condos).

I'm going to assume that Dr. Smith would like to maximize the size of his after-tax estate that will be passed to his heirs. Just like the "Liquidate and Leverage" solution, Dr. Smith will choose to gift money to an Irrevocable Life Insurance Trust (ILIT). In this example, I'm going to assume Dr. Smith will use $484,000 of his $684,000 profit from the sale of the home to gift to an ILIT.

Once the money is in the ILIT, a large death benefit life insurance policy will be purchased on his life, which will pass the maximum amount of wealth to the heirs income-tax and estate-tax free.

One main issue Dr. Smith will have to deal with is the gift-tax problem of repositioning the $484,000 into the ILIT. Dr. Smith and his spouse can gift $12,000 per spouse per child to the ILIT every year without gift taxes. They have two children and four grandchildren, and, therefore, they can gift up to $144,000 a year to the ILIT every year without incurring gift taxes.

In this example, at $144,000 a year, Dr. Smith can gift the money into the ILIT in just over three years.

How much death benefit can Dr. Smith purchase with a $484,000 premium? **$3,000,000**.

Therefore, if Dr. Smith dies tomorrow, next week, next year, or when he's 85 or more years old, $3,000,000 will pass income-tax and estate-tax free to his heirs.

Remember the numbers from the earlier do-nothing scenario? If Dr. Smith did nothing, the $500,000 IRA balance would grow and be taxed at 80%. If Dr. Smith died at age 70, the heirs would receive **$189,830** after taxes. Whenever Dr. Smith dies in this example, his heirs will receive **$3,000,000** after taxes.

There is no doubt that readers who have "trapped" money in IRAs can use this type of solution to significantly increase the size of their after-tax estate for the heirs.

WHAT WOULD DR. SMITH NORMALLY HAVE DONE WITH THE PROFIT FROM THE SALE OF THE PRIMARY RESIDENCE?

Let's assume Dr. Smith still wants to downsize the current house and buy a smaller house locally and one in a nice vacation spot. Furthermore, let's assume he knows nothing about IRA rescue techniques.

Where does everyone else normally reposition money after taking profits from the sale of real estate? Normally, in **stocks and mutual funds**.

If the profit from the sale of the home were invested in stocks and mutual funds, then Dr. Smith would have to deal with dividend taxes, capital gains taxes, mutual fund expenses, and, if a professional money manager is involved, money management fees.

If such investments are chosen, Dr. Smith has 100% risk of loss (so if another 9-11 market crash happens, Dr. Smith is in big trouble), not to mention that the funds would also be inside Dr. Smith's estate.

Many clients, as they get older, will use annuities as a part of their portfolio. If the profits from the sale were invested into

annuities, the money would grow tax free; but when removed, all the growth would be income taxed. Many annuities have guaranteed income benefits, which also help clients protect their wealth in retirement.

What about **life insurance**? That's the reason financial planners and insurance advisors flock to the Equity Harvesting concept. Sure, Dr. Smith could reposition the profit into a cash building life insurance policy.

If you remember from Chapter 2, I had in that chapter an actual e-mail from the TEAM of one of the authors of a "marketing" book on Equity Harvesting. The e-mail offered for sale a lead on a potential client who happened to be **66 years old**. It did not appear that the client had any money in a qualified plan, and the lead suggested that the potential client had $500,000 of equity to reposition into cash value life insurance for "retirement planning."

As I've discussed, the problem with Equity Harvesting for readers who are at or over the age of 60 is that health becomes a significant issue, as do the annual costs of insurance. It is very difficult for someone at or over the age of 60 to use Equity Harvesting as a wealth builder through the use of tax-free loans from a cash value life insurance policy. An insured really needs to wait 10 years before expecting to borrow any significant amount of money from a life policy, and most 60-year-olds do not want to or can't wait that long.

Let's look at a comparison among using life insurance, annuities, and the stock market to see which one works out the best to generate **retirement income**.

LIFE INSURANCE

If Dr. Smith purchased an equity-indexed life insurance policy on his life, where he was considered "standard" health for underwriting purposes, and repositioned only **$420,000** of the $684,000 left after the sale of the old house, he could borrow income-tax free from the life policy **$35,000** a year from ages 70-84 (I assumed a **7.5%** rate of return in the indexed life policy). ($420,000 is an arbitrary number I chose for this example).

EQUITY-INDEXD ANNUITIES (EIAs) (ALSO KNOWN AS FIXED INDEXED ANNUITIES (FIAs)

What if Dr. Smith repositioned the $420,000 into equity-index annuities (EIAs)? If the annuities returned a reasonable **5.5%** annually, then he would be able to withdraw **$67,747** a year for the same 15-year period (70-84). If the annuity was annuitized, Dr. Smith would have the following left after taxes: **$51,314** in the 40% income tax bracket, **$55,422** in the 30% bracket, and **$61,585** in the 15% bracket. Remember that with an annuity, Dr. Smith only has to pay income taxes on the growth.

All of the after-tax withdrawals from of the annuity beat the tax-free income from the life insurance policy.

STOCK MARKET

What if Dr. Smith repositioned the $420,000 into the stock market earning the same 7.5% as the equity-indexed life insurance policy? If we assume a 20% blended capital gain/dividend tax rate annually on the growth and a 1% mutual fund expense (no money management fee however), Dr. Smith could remove **$62,773** after taxes from the brokerage account every year for the same 15-year period (ages 70-84).

This is more than the amount that can be removed from the EIA; but in the stock market, there is **NO protection** if the stock market tanks With the EIA, Dr. Smith has principal protection (and maybe even a guaranteed payout, depending on the product)

FYI, if we assumed Dr. Smith was in "preferred" health for the underwriting of his cash value life insurance policy; he could borrow **$43,000** income-tax free every year from age 70-84.

My point with this discussion is that Equity Harvesting for retirement income is difficult to make work for someone who is at or over the age of 60 years old. Nonetheless, I've seen several illustrations on Equity Harvesting proposed for clients who range from 60 to upwards of 70 years old.

My opinion is that advisors who stick to a strict adherence to Equity Harvesting as a cure-all to solve a client's retirement shortfall will be doing their clients a disservice if they are manipulating the numbers to make a client over the age of 60 think the concept is likely to perform better than other options available. Again, if clients are willing to wait 10-15 years to access the cash in the policy, the number can work for certain individuals (although most will not want to wait that long to access the money).

SUMMARY ON USING HOME EQUITY MANAGEMENT TO RESCUE MONEY FROM AN IRA OR QUALIFIED RETIREMENT PLAN.

Using Home Equity Management to remove money from an IRA or a qualified retirement plan can work very nicely **IF you sell your home**, take profits, and buy a new home with a deductible home mortgage.

As the numbers indicate, using the strategies discussed in this chapter to create more retirement income through the use of cash value life insurance is a very difficult task if you are over the age of 60.

For those with estate tax problems who are also looking to maximize the size of their after-tax estate that will be passed to the heirs at death, using Home Equity Management as discussed in this chapter can increase the size of your after-tax estate by sometimes millions of dollars.

I know this chapter is not the easiest to understand as the subject matter is new to most and the concepts discussed are not the easiest to explain in a book.

Having said that, I put this chapter in the book to make those who have estate tax problems and money in an IRA or qualified retirement plan aware of the double tax dilemma and the few options available to them to mitigate the problem using Home Equity Management.

After reading this chapter, you should be able to determine if you can benefit by the solutions discussed. If you have questions that your local advisors cannot answer, please feel free to e-mail me at info@thewpi.org; and I'll do my best to be helpful.

Chapter 10
Reverse Mortgages

This Chapter of the book was created to teach readers about how Reverse Mortgages are used in the context of Home Equity Management. Let me preface this chapter by saying that I went overboard to give you details about how a Reverse Mortgage works. Reverse mortgages can be very confusing and can be abused by advisors selling them; and while you don't need to be an expert in the subject matter to determine if one can be beneficial for you or a loved one, the material in this chapter will give you enough information to "fully" understand the details of Reverse Mortgages.

You won't see much about Reverse Mortgages in "sales" books that pitch the concept of Equity Harvesting; but since this book is an educational book on Home Equity Management, the topic of Reverse Mortgages must be covered.

There are tens of thousands of Americans who use Reverse Mortgages to manage the equity in their homes and improve their lives in retirement. The number of people using Reverse Mortgages dwarfs those who are using Equity Harvesting to build wealth for retirement.

Using a Reverse Mortgage, for many people, can be a life-altering event that can help them sustain a certain lifestyle in retirement.

Having said that, my guess is that 95% of the people who purchased this book are under the age of 62 and are looking to build wealth for retirement.

Reverse Mortgages are **only** for readers who are over the age of 62. If you are not over the age of 62, you could choose to skip this chapter because you can't use a Reverse Mortgage until you turn 62.

However, I don't recommend skipping this chapter. Why? Because nearly everyone who purchased this book who is not yet 62 years old will have parents, and many of them will be over the age of 62. Many of those parents will have a need for more money in retirement; and through a Reverse Mortgage, they can obtain that needed money. Therefore, I recommend that you read this chapter so that you can be more informed about a topic that can be a useful retirement tool for someone in your family (and maybe for you when you reach the age of 62).

INTRODUCTION

This chapter will focus on what a Reverse Mortgage is, how it works, why it works, and why it should be considered for many readers over the age of 62. This material will compare the various Reverse Mortgage programs to each other and will also dissect some case studies that highlight the salient elements of each program.

The Reverse Mortgage industry is undergoing a cataclysmic change. Investors and lenders now understand that this market has tremendous upside potential. While the amount of closed loans has increased over 500% since 2001, market penetration is a fraction of one percent. In the years to come, the Reverse Mortgage landscape will not be recognizable.

In the past, the industry had few programs and a one-size–fits-all mentality. The programs of the future will take into account the varying needs of our elders. There will be new programs, with different types of interest rate structures and with different cost variations. These changes will put more money into the pockets of our elders and in a more flexible and client-friendly manner.

The examples and case studies contained in this chapter are for didactic purposes only. Because the Reverse Mortgage industry updates interest rates on a weekly basis, it is impossible to track these changes in this book. More importantly, this material will provide you with the key concepts that the industry uses to arrive at a given result.

Reverse Mortgages can act as an emergency investment vehicle, an estate-planning device, or a retirement facilitator. In order to begin a discussion on this topic, it will help to have a good definition of just what a Reverse Mortgage is.

WHAT IS A REVERSE MORTGAGE?

A Reverse Mortgage is a special and different kind of loan that is easy to obtain if you are at least 62 years of age and own your own home, condo (PUD) or co-op (only in New York). A Reverse Mortgage converts a portion of the value (equity) of a home into instant cash. The pool of money that is created by a Reverse Mortgage can be received by a senior homeowner(s) in a variety of ways.

One of the key features to a Reverse Mortgage is that the borrower is NOT required to pay monthly mortgage payments. Additionally, there is NO personal liability attached to the loan. A Reverse Mortgage loan is nonrecourse, except that the borrower's home does serve as collateral.

One other key feature to a Reverse Mortgage is that there are **no income, asset, or credit requirements** to obtain the loan. That means a borrower who has poor credit, no income, and no other assets besides a home with equity could still obtain a Reverse Mortgage to raise money for a variety of needs.

The concept of Reverse Mortgages is easy to understand, and borrowers over the age of 62 who learn about how they work gravitate to them because of the tremendous and immediate benefit provided without having to put up significant assets.

WHO CAN USE A REVERSE MORTGAGE?

Age 62 is one of a few "magic numbers" you will see in this book. Each homeowner must be at least 62. If one spouse is 62 and one is not, then the "couple" cannot obtain such a loan.

On the other hand, should the younger spouse be removed from the title, the older spouse can obtain the Reverse Mortgage. Caution needs to be taken with this strategy, and I personally do not recommend it.

Let's look at an **example**:

A husband and wife are 68 and 60, respectively. If the husband dies before the wife turns 62, the Reverse Mortgage loan must be paid back. (Remember, in order to obtain a Reverse Mortgage for this couple, they had to take the 60-year-old spouse off the title and the mortgage. Therefore, when the older spouse dies, the mortgage, which is tied to husband's death, must be repaid via the terms of the Reverse Mortgage).

Usually to pay back the loan, the surviving spouse, who inherited the entire home, is forced to sell the home. However, that is not always the preference for paying back a Reverse Mortgage.

Many Reverse Mortgages are sold with the incorporation of life insurance, which is used to pay off the mortgage after one or both spouses die. Life insurance, if used in the above example, would be used to pay off the mortgage. This would be the ideal situation since the 60-year-old spouse would have the money (liquid and tax-free) to pay off the mortgage and would not have to move out of her residence. This is explained in more detail later.

Home ownership can be accomplished in a variety of ways. A home that is a primary residence can be owned in severalty (individually), jointly, in trust, or with a life estate.

If one sets up a revocable trust, a Reverse Mortgage can still be an option provided the beneficiaries are the seniors. The children can be beneficiaries upon the death of the surviving parent. Title to the property must be in the name of the trustees, and the trustees do not have to be the borrowers (seniors). The trust will be amended at closing to permit a Reverse Mortgage.

An irrevocable trust, on the other hand, is more troublesome. Typically, such a trust is created as an asset protection device or an estate transfer tool. Whenever such a trust is used, it generally precludes the senior from accessing the corpus (assets) of the trust. Accordingly, drawing down the proceeds from the Reverse Mortgage would be a prohibited activity.

The amount of money that can be created or manufactured (as a salesman would say) from a Reverse Mortgage is dependent upon the program used. Generally speaking, it can be said that three factors will determine how much a borrower can receive from a Reverse Mortgage:

1. The age of the youngest borrower.

2. The value of the home (up to a certain limit for some programs).

3. The interest rate (for some programs). We will get into the specifics of each program when we look at the case studies.

The pool of money that is created from a Reverse Mortgage can be received in a variety of ways. Again, the ways will vary under the different programs. The options that may be available are lump sum, partial lump sum, monthly payment, line of credit, or any combination of these.

One of the key features that sets a Reverse Mortgage apart from any other kind of loan is that it is a **nonrecourse loan**. There is no personal liability to the borrower, their estate, or to their heirs.

Let's look at a worst case scenario.

Assume for a moment that the amount that ultimately becomes due on the Reverse Mortgage is greater than the value of the home. (This could happen due to extra ordinary interest rate increases, if the property significantly decreased in value, or if the client just happened to live much longer than anticipated).

When the house is sold by the estate, it nets, let's say, $300,000. Let us also assume that the amount due on the loan is $400,000. The difference of $100,000 **does not** become a liability of the estate.

ENTERING INTO A PARTNERSHIP WITH YOUR HOME

Another key feature that makes a Reverse Mortgage loan special and different is that **monthly mortgage payments are <u>not</u> required** because interest and servicing fees accrue over time. Just like any other negative amortization loan, the loan balance will increase if mortgage payments are not made.

HARNESSING THE POWER OF REVERSE MORTGAGES

A Reverse Mortgage is nothing short of a life-changing event for many people. For some, the weight of the world will have been lifted from their backs. Many seniors did not make the best investing or financial decisions throughout their earning years. Their need for immediate money can be satisfied with this program. They get the best of both worlds: their equity is transformed into cash AND they **<u>can still stay in their home</u>.**

PRELIMINARY OBSERVATIONS

Many Americans never expected to live as long as they have. As a population, we are living longer. The birth rate as a percentage of the population has been down for many years. It is estimated that over the next 16 years, the population over age 50 will grow by 74%, while the population under age 50 will grow by a small fraction of that amount. No state currently has a senior population greater than 17%. In the next 20 years, 30 states will have a senior population that exceeds 20%.

Social Security is not getting our seniors where they need to be. Ida Mae Fuller was the first recipient of Social Security. Over a few years of work, she contributed about $30 per month. She received back over $23,000. Sara Knauss lived to be over 115. Among her, a daughter, and a grandson they collectively received Social Security for over 100 years. Imagine what will happen when we have tens of millions of Saras and Ida Maes receiving these benefits. Many of us will wish we would have done things differently; but each one of us will be thankful that we have a home that we can depend on.

Medicare has done wonderful things. It has kept a substantial number of people out of poverty. However, its goal of protecting our older citizens from facing catastrophic medical bills has not been fully realized.

Medicare is the government's answer to healthcare insurance. Because it is insurance, the government pays only a portion of a claimant's bill. Each insured is responsible for the yearly deductible, the daily co-insurance under Part A, and the remaining 20 percent of the doctor bills under Part B.

It is important for individuals to purchase private health coverage for the part that the government does not pick up. Medicare's payments to the hospitals are diagnosis-based. This means that the hospital gets paid the same whether the patient is in the hospital two or seven days. There is a great incentive for hospitals to discharge patients as quickly as possible. The need for long-term care becomes critical.

Question: How does this become affordable for people who live only on Social Security benefits and/or a modest pension benefit?

Many seniors believed that the stock market was infallible. They were wrong. Many investors have lost a significant amount of their portfolio in retirement. They do not like the insecure feeling that comes along with their error in judgment but are now forced to deal with the reality that their "nest egg" is not big enough to live in a manner that is acceptable to them and their children.

As you know after reading the first part of this book, many people have never considered financial and/or estate planning.

BRUTAL FACTS OF REALITY

We have many seniors who live in big homes but have little savings (which is something you'll want to avoid and one of the reasons to educate yourself on Equity Harvesting). Typically, older clients, even those who do not have a sizeable liquid estate, have figured out a way to pay down the debt on their personal residence, many times to zero.

While such clients have no or little debt on their house, many still have trouble paying their monthly bills. They are, many times, unable to realize their life's hopes and dreams due to a lack of money. So whether we are talking about a person living in a $200,000 home or someone living in a home valued at greater than a million dollars, a Reverse Mortgage can satisfy diverse needs. There is a special proprietary program specifically created for those who live in high value homes, and a great deal of money can be extracted from the value of these homes.

Question: What financial program can ameliorate years of wrong financial decision-making? Potentially, a Reverse Mortgage.

REVERSE MORTGAGE ADVANTAGES

In just a few pages, I've covered a wide area. Let me take a moment to recap the huge advantages of this unique program.

A senior will never make a monthly mortgage payment to a lender. In fact, the opposite is true. The senior will have a choice (these options vary from program to program) of how they will receive their funds when they convert a portion of their home value into a pool of cash. The senior will always remain the owner of the home. The senior borrower can use the money just about any way he or she would like. The use of funds is limited by the creativity of the borrower. This important economic weapon will allow seniors all over the country to realize their hopes and dreams.

THE THREE REVERSE MORTGAGE PLANS

As of this writing, there are three national Reverse Mortgage programs. The original model program, upon which the other two are based on, was created and authorized by Congress in 1989. This is the FHA (Federal House Adminstration) or HECM (Home Equity Conversion Mortgage) or HUD Reverse Mortgage. All three designations refer to the same (federal) government-insured loan program. This program comprises over 90% of the Reverse Mortgage market.

In 1996, Fannie Mae came out with their HomeKeeper Reverse Mortgage program. It is the only program that one can use to purchase a home. (It is rumored that the FHA will be coming out with a similar program). On the other hand, for the time being, the FHA requires the client to buy the home in cash before it will sell the Reverse Mortgage. Instead, with Fannie Mae, a borrower is allowed to buy a new home with some amount of debt, and then use the Homekeeper program to get the equity out via a Reverse Mortgage. The purpose of HomeKeeper program is to get a borrower into a home without having him or her having to make home mortgage payments.

Finally in 2001, Lehman Bros. developed a proprietary Reverse Mortgage program. Many advisors call it the "Jumbo" Reverse Mortgage program. This program was updated and revised in 2006, and is now called the Cash Advantage. The name change reflects a change in the margin, which was lowered to 3.5 per cent from 5 per cent. This change provides an additional source of funds to the senior borrower. It also contains some unique features that we will discuss when we review the case studies.

REVERSE MORTAGES ARE HERE TO STAY

Reverse Mortgages are here to stay because they fulfill a pressing need; the need is pressing because expenses are increasing (especially health care and long-term care) at a rather alarming pace and because most seniors did not expect the longevity train to take them for such a long ride. Additionally, because most basic financial and estate planning was and continues to be ignored by the general public, there will continue to be a need for people to trade a portion of the value of the home for cash to pay for their living needs.

Let's take a quick look at the effect that an aging population can have on a family. Consider this: eighty-five percent of seniors who are age 65 or over have one chronic illness. Thirty percent of those over age 85 have 3 chronic illnesses. Ten percent of those who reach age 65 suffer from Alzheimer's or some form of dementia. This figure is almost 50% for those age 85.

Take into account that Medicare **will not** pay for custodial care and will only pay for 100 days of skilled nursing care per benefit period only if the person is improving in health. It will cover 100% of the costs for the first twenty days. For days 21-100, it will not cover the daily co-insurance amount. This amount alone could grow to over $8,000. Seniors are wrong to believe that their government will pick up the total cost for their skilled nursing care.

The financial and emotional toll of aging can cause havoc within the family. Children who have children of their own have the added financial and, sometimes, physical burden of meeting the needs of a parent. Children are sometimes forced to become caregivers because funds are scarce. About 20% of family caregivers spend 40 hours per week caring for their loved ones. Sometimes children will sacrifice promotions at work, or may have to quit their job to care for a parent(s). It is not unusual for a child to suffer from burnout soon after taking on this responsibility. If another sibling is not available to lend a hand, or if respite care is not available, it is a recipe for disaster. Many of the baby boomers will spend more time providing eldercare than childcare.

Question: How can parents regain their independence and release their children to live their own lives?

July 1983 marked a watershed moment in our history. It was the first time ever that the number of seniors exceeded the number of teenagers. In 1900, 1 in every 25 person reached their 65th birthday. That number is now just less than 1 in 8.

WHY A REVERSE MORTGAGE WORKS

It works because we are dealing with an asset (the home) that has appreciated over the years. Now, after growing in value, the home is going to return the love to the owner. Part of the value of the home will be use to pay off most of the closing costs of a Reverse Mortgage. If the client chooses, the only out-of-pocket expense will be $450-$600, depending upon the program. In return, a pool of money is created for the owner. With a Reverse Mortgage, it is the home that ultimately becomes responsible for paying the loan back--remember, it is a nonrecourse loan.

MOVING IN REVERSE

Many seniors are told to sell their homes and/or to go to their neighborhood bank to get a conventional loan if they need extra income. How many of you know elder people who have sold their home? Even when everything goes well, it is not a pretty picture for many. The emotional toll on a senior also needs to be considered when considering a Reverse Mortgage. AARP, in survey after survey, has shown that a majority of our elders do not want to move; they want to stay in their homes. Their goal is to stay in the environment that contains much of their family and personal history. Usually, they want to remain in an area that is familiar to them. Their house is the story of their lives.

Question: What is a client to do if he/she **doesn't want to sell** or if he/she can't or chose not to obtain a conventional loan?

RISK REVERSAL

This concept is not spoken about enough. A Reverse Mortgage is 100 percent risk-free. First, no document requires that a borrower continue the process if they subsequently have a change of mind. **Second, every Reverse Mortgage has a counseling component to it.** The purpose of the independent counseling is to insure that every senior understands the concept and is not coerced into action. Third, federal law provides that even after signing the closing documents, every senior has three days to reconsider. If at that time they change their minds, then any funds that they paid out must be returned. This is a 100% risk-free loan.

OUR "SENIOR PIONEERS" – A BIT OF A REVIEW AND SOME THINGS NEW

Once again, seniors are blazing new financial trails--this time with Reverse Mortgages. Earlier, many of today's seniors and/or their parents also pioneered the concept of a thirty-year loan.

In the early 1900's, it was quite difficult for individuals to obtain mortgages. A down payment of 50% was usually required. The mortgage then was a 5-year, interest-only balloon mortgage.

The Great Depression cataclysm marked the end of unregulated mortgage banking in this country. Many homeowners could not repay their debt or refinance their existing loans. Banks lost the ability to lend when their depositors withdrew their funds.

Roosevelt's New Deal helped to restore the public's confidence in the mortgage banking industry. Soon the thirty-year amortized loan became available, along with standard interest rates and standard underwriting guidelines. Loans were securitized. This added liquidity to the mortgage financial markets.

Seniors were doing things no one had done before. They were signing newly created documents. Today, these very documents are considered "standard." Back then, seniors were taking on 30 years of monthly payments. At the time, this was unheard of. Back then, a thirty-year loan was a vastly different concept. Today, this is considered standard.

Back then, the United States government insured these thirty-year loans. This was historic. Today, this is standard.

Years ago, people were warned that they would lose their homes and that they would go broke if they signed these hard-to-understand mortgage documents. Imagine that.

Now let us fast forward to the present. There is this new financial concept that many seniors are now exploring. While Reverse Mortgages have been around since the early 1960's, they were unregulated, took on many forms, and were called by different names. Relatively few were purchased. As mentioned before, it wasn't until 1989 that Congress authorized the first government–insured, standardized Reverse Mortgage. Who says that history does not repeat itself?

Now, seniors are being asked to sign documents that attorneys, accountants, and financial planners have not seen before. Seniors are being told that if they get a Reverse Mortgage, they will lose their home. Imagine that. It's shocking to think that a CPA/accountant or attorney would simply tell a client that a concept like Reverse Mortgages is risky, even though the advisor doesn't really understand the concept.

The bottom line is this; conventional financing permitted seniors to raise their family in the home of their choosing, and after many years of value appreciation, the Reverse Mortgage is permitting many seniors to stay in their home AND live the life they were, up until now, only dreaming about living.

The following is worth repeating: a Reverse Mortgage is a special kind of loan for many reasons.

It is special because the senior, who is at least 62 years of age, never has to make monthly mortgage payments.

It is also special because all Reverse Mortgage loans are nonrecourse loans. This means that there is no personal liability. If the amount that eventually becomes due is greater than the value of the house (assume that the home depreciated in value during the term of the Reverse Mortgage), then the most the bank can receive is the value of the home. This is an incredible feature. Compare this to the loan that you have on your home now. If the same scenario happened with that loan, your bank would sue you personally for the difference. This could never happen with a Reverse Mortgage.

Also, it is special because it frees up a portion of the value of a senior's home that he or she can convert into cash. It provides a senior with a wonderful way to tap this equity without selling his or her home and without obtaining a loan with monthly payments. Many surveys indicate that a majority of seniors prefer to remain in their homes.

Another reason it is a special loan is because it can become a lifesaver for both the children and the parents. Over two billion dollars a month are spent in this country by people to help their aging mom and/or dad. Many cannot do it anymore. The adult children have to put money away for their own retirement and for the college education of their own children.

The parents, on the other hand, by obtaining a Reverse Mortgage, can reclaim their independence and their dignity. In essence, the Reverse Mortgage can transfigure a strained relationship between a senior parent and an adult child into an emotional loving relationship that is free of "required" financial obligations.

Finally, a Reverse Mortgage is special because our seniors can receive the proceeds in a variety of ways. They can receive money each month, take a lump sum or a partial lump sum, or put the money in a Reverse Mortgage line of credit. Once they make a choice, they can always change their minds. They are never locked into a particular way to receive their money.

Professionals today will echo the negative caveats of their colleagues of years ago. Seniors will be told not to go through with the Reverse Mortgage because it is a scam. Yes, a Reverse Mortgage is different but it certainly is not a "scam." The government is insuring these loans and assuring seniors that they will receive every penny they are due, even if the lender goes out of business. In other words, they do not have to worry about a bank closing its doors.

THINGS YOU MAY BE TOLD BY ADVISORS WHO DO NOT UNDERSTAND REVERSE MORTGAGES

This section is very important. Once you put down this book and start looking for help on Reverse Mortgages, you'll run into many advisors who simply do not know the subject matter. That means you'll probably be told all sorts of things about Reverse Mortgages that are simply wrong. This section will point out the more salient misconceptions and rumors that are typically repeated by advisors and non-advisors who do not know what they are talking about.

RUMOR: You will be told that you will have to make monthly mortgage payments.

TRUTH: You will never have to make monthly mortgage payments.

RUMOR: You will be told that the bank will own the house.

TRUTH: You will continue to own the house. The bank will never own the home while you are living in.

RUMOR: You will be told that your heirs could become responsible for paying this loan back.

TRUTH: It is a nonrecourse loan. There is no personal responsibility for the borrowers, their estate, or their heirs.

RUMOR: The loan is due and payable when the first borrower dies.

TRUTH: The loan is not due and payable until the last surviving borrower dies, sells the home, or does not use the residence for 365 consecutive days. The loan must be paid in full when the youngest borrower reaches his/her 150th birthday.

RUMOR: Reverse Mortgages are only for seniors who are poor.

TRUTH: Seniors from every economic level and from all walks of life are taking advantage of the benefits offered by a Reverse Mortgage. Clients range from those who own modest homes to those who own multimillion dollar homes.

RUMOR: A senior must enjoy good health to qualify for a Reverse Mortgage.

TRUTH: This is wrong. Unlike long-term care insurance, or life insurance, Reverse Mortgages are not medically underwritten.

One of the most pressing issues facing our growing senior population is how to effectively finance the out-of-control costs of long-term care. Reverse Mortgage proceeds can be used either as a sole payment source for a healthcare aide or as a supplement to the hours received for home-care benefits through Medicaid. Taking into account all the Reverse Mortgage benefits, seniors may very well be able to live their final years at home and avoid placement in a nursing home. This allows seniors to maintain their independence, their dignity, and control over their long-term care. Reverse Mortgages are especially effective in New York, where the proceeds from a Reverse Mortgage are not considered a countable resource for Medicaid purposes.

CASE STUDIES

We will begin by looking at the Cash Advantage Reverse Mortgage program. This program is designed for high value homes. The borrower's age is a major factor in determining just how much of the value of the home can be converted into cash. The older the borrower is, the greater the pool of money available to him or her. For these and all other illustrations, the closing costs are based on typical New York City metropolitan area costs.

Assume a couple has a home that has a value of $1,500,000 and that it is fully paid off. The age of the younger, or "nearest," spouse is 75. (Unlike the HECM program, the borrower's age and the value of the home determine the Principal Limit (the starting point) of the Cash Advantage program).

The couple has 3 options for receiving the funds from the Cash Advantage Reverse Mortgage program: lump sum distribution, a line of credit/monthly payments, or a combination of the two.

The first option is a lump sum distribution. The couple could realize $709,500 with this option with no closing costs. Under the <u>original</u> Jumbo program, they would have only realized $484,000. So as you can see, the Cash Advantage program introduced in 2006 is a significant improvement over the original Jumbo program.

The second option is the new Combo Plan. Under this plan, the proceeds will be in the form of a lump sum distribution and a line of credit or monthly payments. The origination fee is paid by the lender in this plan. The Combo Plan stipulates that 75% of the amount that can be realized <u>must</u> be taken in one initial payment. The balance of the funds can be placed in a Reverse Mortgage line of credit, where these funds will grow tax-free at a guaranteed rate of 5%. Alternatively, the balance can be received as monthly payments.

Both of these options have a prepayment bar for 5 years. A prepayment bar is not a prepayment penalty; rather, it is a clause that simply "bars" the borrower from making ***voluntary prepayments.*** Sale of the home, death of the borrower, and not using the home as a primary residence are all typical maturity events that would not violate the 5-year prepayment bar.

The third plan or option is now called the Credit Line. It has a total closing cost of over $22,000 (not insignificant). Under this plan, the amount that could be realized is less than the previous two. However, the difference here is that the borrower <u>could take as much or as little as they want from the Reverse Mortgage</u>. There is no prepayment bar, and the borrower could receive monthly payments and/or put all or some of the proceeds in a Reverse Mortgage line of credit. Again, the amount placed in the line of credit will grow at a guaranteed 5%.

The question of making a prepayment or an interest payment often arises with this program, as well as with the HECM and the HomeKeeper plans. You cannot make an interest payment **and** get a tax deduction. See IRC section 163(a). The reason for this is that the Reverse Mortgage balance is increasing each month due to the unpaid interest being added to the unpaid balance, and one can argue that the loan is paying itself interest each month (by subtracting it from the home's equity). Therefore, an interest payment on a Reverse Mortgage amounts to a reimbursement of the home's equity, rather than a deductible interest payment. Also, note that the line of credit is a revolving line of credit. Therefore, the IRS would not look kindly upon an "interest" payment being made when the result would be an increase in the amount of money the borrower could take out from the Reverse Mortgage.

The interest rate on a Cash Advantage program is based upon the 6-month LIBOR Rate (London Interbank Offered Rate). The rate is discounted by 50 basis points for the first six months. Afterwards, the borrower will receive the fully indexed rate, whatever it may be at that time.

The following is a **real live illustration** that goes with the previous explanation.

Estimates For: John Smith Roslyn Heights, NY		Nearest Age **75**	Age **75**
	Credit Line Cash Advantage	Combo Cash Advantage.	Cash Out Cash Advantage.
Initial Interest Rate	8.40%	8.40%	8.40%
Expected Interest Rate*	8.90%	8.90%	8.90%
Interest Rate Cap	14.90%	14.90%	14.90%
Monthly Service Fee	$20	$20	$20
Estimated Home Value	$1,500,000	$1,500,000	1,500,000
Lending Limit	$1,500,000	$1,500,000	$1,500,000
Percentage	100.00%	100.00%	100.00%
Credit line Growth Rate	5%	5%	5%
Principal Limit	$709,500.00	$709,500.00	$709,500.00
Service Set-Aside	$0.00	$0.00	$0.00
Available Principal Limit	$709,500.00	$709,500.00	$709,500.00
Initial Mort. Ins. Prem.	$0.00	$0.00	$0.00
Financed Origination Fee	$14,190.00	$0.00	$0.00
Other Financed Costs	$8,481.28	$8,481.28	$0.00
Net Principal Limit	$686,828.72	$701,018.720	$709,500.00
Debt Payoff Advance	$0.00	$0.00	$0.00
Tax & Ins. Set-Aside	$0.00	$0.00	$0.00
Net Available to You	$686,828.72	$701,018.72	$709,500.00
Cash Requested	$0.00	$523,613.72	$709,500.00
Credit line Requested	$686,82872	$177,375.50	$0.00
Remaining Cash	$0.00	$0.00	$0.00
	Or	or	Or
Potential Tenure Payments	$0.00	$0.00	$0.00
Financed Fees and Costs	$22,671.28	$8,481.28	$0.00
Borrower Paid Costs	$0.00	$0.00	$0.00

If we make the potential client older, you will see that the amount realized will be greater. On the other hand, when there are **two** borrowers under the "Cash Advantage" plan (and the HomeKeeper plan), the amount that can be realized will decrease because the bank must wait for the survivor to pass away before the loan will be repaid. (Under the HECM plan, an additional borrower <u>will not</u> affect the amount available.) The next two charts illustrate these points.

Estimates For: Dr. John Smith Roslyn Heights, NY	Age **85**	Age **85**	
	Credit Line Cash Advt.	Combo Cash Advt.	Cash Out Cash Advt.
Initial Interest Rate	8.40%	8.40%	8.40%
Expected Interest Rate*	8.90%	8.90%	8.90%
Interest Rate Cap	14.90%	14.90%	14.90%
Monthly Service Fee	$20	$20	$20
Estimated Home Value	$1,500,000	$1,500,000	1,500,000
Lending Limit	$1,500,000	$1,500,000	$1,500,000
Percentage	100.00%	100.00%	100.00%
Credit line Growth Rate	5%	5%	5%
Principal Limit	$787,500.00	$787,500.00	$787,500.00
Service Set-Aside	$0.00	$0.00	$0.00
Available Principal Limit	$787,500.00	$787,500.00	$787,500.00
Initial Mort. Ins. Prem.	$0.00	$0.00	$0.00
Financed Origination Fee	$15,750.00	$0.00	$0.00
Other Financed Costs	$8,481.28	$8481.28	$0.00
Net Principal Limit	$763,268.72	$779,018.72	$787,500.00
Debt Payoff Advance	$0.00	$0.00	$0.00
Tax & Ins. Set-Aside	$0.00	$0.00	$0.00
Net Available to You	$763,268.72	$779,018.72	$787,500.00
Cash Requested	$0.00	$582,143.72	$787,500.00
Credit line Requested	$763,268.72	$196,875.00	$0.00
Remaining Cash	$0.00	$0.00	$0.00
	Or	or	or
Potential Tenure Payments	$0.00	$0.00	$0.00
Financed Fees and Costs	$24,231.28	$8,481.28	$0.00
Borrower Paid Costs	$0.00	$0.00	$0.00

Estimates For: Dr. and Mrs. Smith Roslyn Heights, NY		Nearest Age 85 85	Age 85 85
	Credit Line Cash Advt.	Combo Cash Advt.	Cash Out Cash Advt.
Initial Interest Rate	8.40%	8.40%	8.40%
Expected Interest Rate*	8.90%	8.90%	8.90%
Interest Rate Cap	14.90%	14.90%	14.90%
Monthly Service Fee	$20	$20	$20
Estimated Home Value	$1,500,000	$1,500,000	1,500,000
Lending Limit	$1,500,000	$1,500,000	$1,500,000
Percentage	100.00%	100.00%	100.00%
Credit line Growth Rate	5%	5%	5%
Principal Limit	$750,000.00	$750,000.00	$7500,00.00
Service Set-Aside	$0.00	$0.00	$0.00
Available Principal Limit	$750,000.00	$750,000.00	$750,000.00
Initial Mort. Ins. Prem.	$0.00	$0.00	$0.00
Financed Origination Fee	$15,000.00	$0.00	$0.00
Other Financed Costs	$8,312.28	$8481.28	$0.00
Net Principal Limit	$726,518.72	$779,018.72	$750,000.00
Debt Payoff Advance	$0.00	$0.00	$0.00
Tax & Ins. Set-Aside	$0.00	$0.00	$0.00
Net Available to You	$726,518.72	$741,518.72	$750,000.00
Cash Requested	$0.00	$554,018.72	$750,000.00
Credit line Requested	$726,518.72	$187,500.00	$0.00
Remaining Cash	$0.00	$0.00	$0.00
	or	or	Or
Potential Tenure Payments	$0.00	$0.00	$0.00
Financed Fees and Costs	$23,481.28	$8,481.28	$0.00
Borrower Paid Costs	$0.00	$0.00	$0.00

ESTATE PLANNING WITH JUMBO REVERSE MORTGAGES

While the core use of a Reverse Mortgage is to increase the cash flow of a senior who needs money and wants to remain in his/her home, using a Reverse Mortgage in a large estate plan can also make a lot of sense.

Think about the following: if a client (widow) has an estate of $7,000,000, and if a $1,000,000 home (no debt) made up part of the total value of the estate, the client has a pretty big estate tax headache.

With this type of client, classic estate planning says to take out a large Reverse Mortgage and have the client gift the borrowed funds to an Irrevocable Life Insurance Trust (ILIT), where the largest possible death benefit life insurance policy can be purchased.

Once the policy is inside an ILIT, the death benefit will pass **income and estate tax-free** (unlike the house, which will be estate taxed at 55% (if the client's death is after 2010)).

Almost universally with this strategy, the client will be able to buy a policy with a death benefit high enough to pay off the debt on the home from the Reverse Mortgage and still have several hundred thousands of extra death benefit that will pass income and estate tax-free to the heirs.

One reason people get concerned about using a Reverse Mortgage is because of the high debt that is piled onto the house (a house that many would like to pass to the heirs). When using life insurance in conjunction with a Reverse Mortgage for a client with an estate tax problem, the client can pass more after-tax wealth to the heirs than in the "do-nothing" alternative, where the IRS gets to keep 55% of the home's value through estate taxes after 2011.

The **next set of charts** illustrate the **HECM and the HomeKeeper Programs**. Unlike the Cash Advantage and HomeKeeper programs, the HECM has three factors that determine how much money the borrower can get. These are the age of the youngest borrower, the value of the home (up to the FHA lending limit for that area), and the Expected Interest Rate.

The Expected Interest Rate represents the yield on the 10-year bond plus a margin. The monthly adjustable Expected Interest Rate has a margin of 1.5%, whereas the annual adjustable has a 3.1% margin. In short, what all this means is that you can have two clients of the same age and with identical value homes living in areas that have different FHA lending limits; and the client who lives in the area with the higher FHA limit will have access to more funds than the client in the area with the lower limit. Notice the difference in the numbers in the next two charts.

Estimates For: Dr. John Smith Maryland, NY		Nearest Age 75	Age 75
	FHA/HUD Monthly Adj.	**FHA/HUD** Annual Adj.	Fannie Mae Standard
Initial Interest Rate	6.60%	8.20%	8.75%
Expected Interest Rate*	6.36%	7.96%	8.75%
Interest Rate Cap	16.60%	13.20%	20.75%
Monthly Service Fee	$30	$30	$30
Estimated Home Value	$400,000	$400,000	400,000
Lending Limit	**$200,160**	$200,160	$417,000
Percentage	50.04%	50.04%	100%
Credit Line Growth Rate	7.10%	8.70%	0%
Principal Limit	$131,705.28	$107,485.12	$166,528.00
Service Set-Aside	$4,323.35	$3,764.52	$3,468.21
Available Principal Limit	$127,381.93	$103,721.40	$163,059.79
Initial Mort. Ins. Prem.	$4,003.20	$4,003.20	$0.00
Financed Origination Fee	$4,003.20	$4,003.20	$8,000.00
Other Financed Costs	$3,422.85	$3,422.85	$3,482.39
Net Principal Limit	$115,952.68	$92,292.15	$151,577.40
Debt Payoff Advance	$0.00	$0.00	$0.00
Tax & Ins. Set-Aside	$0.00	$0.00	$0.00
Net Available to You	$115,952.68	$92,292.15	$151,577.40
Cash Requested	$0.00	$0.00	$0.00
Credit line Requested	$0.00	$0.00	$0.00
Remaining Cash	$115,952.68	$92,292.15	$151,577.40
	or	Or	Or
Potential Tenure Payments	$804.60	$735.49	$1311.14
Financed Fees and Costs	$11,479.15	$11,479.15	$11,482.39
Borrower Paid Costs	$0.00	$0.00	$0.00

In the above chart, the lending limit of an FHA/HUD monthly adjustable Reverse Mortgage for a $400,000 home is

$200,160. The same type of Reverse Mortgage for the same $400,000 home in a different part of the country (see the next chart) has a lending limit of **$362,790**.

Estimates For: Dr. John Smith **Roslyn Heights, NY**		Nearest Age 75	Age 75
	FHA/HUD Monthly Adj.	FHA/HUD Annual Adj.	Fannie Mae Standard
Initial Interest Rate	6.60%	8.20%	8.75%
Expected Interest Rate*	6.36%	7.96%	8.75%
Interest Rate Cap	16.60%	13.20%	20.75%
Monthly Service Fee	$30	$30	$30
Estimated Home Value	$400,000	$400,000	400,000
Lending Limit	**$362,790**	$362,790	$417,000
Percentage	90.7%	90.7%	%
Credit line Growth Rate	4.89%	6.49%	0%
Principal Limit	**$238,715.82**	$194,818.23	$166,528.00
Service Set Aside	$4,323.35	$3,764.52	$3,468.21
Available Principal Limit	$234,392.47	$191,053.71	$163,059.79
Initial Mort. Ins. Prem.	$7,255.80	$7,255.80	$0.00
Financed Origination Fee	$7,255.80	$7,255.80	$8,000.00
Other Financed Costs	$4004.45	$4,004.45	$3,451.37
Net Principal Limit	$215,876.42	$172,537.66	$151,608.42
Debt Payoff Advance	$0.00	$0.00	$0.00
Tax & Ins. Set-Aside	$0.00	$0.00	$0.00
Net Available to You	$215,876.42	$172,537.66	$151,608.42
Cash Requested	$0.00	$0.00	$0.00
Credit line Requested	$100,000.00	$100,000.00	$100,000.00
Remaining Cash	$115,876.42	$72,537.66	$51,608.42
	or	or	or
Potential Tenure Payments	$804.09	$578.08	$446.41
Financed Fees and Costs	$18,513.80	$18,513.80	$11,451.37
Borrower Paid Costs	$0.00	$0.00	$0.00

You will also notice that the FHA program has 2 different types of interest rates. The first one is called the initial interest rate. This is just like the note rate on any mortgage. The second rate listed in the chart is the Expected Interest Rate. It has one function: to determine how much money a senior can realize. Since the bond market fluctuates everyday, you will never know exactly how much money will be available until you get closer to the closing date. After the closing, the subsequent fluctuation in the bond market no longer has any effect. The Expected Interest Rate is now etched in stone because the loan is closed.

The Lending Limit of the last chart is for the downstate New York Metropolitan area. Your lending limit will probably be different. It is important to know just what it means. In the world of Reverse Mortgages, the location of the home will determine whether $362,790 or $200,160 of the $400,000 home value (using the figures from the last 2 charts) is potentially available to you. This means that your age, the lending limit I just discussed, and the Expected Interest Rate provides you with a beginning point. This beginning point is called the Principal Limit. It is from this Principal Limit that all expenses are deducted

Because you will never make a mortgage payment, the lender that services this loan provides you with a statement each month that tracks the amount of funds used. The lender needs to charge a fee for this service. This fee can be either $30 or $35. In our example, it is $30 and appears as "Monthly Service Fee" in the chart above. Actually, Fannie Mae makes these payments to the lender. Fannie Mae makes the payments because they actually purchase all the FHA paper.

The amount that is put aside in this illustration is based on mortality tables and upon the Expected Interest Rate. The reason for this cushion is because Fannie Mae wants to be assured that, when the loan is paid off, there is an amount that can be charged as reimbursement to Fannie Mae for paying the lender the monthly service fees during the time this loan was in place. Because this Service Set Aside amount remains the property of the borrower, interest is not being charged or accrued against this sum of money.

The closing costs are deducted from the available Principal Limit.

269

The mortgage insurance premium makes up a substantial part of the closing costs. The purpose of the mortgage insurance is to insure that all seniors get every dime that is owed to them. The government stands behind every loan. In addition to this, the government will also protect the lenders as well. In the event that a sale does not bring in enough funds to pay the negative amortized balance, the government will make the lenders whole, up to the FHA lending limit for that area.

The next cost listed in the charts is the origination fee. This fee, along with mortgage insurance amount, is determined by multiplying the Maximum Claim Amount by 2 percent. The Maximum Claim Amount is the lesser of the appraised value or the FHA lending limit. In the example above, multiply the FHA lending limit by 2% to arrive at the value of these fees.

The balance of the charges listed in the illustrations are an assortment of typical closing fees, with the bulk going to title insurance and title-related charges as they exist in the New York Metropolitan area. When all is subtracted, you will see that the monthly adjustable option provides significantly more money than the other two options. If you reside in an area that has a low FHA lending limit, you will find that the HomeKeeper will usually provide more funds than the HECM program. Head to head in a jurisdiction with the maximum FHA lending limit, the FHA program will always provide more access to funds than the HomeKeeper. This is because the internal calculations in the HomeKeeper program are more conservative, notwithstanding the current single national limit of $417,000.

You will also notice that the annual adjustable option has an interest rate cap of about 5% above the initial interest rate, while the monthly adjustable option has a cap of 10%. However, most purchasers really look toward the program that provides them with the most funds, not the lowest interest rate.

The FHA is a very flexible program. The 75-year-old client living in Roslyn Heights can receive $1,498 per month under what is called a tenure plan. This means that the money will never stop flowing to the borrower as long as the borrower is using the home as his/her primary residence. This means that the money will not stop even if they received a sum total greater than the $215,876.42.

The money will never stop, even after many years have passed and there is no more equity in the home.

If you need more than this amount per month, you could get it. For example, let's say that you need $2,000 per month. You could receive that amount of money for 166 months. After that period of time, the flow of money will stop.

You could even take a lump sum of $215,876.42 or a partial lump sum.

You can even combine payment options. You could take, say, about $800 per month for yourself and put about $100,000 in the Reverse Mortgage line of credit. The money that is in the line of credit will grow at 50 basis points above the current note interest rate, tax-free. While it is easier to suggest that the money automatically grows at a predetermined rate, what is actually happening is that the credit limit is merely increasing. These funds are not invested and earning money for the borrower.

It is important to remember that the margin on the standard FHA program has decreased to 1 point (from 1.5%). This means that FHA borrowers could receive even more funds now. Typically, a borrower could receive from $10,000 to $25,000 more, depending on his or her age.

In contrast to the FHA program, the HomeKeeper program has a credit line option without the growth factor. You could not choose a term payment option either. The one thing that is unique to the HomeKeeper program is that it can be used for a home purchase.

IN REVIEW

A Reverse Mortgage is the only way you can turn your home's equity into cash while staying in the home that you love and not having to pay an interest payment on the loan. A Reverse Mortgage oftentimes is a lifesaver for clients and their families. I've discussed the sacrifices the adult children are making on behalf of their parents and in-laws. The Reverse Mortgage can prevent the emotional family volcano from exploding. Parents hate having to go to their kids to ask for money. With a Reverse Mortgage, the parents would be able reclaim their independence and their dignity, while allowing the adult children to focus on their own family.

Because we are living longer these days, we must prepare for the unique challenges all of us will eventually face. We are probably past the point where we can depend on the government to take care of us. It is a time for becoming proactive. Beginning in the year 2012, 10,000 Americans per day will be turning 65. In the good old days, one became old, then sick, and then died. That is no longer happening. There is a new paradigm. Now, we grow old, get sick, and survive....for many more years.

A National Council on Aging study shows that Reverse Mortgages can help keep millions of our seniors in their homes. Not only will it free up funds for home-care, but it will allow millions of our elders to make needed improvements to their homes. This will enable seniors to stay in their homes. In fact, it is estimated that over half-a-trillion dollars can be extracted by over 13 million seniors who suffer from some kind of physical impairment. A significant number of seniors suffer from macular degeneration or another malady that requires that they stay in their homes, and, many times, that also requires that they make improvements to the home that will allow them to stay there. As the saying goes, "money does not grow on trees."

Seniors do not buy long-term care insurance because it is too expensive. A Reverse Mortgage will make that which was not affordable very affordable.

There are about 22 million senior households in this country. About 17 million of these households own their home mortgage-free. The home will continue to represent the biggest untapped source of equity for these households. Many of our elders are sitting on a gold mine. By learning this topic, you or your parent can easily and safely extract your home's equity, convert it into cash, and use the proceeds for any purpose, while never having to make a mortgage payment. A Reverse Mortgage can be a life-altering event for those who want to stay in their homes and not reduce their quality of life in retirement.

I'd like to give a special thanks to Dennis Haber, JD, who helped me with this extensive material on Reverse mortgages.

Chapter 11
The Home Equity Acceleration Plan (H.E.A.P.)

I'd like to thank John Steinke of Pier Financial Group for his contribution to this chapter. John is the co-creator of H.E.A.P.

INTRODUCTION

If you've turned first to this chapter of the book, you must be more interested in paying off the debt on your home instead of using your home's equity to build wealth in a tax-favorable manner for retirement.

If you read Chapters 1-10 first, I hope you came away from doing so with the understanding that using a home's equity to build wealth can be very beneficial when trying to create the largest possible retirement nest egg.

This chapter is the polar opposite to the rest of this book. This chapter discusses and explains the various plans you can use (without affecting your cash flow) to pay off the debt on your home literally years earlier than you would by simply paying your monthly 15- or 30-year mortgage payment.

SALES BOOKS VS. EDUCATIONAL BOOKS

As I've stated repeatedly in the other chapters of this book, there is a fundamental difference between books that educate and give full disclosure on topics and those that are written with fuzzy math and lack full disclosure on important issues.

Sales books try to drive the reader to a predetermined conclusion that the author wants the reader to come to and are written to motivate the reader to implement the concepts discussed in the book.

Sales books that discuss building wealth via Home Equity Management not only do not have a chapter telling readers how to pay off their home early but chastise the reader for even having such a thought.

The sales books give readers multiple reasons for not paying off the debt on their homes. While I fundamentally don't disagree that building wealth by using the equity in your home is a good idea for many readers, I fully understand that some people just don't like debt and, if they had the ability, would pay off the debt on their home as soon as possible.

If my main goal with this book is to manipulate and motivate every single reader to borrow money from their homes and build wealth by repositioning it into a tax-favorable, wealth-building vehicle, I would not have put this chapter in the book.

Why? Because many readers will read this chapter and not be motivated to Harvest Equity for wealth-building: instead, they will be excited that they finally found a plan that can be used to help them pay off the debt on their home years earlier without affecting their cash flow.

I'm fine with either decision for readers so long as a decision is made to move away from the "do-nothing" position that most people take in their lives and instead take action that will positively affect their lives in a positive financial manner.

THERE ARE TWO TYPES OF PEOPLE IN THIS WORLD

Is it a fair statement to say that there are two types of people in this world? There are those who want to use the equity in their homes to build a tax-favorable retirement nest egg and those who want to pay off the debt on their home as soon as possible.

I think that's a true statement. If you asked 100 people whether they would be interested in paying off their home loan years earlier through a simple plan, how many would say that they would rather just slowly pay off their 30-year home loan over 30 years? Not many.

If you've read Chapters 1-10, you are armed with the knowledge of how powerful Equity Harvesting can be to help grow your wealth in a tax-favorable and conservative manner. After reading this chapter, you will know how to pay off the debt on your home years earlier through simple plans that will not alter your spending habits or lifestyle.

CRITICAL CAPITAL MASS (CCM)

Many readers have a goal of reaching "critical capital mass" so someday they will be able to retire (hopefully sooner rather than later). As the name implies, critical capital mass means that you've amassed enough assets so you do not have to work and so you do not have to change your lifestyle in retirement (for however long you live).

Until people reach critical capital mass, they exist in a budgeted life style with a mortgage, a car loan, and a couple of credit cards. Then, hopefully, with the little bit they have left over after bills each month, they can invest some of it to reach their ultimate retirement goal.

Today there are hundreds of books and articles with advice on the best ways to become rich: get rich quick, get rich slow, get rich off real estate, get rich off your kids, etc. These books are full of great information, charts, graphs, and advice that may or may not be simple and straightforward. There are also back-to-back infomercials on TV, with real people giving testimonials on how they increased their wealth in just a few weeks, while the small print on the bottom of the screen reads how these results are not typical. All the while, the typical person tries to figure out the best way to get ahead.

The sales books out there that discuss Home Equity Harvesting cover similar strategies as this book but warn of recessions, job insecurity, and even the eventual demise of Social Security. They discuss these topics seemingly to scare readers into implementing the concepts discussed in their books.

Although it is true that the current Social Security system is in trouble, it is unlikely that the government will turn its back on the older members of society. There may be some drastic changes to the system that could reduce benefits but scaring people into using Equity Harvesting is not something I'm interested in doing with this book. I'd much rather have you choose to use Equity Harvesting to build wealth out of greed instead of out of fear.

While using Equity Harvesting to build your wealth (and if you have not read the chapter on Equity Harvesting, you should do so before continuing with this chapter) can be a great way to reach critical capital mass, paying down the debt on your home as discussed in this chapter will also help you build wealth by reducing debt.

After eliminating the debt on your home, your residual income will increase providing you with the opportunity to significantly boost your ability to build wealth outside of the value of your home.

The objective of this chapter of the book is to lay out the Home Equity Acceleration Plan (H.E.A.P.) as simply and as straightforward as possible and to give you the education and so you can determine if the plan is one that you should use in your wealth-building plan. This is a plan that you can be in complete control over and can track the progress weekly and within a very short period of time see the results and know that it truly is working.

Like any kind of wealth-building plan, the Home Equity Acceleration Plan may not work for everyone because there are some qualifying elements that are required (which will be discussed in the following pages).

Finally, as you read through this chapter, plug in your own numbers in some of the examples to see if there is any way the Home Equity Acceleration Plan can work for you. The goal of the chapter is to make the math simple enough to understand so that you can apply the calculations to your own situation.

THE BASICS OF MORTGAGE INTEREST

Since most of the chapter is about reducing mortgage debt, it is most important that you first understand how a mortgage is put together.

What is a residential home loan?

Generally speaking, it's when a lender agrees to lend money to a borrower using a home as collateral for a specific period of time at a specific interest rate.

Based upon the terms, a monthly payment is established so that the loan will be completely paid off at the end of the term of the loan.

If the interest rate chosen is an adjustable rate, the monthly payment may change periodically because it is recalculated when the interest rate changes.

Each loan payment has a principal and interest component to it. In the early years of paying back a loan, the majority of the payments are allocated to interest. In the last few years of a home loan, the majority of each of the payments is allocated to paying down the principal loan balance. Therefore, the lender makes the majority of its income from a home loan in the early years and not much towards the end of the lending term.

Mortgage calculations

While most of you know the math, you can see very simply how a monthly mortgage payment is calculated.

For example, a $200,000 loan at a rate of 6.5% would accrue approximately $1,083.33 of interest in the first month:

$200,000 x .065 = $13,000 (annual interest) / 12 (months) = $1,083.33

The payment schedule for this loan over 30 years would require a monthly payment of $1,264.14 in order to pay off the loan in full by the end of the term of the loan.

What most people try not to think about is the fact that in the early years of the loan very little of the loan balance is reduced.

For this example, after the first monthly payment was made, there would be a remaining principal balance of $199,819.19

$1,264.14 (payment) − $1,083.33 (interest charged) = $180.81 that is applied to paying down the principal loan balance.

$200,000 (original loan balance) − $180.81 (amount of payment that is applied towards principal balance) = 199,819.19 (new balance).

Going into the second month, the interest charges are calculated on the remaining balance. So the math is:

$199,819.19 (balance) x .065 (interest rate) / 12 (months) = $1,082.35 (interest for 2nd month).

That means the payment of $1,264.14 would pay $181.79 towards the balance (98 cents more than the previous month).

$1,264.14 (payment) – $1,082.35 (interest) = $181.79 (amount of payment applied to the remaining loan balance).

Based on these calculations, you can start to see how over time the balance is slowly reduced in the early years of a mortgage. Since the interest is calculated on the remaining balance, the interest charges reduce over time. Since the monthly payment amount remains the same, over time, the amount applied towards interest shrinks, while the amount applied to principal increases.

Take a look at the following amortization schedule. The schedule represents the annual amounts paid towards interest and principal. It also shows the remaining balance at the end of each year.

Loan Balance: $200,000; Interest Rate: 6.5%
First Payment: Jan.1, 2007 Monthly Payment: $1,264.14

Year	Total Payment	Interest Due	Applied to Principal	Remaining Balance
2007	$15,169.68	$12,934.23	$2,235.45	$197,764.55
2008	$15,169.68	$12,784.52	$2,385.16	$195,379.39
2009	$15,169.68	$12,624.78	$2,544.90	$192,834.48
2010	$15,169.68	$12,454.34	$2,715.34	$190,119.14
2011	$15,169.68	$12,272.49	$2,897.19	$187,221.95
2012	$15,169.68	$12,078.46	$3,091.22	$184,130.73
2013	$15,169.68	$11,871.43	$3,298.25	$180,832.49
2014	$15,169.68	$11,650.55	$3,519.13	$177,313.35
2015	$15,169.68	$11,414.86	$3,754.82	$173,558.54
2016	$15,169.68	$11,163.40	$4,006.28	$169,552.25
2017	$15,169.68	$10,895.09	$4,274.59	$165,277.66
2018	$15,169.68	$10,608.81	$4,560.87	$160,716.79
2019	$15,169.68	$10,303.36	$4,866.32	$155,850.47
2020	$15,169.68	$9,977.45	$5,192.23	$150,658.24
2021	$15,169.68	$9,629.72	$5,539.96	$145,118.28
2022	$15,169.68	$9,258.70	$5,910.98	$139,207.30
2023	$15,169.68	$8,862.83	$6,306.85	$132,900.45
2024	$15,169.68	$8,440.45	$6,729.23	$126,171.22
2025	$15,169.68	$7,989.78	$7,179.90	$118,991.32
2026	$15,169.68	$7,508.93	$7,660.75	$111,330.57
2027	$15,169.68	$6,995.887	$8,173.81	$103,156.76
2028	$15,169.68	$6,448.46	$8,721.22	$94,435.54
2029	$15,169.68	$5,864.38	$9,305.30	$85,130.24
2030	$15,169.68	$5,241.19	$9,928.49	$75,201.75
2031	$15,169.68	$4,576.26	$10,593.42	$64,608.32
2032	$15,169.68	$3,866.80	$11,302.88	$53,305.44
2033	$15,169.68	$3,109.82	$12,059.86	$41,245.58
2034	$15,169.68	$2,302.15	$12,867.53	$28,378.06
2035	$15,169.68	$1,440.39	$13,729.29	$14,648.77
2036	$15,169.68	$520.91	$14,648.77	$0.00

Take a little closer look at the amortization schedule. In the first year, the total monthly payments equal $15,169.68.

$1,264.14 (monthly) x 12 (number of payments) = $15,169.68.

Of the total payments made, $2,235.45 is applied to pay down the principal loan balance and $12,934.23 is paid as interest.

Now skip down to year 2017, which is the tenth year of the loan. The same amount of $15,169.68 is paid that year; however, $4,274.59 is applied to principal and $10,895.09 towards interest.

Now that we understand the math, let's try to calculate how much interest is due in 2018. Using a simple interest calculation, a reasonable estimate of how much interest is due in 2018 can be determined.

$165,277.66 (balance at end of 2017) X .065 (interest rate) = $10,743.05

Is the calculation correct?

Looking back at the chart, the actual interest charges for 2018 are $10,608.81, not $10,743.05. Why is the actual amount a little less than what we manually calculated? Because the manual calculation was for an **annual amount**.

Remember that the payments are applied monthly; each month that a payment is made, the principal balance is slightly reduced; and, therefore, the interest charges are also slightly reduced.

Let's look at each month of the year 2018 and how these payments are applied towards interest and principal.

Date	Interest	Principal	Balance
Jan, 2018	$895.26	$368.88	$164,908.78
Feb, 2018	$893.26	$370.88	$164,537.90
Mar, 2018	$891.25	$372.89	$164,165.01
Apr, 2018	$889.23	$374.91	$163,790.10
May, 2018	$887.20	$376.94	$163,413.16
Jun, 2018	$885.16	$378.98	$163,034.18
Jul, 2018	$883.11	$381.03	$162,653.14
Aug, 2018	$881.04	$383.10	$162,270.05
Sep, 2018	$878.97	$385.17	$161,884.87
Oct, 2018	$876.88	$387.26	$161,497.61
Nov, 2018	$874.78	$389.36	$161,108.26
Dec, 2018	$872.67	$391.47	$160,716.79

The above chart also might get you to think of how little the person in the example has paid down the principal loan balance after paying the $1,264.14 payment every month for 12 years. The person in this example paid 144 payments (12 years x 12 payments per year) for a total of $182,036.16. That's a lot of money to only have a debt reduction of only $39,283.21.

$200,000 (beginning balance) - $160,716.79 (balance 12/2018) = $39,283.21.

This means that over the 12-year period, the borrower paid $142,752.95 in interest.

$182,036.16 (total of all payments through 2018) - $39,283.21 (amount applied towards principal) = $142,752.95.

Because most borrowers understand that paying a home mortgage is making a bank a lot of money through interest payments and removing money from his/her pocket, many are motivated to pay off the debt on their home as early as possible.

Now let's look at the year 2026. This year would represent the 20th year of the 30-year loan. Notice anything special about 2026?

Date	Interest	Principal	Balance
2025	$7,989.78	$7,179.90	$118,991.32
2026	**$7,508.93**	**$7,660.75**	**$111,330.57**
2027	$6,995.87	$8,173.81	$103,156.76

2006 is the first year that the amount applied towards principal is more than the amount paid in interest. And it only took 20 years! 20 years is a long time. Think about what you were doing 20 years ago. It seems like a lifetime ago. With that thought in mind, I repeat: it took 20 years to get to the point in your home loan term where the mortgage payment finally allocated more money towards paying down principal than to paying interest.

Before moving on, let's look at one more number.

$455,090.40

This number represents the future value of the loan for the lender

$1,264.14 (monthly payment) x 360 (number of payments) = $455,090.40. This is the grand total of all the payments over the 30-year period.

Keep this figure in mind as you read through the rest of this chapter.

MORTGAGE INTEREST AS A DAILY AMOUNT

So far, this chapter has covered the basics of mortgage math. Using some basic arithmetic, you can come up with a fairly reasonable estimate of the interest that would be charged annually and monthly on a mortgage.

Balance x Interest Rate = Annual Interest

Annual Interest / 12 = Monthly Interest

These calculations can now be taken one step further to calculate the amount of interest that is charged **each day** on a home loan. Understanding this should make it easier to understand how the Home Equity Acceleration Plan works to help you pay off your home loan years earlier.

Balance x Rate = Annual Interest

Annual Interest / 365 days a year = Daily Interest

For our example, it would look as follows:

$200,000 (balance) x .065 (rate) = $13,000 (annual interest)

$13,000 (annual interest) / 365 days = $35.62 per day in interest charges.

Key Point: Interest accrues daily on the outstanding principal balance.

Everything that you have read and learned so far indicates that every time a mortgage payment is made, it first pays for the interest charges that have accrued <u>since the last payment</u>; after paying for those interest charges, any left-over amount is then applied towards the principal balance. If regularly scheduled payments are made, the future value of the loan will be realized by the lender at the end of the term.

Now it's time to reveal a little more about the key point. Remember that monthly interest is calculated by the following equation:

Balance x Interest = Annual Interest

Annual Interest / 12 = Monthly Interest.

This is a good simple way to figure out the average interest per month. But what about February? February only has 28 days, so do you pay the same amount of interest in February as you do in March, which has 31 days?

The answer is no. Lenders take the interest calculation one step further and calculate the **daily interest**. To find the daily interest, the calculation would look like the following:

Balance x Interest = Annual Interest

Annual Interest / 365 = Daily Interest

Using the current example, the daily interest would be calculated as follows:

$200,000 (balance) x .065 (rate) = $13,000 (annual interest)

$13,000 (annual Interest) / 365 (days per year) = $35.62 (**Daily interest**)

Having an understanding of daily interest is key to understanding how to efficiently accelerate the payoff of a mortgage.

There are several programs people utilize in an effort to reduce the length of their mortgage. The following pages will take a closer look at the three most common programs and their effectiveness, their ease of use, and the ability to budget them into your current lifestyle. After learning about these three programs, you will be introduced to a fourth program, which is by far the most effective, easy to use, and affordable program. It is called the Home Equity Acceleration Plan.

For all four plans, the following mortgage scenario will be used:

Original Loan Amount: $200,000
Loan Closing Date: December 31, 2006
First Payment Date: February 1st, 2007
Interest Rate: 6.25%
Term: 30-Year Fixed
Payment: $1,231.43

---

1) ROUNDING UP

When you buy gasoline, do you try to squeeze the pump a few extra times in order to pay an even dollar amount?

For many, paying $39.68 doesn't affect them any more than paying $40.00 to fill up the automobile.

What about leaving a tip for your favorite server at a restaurant? If 15% of the bill comes out to $14.40, isn't it just easier to leave a $15.00 tip? Does leaving an extra 60-cent tip affect someone's daily life? Of course not.

This same mentality holds true for millions of people every month when they sit down to write the check for their mortgage payment.

Possibly the most common way people try to accelerate paying off their mortgage is by "Rounding Up" their payment to the nearest denomination of $10, $50, or $100. Although this plan is both easy and affordable for most, it is the least structured of all the acceleration plans discussed in this book because the extra payment amount is not required. It is merely a choice made each month as the payment check is filled out. If homeowners utilize direct withdrawals from their checking account(s) to pay their mortgage, they may choose to add the extra amount when they set up the payment amount.

Most people who use this plan aren't really considering the exact effect it will have on their payoff date. It just seems like a good way to knock a few months off the term of the loan, and it isn't painful because of the low dollar amounts typically involved in Rounding Up.

When considering the use of Rounding Up as a way to reduce the term of your mortgage, remember what you learned earlier about how interest is charged in arrears and how payments are applied when they are received by the bank. Using the current mortgage example, let's analyze the effect that "Rounding Up" the payments would have on the overall length of the term. First, let's take a look at the interest accrued in January 2007 and how much of the first payment would be applied towards the balance when **not** using Rounding Up:

Balance = $200,000

Daily interest = $34.25

Days in month = 31

Total Interest = $1,061.64

Payment = $1,231.43

Amount Applied to Principal = $169.79
($1,231.43 – $1,061.64)

New Balance = $199,830.21 ($200,000 - $169.79)

Now remember that any **extra** payment amount will directly reduce the principal balance of the loan, which, in turn, reduces the amount of interest that will accrue and be charged each day of the next month.

This means that more and more of the payment will be applied toward the principal earlier in the loan term, and, as you will soon see, paying extra towards a mortgage early in the life of the loan significantly affects the total amount of interest paid over the life of the loan.

In the current example, a monthly payment of $1,231.43 on a $200,000 loan would pay off the loan as scheduled in 30 years. By simply rounding up the monthly payment to $1,240, $1,250 or $1,300, the borrower would be paying an additional amount of $8.57, $18.57, or $68.57 per month, respectively.

These amounts would be applied directly towards the principal loan balance, thereby reducing the interest charged in subsequent months and, ultimately, reducing the term of the loan.

The chart below shows how the additional payments would affect the term of the loan. Remember, this loan has its first payment due on February 1, 2007.

Monthly Payment	Additional Payment	Payoff Date	Total Interest Paid	Interest Saved
$1,231.43	$0.00	2/1/2037	$243,316	$0
$1,240.00	$8.57	7/1/2036	$237,514	$5,802
$1,250.00	$18.57	11/1/2035	$231,139	$12,177
$1,300.00	$68.57	2/1/2033	$204,368	$38,948

As you can see, simply rounding up the payment each month reduces the loan term and total interest charged. If the borrower chooses to round up to a $1,300 monthly payment, the additional payments would add up to approximately $822.84.

However, this cost spread out over the period of a year is affordable and easy to budget.

While the additional amounts paid each month are not significant, you can see the power of paying just a few extra dollars each month and how it affects a long-term loan. In the example, if the client pays just $68.57 extra a month over the life of the loan, the loan would be paid off four years earlier; and the amount of interest saved is nearly $40,000.

As mentioned earlier, Rounding Up is very affordable and simple. Paying an extra $8.57 or even $18.57 should not require any changes to most peoples' monthly budgets. Even an additional $68.57 is affordable for most. Think about it. You can't even go to dinner today at a nice restaurant with your spouse and one or two children and drop less than $60.00.

As we mentioned in the beginning of the chapter, the goal is to show and teach you the "real" math so that you can make decisions about which concepts in this book are best for your individual situation. With this being said, let's take a closer look at the actual dollars spent and the dollars saved for each of these rounded up payment options.

Monthly Payment Amount	$1,231.43	$1,240	$1,250	$1,300
Number of Payments	360	353	344	312
Total Of ALL Payments	$443,314.80	$437,720	$430,000	$405,600
Actual Savings	**$0.00**	**$5,594.80**	**$13,314.80**	**$37,714.80**

Rounding Up is an easy, inexpensive way to reduce the total term and the total payments of your mortgage. Millions of people do it every month without even knowing the exact effect it will have on their loan.

Should you be using Rounding Up to reduce the term of your mortgage? It depends. The other strategies you will read about in this chapter are better than Rounding Up for accelerating your mortgage, and Equity Harvesting is a much better way to build wealth than paying down your mortgage; but if the choice is between doing nothing and Rounding Up, you should use Rounding Up.

2) APPLYING THE BONUS

Annually, millions of people receive some type of cash bonus. This could be from an employer, from a rich uncle, a parent who has passed away, or even from the Federal Government in the form of an income tax refund. Although a tax refund isn't truly a bonus, to many people, it feels like one.

For this section of the material, the examples will assume that the borrower will receive an annual income tax refund. No bonus is guaranteed from an employer, the IRS, or other sources; but in order to have an example that makes sense, an assumed annual bonus will be used.

For this example, we will use the same parameters used in our previous example: a $200,000 mortgage at a rate of 6.25%, a 30-year term, and a payment of $1,231.43, with the first one being due February 1, 2007.

Let's also assume the client earns $60,000 a year, and, as a savings plan, has the maximum income tax withheld from his/her paycheck—knowing that there will be a sizable tax refund the following year. Assume that the refund in this example is $1,000 a year and will continue to be a similar amount for the life of the 30-year home loan.

Although the customer would love to spend the entire tax refund amount on new electronic equipment or a vacation, he/she is dedicated to using the refund each year to reduce the term of the home mortgage. Therefore, the client will apply the $1,000 refund towards the mortgage—as an extra payment that will be paid to the lender on May 1 of every year during the term of the loan.

Look what happens to the mortgage when you apply the extra $1,000 payment each year.

Payment	Additional Pmt	Payoff Date	Total Interest Paid	Interest Saved
$1,231.43	$0.00	2/1/2037	$243,316.00	$0.00
$1,231.43	$1,000.00	5/1/2032	$196,968.00	$46,348.00

Uncle Sam, through the tax refund checks, has helped the client reduce the term of the loan by almost five years, which helped the client save over $46,000 in interest charges over the life of the loan.

Now here is an additional consideration for this program. What if the borrower "Rounds Up" **and** applies the bonus? For this scenario, let's assume the same $1,000 annual refund and a monthly payment of $1,250, which is an additional $18.57 each month.

Monthly Payment	Additional Monthly Payment	Additional Annual Payment	Payoff Date	Total Interest Paid	Interest Saved
$1,231.43	$0.00	0	2/1/2037	$243,316.00	$0.00
$1,250.00	$18.57	$1,000	5/01/2031	$189,355.00	$53,961.00

By combining these two simple methods of term reduction and keeping it affordable for the customer, the term would be reduced to 24 years and 4 months; and the total interest saved would be $53,961.

While the Bonus Plan seems simple and certainly can work, what would be better advice for the client?

Assuming the client has the discipline to do so, it would be better for the client to take home as much money as possible from his or her salary paycheck from work and pay down more of the mortgage with that extra money each month (even if this causes the client to owe money to the IRS when the tax return is filed).

Why would anyone want to use an IRS tax refund as a savings plan (and hundreds of thousands of Americans do this knowingly or unknowingly each year)? The IRS does not pay interest on the refund and letting the IRS keep your money throughout the year is not a good financial decision.

Think of the following example.

Assume that our $60,000-a-year salary borrower, instead of missing out on an additional income of $83.33 a month that is being withheld from his/her paycheck, receives that money each month. Furthermore, assume that the borrower changes the amount withheld from his/her paycheck so that he/she will actually owe $1,000 when filing his/her tax return next year. Therefore, the client now has an additional $166.66 in his/her paycheck after taxes.

Now let's assume the borrower adds that extra $166.66 to the mortgage payment each month. By restructuring the withholding amount the borrower currently has and applying that amount directly to the mortgage monthly payment, the interest savings over the life of the loan will be **$75,483**.

The following chart summarizes the savings. The figures in row 2 illustrate how much interest is saved using Rounding Up and applying the $1,000 tax refund bonus each year towards the mortgage. Row 3 shows the effect of having $166.66 less withheld from the client's paycheck without the use of Rounding Up.

Monthly Payment	Additional Monthly Payment	Additional Annual Payment	Payoff Date	Total Interest Paid	Interest Saved
$1,231.43	$0.00	0.00	2/1/2037	$243,316.00	$0.00
$1,250.00	$18.57	1,000	5/1/2031	$189,355.00	$53,961.00
$1,398.09	$166.66	0.00	2/1/2029	$167,832.93	$75,483.45

You may be saying to yourself that the borrower has to find an additional of income to pay the income tax bill each April. That's right, and the following material will show you how to find that money using the Home Equity Acceleration Plan.

3) BI-WEEKLY PLANS

Most mortgage payments are due on the first day of every month. When this payment is made, the previous month's interest that has accrued is paid. Therefore, if the previous month had 30 days, interest on the loan would have been accruing for 30 days.

Since there are twelve months in a year, there are twelve mortgage payments due every year. Going back to our example of a $200,000 mortgage amortized at a 6.25% interest rate, twelve monthly payments of $1,231.43 would add up to an annual payment total of $14,777.16.

Today, many homeowners are utilizing a program that is offered through many loan servicers (and also through many private companies). This program is most commonly known as the Bi-Weekly payment program. This program allows the borrowers to make one half of their required monthly payment every two weeks. So on February 1, instead of paying the typical monthly payment of $1,231.43, a payment of $615.72 is made. Then, two weeks later, another payment of $615.72 is made.

Let's revert to our basic math skills to help us determine how and why this program works to reduce the term of a mortgage.

How many weeks are there in a year? 52. If a payment is made every two weeks, how many half payments are made a year? 26.

Since the payment amount is half of the full amount, how many full payments per year? 13. This is one more payment per year than a borrower would normally pay by making monthly payments.

So the reason the term of the mortgage is reduced is because an extra mortgage payment is made every year. As with Rounding Up or the Bonus Plan, anytime you pay more than is required on your mortgage, it lowers the principal balance and the interest due (which will cut months or years off the term of the loan).

Most of the Bi-Weekly payment programs require direct withdrawal from a bank account to make it easier on the customer and to make sure that payments are received by the day they are to be posted.

Let's compare the numbers.

Payment Program	Monthly Payment	Loan Balance at 5 Years	Total Interest Paid over 30 Years	Interest Saved
Standard Monthly	$1,231.43	$186,674.48	$243,316.00	$0.00
Bi-weekly	$615.72	$179,195.95	$187,475.00	$55,841.00

The above chart details that the Bi-Weekly payment program saved $55,841 in interest charges over the entire term. This interest savings would reduce the length of the term to just over 24 years; that's almost a 6-year reduction.

The chart also details the balance after Year 5. The reason this number was included is that, although most people want to aggressively pay off their mortgage, they will, in all likelihood, sell their home or refinance the mortgage. In the US, mortgages are kept for an average of 3-5 years. With this in mind, it is just as important to identify the five-year savings as it is to identify the savings over the entire term.

The chart above shows that the borrower utilizing the Bi-Weekly payment program owes $179,196 at the end of the 5th year, whereas the borrower using the standard monthly payment program would owe $186,674. This means that the client would have about $7,500 (not including appreciation) of additional equity.

If you get a calculator out, you will see that 26 payments of $615.72 total annual payments of $16,008.72 or an additional $1,231.56. This equates to almost one additional payment per year. However, the bi-weekly program **works better because the client would be applying principal twice a month**, which reduces the interest paid every time a payment is posted.

Using the same example, the interest on the original $200,000 mortgage would be accruing at approximately $34.25 ($200,000 x .0625 (rate) / 365 days/year = $34.25) per day during the first month. By paying $615.72 (half of the normal monthly payment) on the 15th of the first month, the accrued interest of $513.75 ($34.25 x 15) would be paid, and $101.97 ($615.72 – $513.75) would be applied to the principal.

This means that for the remaining days of the month, interest would only be charged on $199,898.03, rather than the full $200,000, reducing the daily interest charged. In other words, instead of the interest accruing for 30 days on $200,000, it only would only accrue for two weeks on $200,000; then, when the $615.72 payment is made, the interest would begin to accrue on the smaller principal balance of $199,898.03 for the next two weeks. When the next payment is made, that payment would slightly reduce the principal balance again. As the borrower would continue to do this every two weeks, it would slowly reduce the overall debt, which in turn would reduce the daily interest charged, that over time would increase the speed at which the loan is paid in full. Although the reduction of the principal balance is minimal, the compounding effect over time is significant and makes the plan beneficial to borrowers who use the program.

Applying the funds

Earlier, it was mentioned that there are many private companies who offer this service (most at a minimal charge). These companies handle the setup and the general accounting for customers who want to take advantage of it.

Some of these companies will not apply the funds immediately to the mortgage account and will instead wait until the end of the year and then apply the extra payment. This will shorten the term of the loan as well (simply because you are making an extra payment each year), however, not by as much as if the payments were applied immediately. If the extra payments aren't applied immediately, the interest will continue to accrue on otherwise higher principal balances. These higher principal balances will persist until the extra payment (and the resultant principal reduction) is made.

The point being made here is that, if the borrower opts for a program like this, he/she should know when the company applies the payments and should even go as far as to ask for the amortization schedule and the annual accounting statement from the company. This annual accounting statement should show their account activity for the most recent periods. This information will tell the borrower whether the payments are being applied immediately.

It is good to know that there are several variations of this program; some have even set the program to run weekly. What you'll find interesting is that there is virtually no difference between making weekly and bi-weekly payments. If you make weekly payments, you would make 52 payments annually of $307.86, which adds up to $16,008.59. Since the payment is ¼ of the monthly payment, the borrower is still only making the equivalent of 13 full monthly payments (52 / 4). The annual payment amount is only a few cents more than the bi-weekly annual payment of $16,008.72. Therefore, the term is virtually identical when comparing the weekly payment to bi-weekly plan would.

As I mentioned earlier, most of these plans require a system of direct withdrawals from a checking or savings account. Should there ever be a significant change in your income, you would have to notify the company handling the transactions and have the payments stopped. However, you would still need to continue making at least the monthly payments that are due.

SUMMARY ON THE "COMMON" MORTGAGE ACCELERATION PLANS

So far, we have covered the three common mortgage acceleration plans. We have covered the Rounding Up method in which the customer adds a few extra dollars each month to their mortgage payment, which can reduce the mortgage term by a few years (which is better than doing nothing).

We have also covered how applying a one-time payment per year ("Applying the Bonus") utilizes a lump-sum approach which can reduce the term once again by a few years (again better than doing nothing and can be used in combination with the Rounding Up method).

The bi-weekly payment method also reduces the term by essentially making an extra payment throughout the course of the year by paying every two weeks and by reducing the principal balance more frequently.

All of these plans, although easy to budget, will only reduce the term of the mortgage by 2 – 7 years. While paying off a home loan in 23-28 years is better than in 30 years, what if there was another plan that allowed a borrower to cut the term in half (or more) without altering their spending habits?

4) HOME EQUITY ACCELERATION PLAN (H.E.A.P.™)

H.E.A.P. is not a new concept, but it is relatively unknown. Why it is unknown is a bit of a long story, but generally speaking, mortgage professionals are not taught this program in the educational programs available in the marketplace (that is until The WPI rolled out the Master Mortgage Broker (MMB™) certification course in early 2007).

Traditionally speaking, mortgage professionals sell mortgages; they do not craft plans or help clients figure out ways to reduce the term of their mortgage. Since the vast majority of financial planners, insurance agents, CPAs/EAs/accountants, and attorneys know very little about mortgages in general (let alone mortgage acceleration plans), the consumer is not receiving information on this very unique and simple mortgage reduction plan.

When I decided to write this book, I knew that it would have crossover appeal for readers who wanted to build wealth through Equity Harvesting and also appeal to those who were constantly looking for the most useful and best way to pay off their home mortgage debt early.

As much as I believe Equity Harvesting is a much better way to grow wealth than paying off a mortgage for many clients, I must admit that the material on H.E.A.P. is very compelling.

Ask yourself the following question:

If you could pay off your mortgage substantially sooner than 30 years (assuming you have a 30-year mortgage) and you wouldn't have to alter your spending habits – would you?

The question is more of a rhetorical question as the obvious answer is "yes." If one of your advisors asked you this question, I'm sure you would follow up the question with, "Can you show me how to do that?"

How in the world can a homeowner pay off their mortgage "substantially sooner" and not change their spending habits? It can be done through the creative use of a **home equity line of credit**.

HOME EQUITY LINE OF CREDIT

A **home equity line of credit** (HELOC) is similar to a revolving line of credit (credit card). A borrower goes to a lender and uses the equity in their home to receive a "line of credit."

Besides a small annual fee in some cases, if the borrower is not paying off an existing second mortgage, the beginning balance on the HELOC is $0. Since the monthly payment due on a HELOC is based on the outstanding balance, if the HELOC has a balance of $0, there will be no monthly payment due.

A borrower is literally given checks that can be used to access the HELOC. In the traditional use of a HELOC, a borrower who is fixing up his/her house and doesn't have the cash to do so might go down to the local hardware store to buy fixer-upper supplies and would use a check from the HELOC to pay for the supplies. When the checks are used, interest starts on the HELOC and a monthly payment is then due based on the amount of money borrowed.

If the HELOC balance is $10,000, the monthly payment is calculated by using the current interest rate and the number of days in the period.

If the interest rate is 8.25%, the payment for a 30-day month would be calculated as $10,000 x .0825 = 825 / 365 x 30 (days in current month) = $67.81.

This would be the interest due for the month. Some accounts have a 1% minimum, which would require a payment of $100.00 ($10,000 x .01). In this case, if $100 were paid, $32.19 would be applied to principal leaving a remaining balance of $9,967.81.

The "available credit" offered by a lender through a HELOC may be drawn when needed. Like a traditional home loan, the borrower must pay monthly payments and is required to pay off the balance over a specified period of time. And like a mortgage, the interest accrues daily on the balance owed. When a payment is made, it is applied first to the interest due; and then any amount in excess of the interest is applied directly to the principal balance.

Many of these accounts are set up with **"interest only"** payment requirements with a limited "draw period" followed by a repayment period. Typical HELOCs have a ten-year draw period, after which normal payments are calculated for paying off the balance over the remainder of the term, which can be up to 30 years.

The interest rate for a HELOC is usually a variable (adjustable) rate. The measuring index or variable portion of the loan will often be the current prime rate. The margin, or the fixed portion, will be a number that the lender adds to the rate in accordance with the risk factors associated with the loan.

For example, a Line of Credit that leaves the borrower with little or no equity will have a higher margin than a line that leaves a large equity position. Generally speaking, a borrower with bad credit will have a higher margin charged to the loan; and someone with good credit can sometimes find a HELOC at the prime rate with no margin (and sometimes even less than the prime rate).

If the prime rate is 8.25% and the margin is zero, the rate on a HELOC at prime + 0 would be 8.25%. The rate on a HELOC is usually higher than that of a conventional fixed-rate mortgage (which does not use prime as a basis for the lending rate).

The following chart represents the historical data of the prime rate since the year 2000. As you can see, the rate has been as high as 9.5% and as low as 4% in the period of six full years. There is no limit as to how long the rate can stay at one point or how often it can change. The prime rate is defined by The Wall Street Journal (WSJ) as *"The base rate on corporate loans posted by at least 75% of the nation's 30 largest banks."* It is not the "best" rate offered by banks.

Date of Change	Prime Rate	Date of Change	Prime Rate
3-Feb-00	8.75%	11-Aug-04	4.50%
22-Mar-00	9.00%	22-Sep-04	4.75%
17-May-00	9.50%	10-Nov-04	5.00%
4-Jan-01	9.00%	14-Dec-04	5.25%
1-Feb-01	8.50%	2-Feb-05	5.50%
21-Mar-01	8.00%	22-Mar-05	5.75%
19-Apr-01	7.50%	3-May-05	6.00%
16-May-01	7.00%	30-Jun-05	6.25%
28-Jun-01	6.75%	9-Aug-05	6.50%
22-Aug-01	6.50%	20-Sep-05	6.75%
18-Sep-01	6.00%	1-Nov-05	7.00%
3-Oct-01	5.50%	13-Dec-05	7.25%
7-Nov-01	5.00%	31-Jan-06	7.50%
12-Dec-01	4.75%	28-Mar-06	7.75%
7-Nov-02	4.25%	10-May-06	8.00%
27-Jun-03	4.00%	29-Jun-06	8.25%
1-Jul-04	4.25%	**8.25% at the time of Printing**	

When a HELOC is mentioned to most borrowers, they will usually think of it as a 2nd mortgage. In fact, that is the way most of them are set up; however, some lenders now do offer first lien Lines of Credit.

Generally speaking, so long as the HELOC loan balance does not exceed $100,000 and the borrower has no other home equity debt on the property, the interest on the loan is tax deductible (except as limited by Section 264(a) of the IRC).

Before securing a HELOC, the borrower needs to be educated on one important factor. By securing a HELOC, they are using available equity of the house. When funds are drawn from the HELOC, the equity of the house is reduced; it can even be reduced to $0.00 if all the equity is accessed.

For example, if the first mortgage on a home is $80,000 and the HELOC balance is $20,000, there would be a $100,000 lien against the home. If the home is valued at $105,000, the borrower would only have $5,000 in available equity. This is not necessarily a negative thing; however, if the borrower's goal is to list and sell the house within a year, it could potentially cost them money to sell the house (because the house would be sold in a negative equity situation when you take into account realtor fees and other closing costs).

In general, a HELOC is a type of mortgage that gives the borrower the flexibility to use available equity when they need it and only pay for what they are using. With a better understanding of how a HELOC works, it will now be easier to understand the concept of H.E.A.P.

HERE IS HOW H.E.A.P. WORKS IN CONJUNCTION WITH A HELOC

First, a borrower sets up a HELOC utilizing the equity in the home. The HELOC is usually a 2nd lien on the personal residence. For our example, it will be assumed that the line of credit is **$25,000**.

The repayment terms are interest only, and the rate is variable tied to prime. Although it is not a realistic assumption, we will assume that prime remains at 8.25% for the term (prime will go up or down over time). We only assume this to make the concept easier to understand. Once you fully understand how H.E.A.P. works, you can vary prime in your calculations and still come up with similar results. As noted in the chart above, the prime rate can fluctuate several times per year. In the past several years, it has been as low as 4% and as high as 9.5%.

Here is the other basic information about our example client you will need to keep in mind while reading through this example and explanation:

-Monthly income (after taxes) = $5,000

-First mortgage balance = $200,000

-First payment due date = Feb 1, 2007

-Mortgage monthly payment at 6.25% = $1,231.43

-All other monthly payments (bills, credit cards, utilities, etc.) = $789.02

-Miscellaneous monthly expenditures (dinners, movies, fuel, etc.) = $800

-Total monthly outlay = **$2,820.45**

For our example, we are NOT going to consolidate the client's other bills. Once clients are fully educated on this plan, most will want to consolidate other debt using the HELOC. Why? Because interest payments on credit cards are NOT deductible, whereas when set up correctly, interest payments on a HELOC are.

Once the line of credit is opened, a comfortable amount of emergency cash is determined. This is the amount of money that the client should have available at ALL times in the line of credit. This amount will then always be available to the borrower in case of emergency.

Therefore, with this example, we'll assume the client should have $15,000 available at all times in the HELOC in case of an emergency. This amount was determined by taking three months of the client's salary. There is no standard amount that is required as a reserve. You will need to determine for yourself what an acceptable reserve amount is considering your own situation. The reserve is really there to pay your bills should you become disabled, lose your job, or have an unexpected expense (like a major health expense).

Having said that, many clients will use three times their after-tax income (in our example, that is $15,000). If the client designates $15,000 of the $25,000 HELOC as a cushion available for emergencies, that leaves him/her with $10,000 at his/her disposal from the HELOC. Therefore, the client will then draw from the HELOC **$10,000 and pay it directly towards the first mortgage**. Remember the plan was designed to help you pay off your primary mortgage several years early, and the money from the HELOC will be used to accomplish that goal.

By paying $10,000 down on the 1st mortgage, the client will obviously reduce the principal of the 1st mortgage (and the interest that would have been paid on the loan over the long term) and shorten the length of their primary mortgage (assume it is a 30-year fixed).

Having made this payment, the client now will have to pay at least the minimum payment on the $10,000 HELOC. The key, as you will see with the H.E.A.P., is how quickly a client can pay down the $10,000 HELOC.

Remember, with H.E.A.P., the client will NOT have to change their spending habits, which is why this is such a useful program.

The "**total**" debt on the home is still the same as the day the HELOC is accessed ($190,000 from the primary mortgage and $10,000 from the HELOC that was applied to pay down the 1st mortgage).

CHECKING ACCOUNTS

It is fair to say that most Americans keep a balance in their personal checking accounts? Absolutely.

Those who don't are not in a positive cash flow situation and should be worried about simply making their monthly mortgage payment rather than trying to find creative ways to pay it off early.

Depending on the person, the average monthly checking account balance is anywhere from $500 to as much as $5,000+. This money is used to pay our monthly bills for our families.

What's the problem with a checking account?

The interest paid on such accounts (if any) is very low, and it is taxable every year.

Getting back to our example, assume the client currently has his/her paycheck directly deposited into a normal checking account that accumulates little or no interest.

The client, after bills, maintains a decent balance in the account and accumulates most of his/her retirement savings through vehicles provided from work (401k, etc.).

HOW H.E.A.P. WORKS TO CONSTANTLY HAVE A CLIENT'S MONEY AT WORK IN THE MOST PRODUCTIVE MANNER

With H.E.A.P., clients, after the HELOC is established and accessed, **will have their paycheck direct deposited into the line of credit account (NOT their normal checking account)**.

How then will clients be able to pay their bills?

Remember that any portion of the HELOC that is not used (i.e., available credit) can be withdrawn at any time. With H.E.A.P., clients will utilize the check-writing ability of the HELOC to pay their bills.

In our example, the $800 in miscellaneous bills are paid from the HELOC by writing a check just as the client would from a normal checking account. The client can choose to write one $800 check to the primary checking account (and then pay the bills using the primary checking account) or by using separate checks for all the bills paid directly from the HELOC.

Let's look at the running balance for the first few months of the line of credit where the client deposits his/her paycheck into the HELOC account.

Assume the client gets paid on the 15th and the 30th of each month. Remember, with this example, the client started out by accessing the HELOC in the amount of $10,000, which was used to pay down the mortgage balance on the primary home loan. This would start the HELOC with a "balance owed" of $10,000 and available funds of $15,000.

Remember, our goal is to keep a minimum of $15,000 available at all times in the HELOC for emergency funds. Also, remember that the client is earning income above what is spent on the normal bills in the household (which creates a positive average balance in a normal checking account that earns virtually no interest each year).

Date	Activity	Amount	HELOC Balance	Available Credit
2/1/2007	First Mortgage Reduction	-$10,000.00	$10,000.00	$15,000.00
2/15/2007	Payroll Deposit	$2,500.00	$7,533.90	$17,466.10
2/28/2007	Payroll Deposit	$2,500.00	$5,059.44	$19,940.56
3/1/2007	Bills	-$2,820.45	$7,879.89	$17,120.11
3/15/2007	Payroll Deposit	$2,500.00	$5,406.61	$19,593.39
3/30/2007	Payroll Deposit	$2,500.00	$2,924.94	$22,075.06
4/1/2007	Bills	-$2,820.45	$5,745.39	$19,254.61
4/15/2007	Payroll Deposit	$2,500.00	$3,264.87	$21,735.13
4/30/2007	Payroll Deposit	$2,500.00	$775.94	$24,224.06
5/1/2007	Bills	-$2,820.45	$3,596.39	$21,403.61
5/15/2007	Payroll Deposit	$2,500.00	$1,108.58	$23,891.42
5/30/2007	Payroll Deposit	$2,500.00	-$1,387.66	$26,387.66

In four months, without changing any spending habits and without using extra money, the client just paid off the $10,000 balance on their line of credit.

Besides smiling due to the fact that the HELOC has been paid off, what does the client do next to continue using H.E.A.P.?

You guessed it—the client will access the line of credit in the amount of $10,000 and pay down the debt on the primary mortgage again. Then the client will continue with life as usual, except the client's paycheck will continue to be deposited in the HELOC.

THE NUMBERS

Understand that the exact numbers are not that important due to the fact that everyone's situation will be different. It's the concept that either does or does not work.

This concept will work for readers who <u>have the discipline</u> to use it and who carry some kind of balance monthly in their checking accounts.

Sure, those who use the H.E.A.P. plan are going to have unexpected expenses or expected expenses that will change the numbers in any given period of time.

The key is that a borrower is always using his/her money in its **best use** and having money sitting in a checking account earning very little or no interest (which is taxable each year) is **NOT** in any borrower's best interest.

Back to the example

Let's go back to the original first mortgage. Realize that the client in our example could access an additional $30,000 per year from the HELOC to pay down the debt on the primary mortgage. They can do this because every four months, the balance of the HELOC is back to zero.

This is not realistic since other expenses always come up. And it is extremely important in order to make the program a success that you anticipate the "other" expenses that you have incurred in the past and budget those into your calculations when using the H.E.A.P. plan.

Therefore, let's assume it takes our example client six months to pay down the line of credit instead of four (which would allow him/her to apply $20,000 per year directly to the first mortgage).

After applying the $20,000 per year to the primary mortgage, the new calculated payoff date of the first mortgage is 2/1/2014. That's **twenty-three years early**.

Remember, this can be done WITHOUT changing spending habits so long as the client has the discipline to stay with the plan.

I know the previous material does not make you a H.E.A.P. expert, but does this concept seem interesting to you?

My guess is that even if you read the first ten chapters of this book and have come to the conclusion that Equity Harvesting is a good way to build your wealth, you probably still have an interest in exploring how H.E.A.P. can benefit you.

Let's go back and make sure you understand the calculations used in the last table.

With a starting HELOC balance of $10,000 and an interest rate of 8.25%, the daily interest (10,000 x .0825 / 365) is $2.26 per day.

The balance on Feb. 15 is calculated as:

Daily Interest x Number of Days + Balance – Payment

$2.26 (per diem interest) x 15 (days) + $10,000 (outstanding balance) – $2,500 (payroll deposit) = $7,533.90.

The biggest critics and skeptics of the program will key in on one fact—that the average American who uses the program will not be depositing ANY money into a savings or brokerage account to build a "retirement nest egg."

In other words, if the client uses H.E.A.P., he/she will not have any other money left over to fund traditional retirement vehicles such as 401(k) plans or IRAs or an after-tax brokerage account. Such criticism is misplaced.

The goal for our example client was to pay off the home as quickly as possible, and they did it in seven years. The client saved $199,917 in interest over the life of the plan. The client also always had at least $15,000 in available cash and is still saving for retirement through a company-sponsored retirement plan.

IF the client still wants to have an additional savings/retirement plan at or outside of work, then that amount needs to be budgeted into the monthly expenses of the client when starting H.E.A.P. (which would reduce the amount that could be allocated to pay down the HELOC).

You need to always keep in mind that the goal of clients who use H.E.A.P. is to pay off their home mortgage as soon as possible. Clients who want to build the largest possible pre- and post-tax retirement nest egg are NOT great candidates for the H.E.A.P. and instead are candidates for Equity Harvesting. As you already know from reading the previous chapters of this book, Equity Harvesting requires a client to allocate dollars to a new interest expense that is created when the client borrows money from the home to reposition into a tax-favorable, wealth-building tool. Equity Harvesting reduces the available dollars (a client has would have on a monthly basis), which then would not be available to pay down the debt on the HELOC.

My position and that of the coauthor of this chapter, John Steinke, are clear on one main point: clients are either candidates to NEVER pay off the debt on their home and have maximum debt so that their money can be used to grow in a tax-free manner for retirement purposes OR they are candidates for H.E.A.P. because they want to pay off their home's debt as soon as possible.

The great thing about H.E.A.P. is that you can tailor it to meet your needs whatever they may be (so long as you currently carry a balance in your checking account on a monthly basis). Clients who use H.E.A.P. can use $5,000 withdrawals from the HELOC, set up a first lien line of credit, have partial direct deposits, and the list goes on and on. Every case will be slightly different; and while the amount of the term reduction will vary per client, the results will be similar in that the original term of the loan on the primary residence is significantly reduced and the client will save thousands of dollars in interest, all while not having to alter his/her spending habits.

Example

Let's take a look at another real life example.

H and W live in a nice new home and maintain a fairly strict budget. Their current mortgage, taken out in November of 2006, is an interest-only mortgage with a $236,000 balance and a $1,202 per month <u>interest-only</u> payment (the full payment amount of $1,700 <u>includes</u> property taxes and homeowners insurance of $498 per month).

They also have a second mortgage with a $39,000 balance and a $300 payment. Their other monthly bills include a car payment, two credit cards, utilities, a gym membership, and insurance. These total $850 per month. Their miscellaneous spending is budgeted to $250 per week and pays for groceries, fuel, and fun. W works part time and H works full time. Together they bring home $1,200 per week after taxes as income.

Creditor	Balance	Monthly Payment
First Mortgage	$236,000	$1,700
Second Mortgage	$39,000	$300
Auto	$11,000	$300
Credit Card	$5,500	$120
Utilities		$200
Gym Membership		$80
Insurance		$150
Groceries, Fuel, & Fun		$1,000
Total Monthly Outlay		$3,850
Total Monthly Income – Take Home (after tax)		$5,200

Currently, at the end of 10 years, the first mortgage will transition from an interest only mortgage to a fully amortizing mortgage, at which time the payment would increase to $1,724 principal and interest ($2,222 with taxes and insurance), which would equate to approximately a $500 increase.

The following are the steps the client would need to take in order to implement H.E.A.P.

<u>Step 1</u>. – Establish a HELOC.

The current second mortgage of $39,000 is a closed-end second mortgage (no draws available). An appraisal verified that the home is currently worth $320,000. A **$60,000** HELOC is established (93% combined loan to value). The interest rate is prime + .25% = 8.5%.

Once the HELOC is established, it would be accessed and used to pay off/replace the current second mortgage of $39,000, leaving them with total monthly expenses of $3,550 ($3,850 (current expenses) – $300 (the old 2nd mortgage). Therefore, the client would not consider the HELOC debt as part of the normal monthly expenses.

Step 2 – Start the plan. The following chart will show the weekly running balance of the HELOC. The first transaction the client would complete is to access the HELOC to reduce the principal mortgage by $11,000, and the emergency fund is set at $10,000. This creates a new HELOC balance of $50,000 ($39,000 + $11,000).

Date	Transaction	Transaction Amount	HELOC Balance	Available Credit
4/1	Mortgage Reduction	-$11,000.00	$50,000.00	10,000.00
4/6	Payroll	$1,200.00	$48,858.22	11,141.78
4/13	Payroll	$1,200.00	$47,737.87	12,262.13
4/20	Payroll	$1,200.00	$46,617.65	13,382.35
4/27	Payroll	$1,200.00	$45,493.64	14,506.36
5/4	Payroll	$1,200.00		
5/4	Bills	-$3,550.00	$47,917.80	12,082.20
5/11	Payroll	$1,200.00	$46,795.91	13,204.09
5/18	Payroll	$1,200.00	$45,672.19	14,327.81
5/25	Payroll	$1,200.00	$44,546.64	15,453.36
6/1	Payroll	$1,200.00		
6/1	Bills	-$3,550.00	$46,969.26	13,030.74
6/8	Payroll	$1,200.00	$45,845.83	14,154.17
6/15	Payroll	$1,200.00	$44,720.56	15,279.44
6/22	Payroll	$1,200.00	$43,593.46	16,406.54
6/29	Payroll	$1,200.00	$42,464.52	17,535.48
7/6	Payroll	$1,200.00		
7/6	Bills	-$3,550.00	$44,883.74	15,116.25
7/13	Payroll	$1,200.00	$43,756.91	16,243.09
7/20	Payroll	$1,200.00	$42,628.24	17,371.76
7/27	Payroll	$1,200.00	$41,497.73	18,502.27
8/3	Payroll	$1,200.00		
8/3	Bills	-$3,550.00	$43,915.38	16,084.62
8/10	Payroll	$1,200.00	$42,786.97	17,213.03
8/17	Payroll	$1,200.00	$41,656.72	18,343.28
8/24	Payroll	$1,200.00	$40,524.63	19,475.37
8/31	Payroll	$1,200.00	$39,390.69	20,609.31
9/7	Payroll	$1,200.00		
9/7	Bills	-$3,550.00	$41,804.90	18,195.10
9/14	Payroll	$1,200.00	$40,673.05	19,326.95

In five-and-a-half months, the available credit would have increased to $20,000; and a principal reduction of $10,000 could have been made again. The question the clients would have to ask themselves is do they want to access the line of credit for another $10,000 (and repeat the process) or do they want to continue to pay down the HELOC.

For that matter, the clients would have to decide if they want to access the HELOC at all until such time as they pay down the HELOC to zero.

Based on the numbers, H and W could pre-pay $20,000 per year on their interest-only first mortgage and pay off the HELOC two times a year so the initial balance of the HELOC does not exceed $39,000 at the end of the year.

Lets' assume they do want to slowly pay down the HELOC to zero. To do that, they will set themselves up to make only one principal reduction per year ($10,000) until the balance of the HELOC reaches $0.00. At that time they could choose to make a $20,000 reduction annually until the primary mortgage is paid off.

After four years, H and W would have paid off the HELOC down to zero while also paying down $10,000 a year on their primary mortgage. After the HELOC reaches zero, H and W would then decide whether to access the HELOC for $20,000 and pay that amount down annually on the primary residence until it is paid off or maintain the annual amount at $10,000, which will free up $10,000 for other expenses (for fun, to buy a new car, start funding a college fund, or for any other expense).

DOES H.E.A.P. WORK FOR THOSE IN THE LOWER INCOME TAX BRACKETS?

Sure, why not? A dollar saved in interest is a dollar saved. Those who make more money and/or have a larger monthly surplus can benefit more than those who don't make a lot of money or don't have much of a surplus; but the bottom line is that, if you carry a balance in your checking account, you can use H.E.A.P.

Whenever you can knock off any amount of money from your primary mortgage, you not only pay down the debt but you also stop the compounding of interest on that money (which is why the previous three mortgage acceleration plans knock a few years off the length of a mortgage).

Abnormal Expense Months

Although many clients will be able to easily maintain their current spending levels, some clients seem to always have a variety of unexpected expenses pop up such as an appliance breaking, a car needing repair/replacing, or kids begging to go somewhere warm for spring break. Most families will find that a few times per year their "normal" monthly expenses are actually rather abnormal. Christmas is a good example of this.

When the plan is set up, these abnormal months need to be considered. Although an amount needs to be set aside for emergencies, these higher cost months shouldn't be considered emergencies.

If you look back at the first example (the one before the last), our client will be able to repay the initial $10,000 in four months by utilizing the plan. This will allow him/her to make three large principal reductions each year. As you may recall, the plan only had the client carrying out two reductions per year instead of the three he/she could afford. This was done to allow for some months where the costs will not be normal.

In the second example, remember that two reductions of $10,000 on the first mortgage could be taken every year; however, we assumed that the clients had decided to only take one until the balance of the HELOC ($50,000) is reduced to $0.00.

The clients could have decided after a short period of time that the H.E.A.P. plan as budgeted was just too strict. Does that mean the plan won't be useful to them? Not at all.

H and W could choose to only reduce the HELOC by $10,000 a year total instead of $20,000. All that means is that the HELOC initial balance will take twice as long to pay off (eight years instead of four at $5,000 a year), and they will only be making a $5,000 annual reduction on their primary home mortgage.

H.E.A.P. is very flexible as the only mandatory payments a client needs to make are the interest only payments of the HELOC. Clients can choose to access the HELOC in varying amounts every single year. However, for examples in a book, it works best to assume a systematic plan so that everyone can understand the math and how the plan works.

Also, don't forget that in both of the earlier examples, an emergency fund will be established and, hopefully, will never have to be dipped into. By taking the abnormal months into consideration during the plan setup, the client should not have to take money from that emergency fund to buy a new washer or dryer (but it is there if they need it).

What happens when you pay off the entire debt on your property through H.E.A.P.?

There will come a point in the plan at which your mortgage balance reaches $0.00. That will be a happy day for you.

What should you do next?

At this point, you will have proof positive that an entire residential mortgage can be eliminated rather quickly because it was just accomplished with H.E.A.P.

My hope actually is that many readers of this book choose to use Equity Harvesting to build wealth rather than use H.E.A.P. to pay down the debt on a home.

Remember, H.E.A.P. isn't for people who want to build the maximum amount of wealth; it's specifically for people who want to pay down the debt on their home (which does build wealth by reducing overall debt and interest payments, but does not build "maximum" wealth).

Once you pay off the debt on your home, a decent amount of money will be freed up due to the fact that there are no future mortgage payments to make. At that point, you have several options. You can use the money normally allocated to the mortgage payment and instead use it to:

-party, travel, and play.

-invest in the stock market in a taxable brokerage account.

-tax-defer more income through a qualified plan at work or an IRA.

-fund a low-expense, high-cash-value life insurance policy.

Realistically, many borrowers do not choose to reposition or invest a lot of their extra dollars. It doesn't seem to be the American way. We are a consumption society where we are always looking to buy that next toy, take that next trip, and buy that bigger house.

While paying off the debt on your home early through H.E.A.P. makes a lot of sense for borrowers, again, implementing an Equity Harvesting plan to build wealth is a more prudent option for many.

Assuming that there are many readers who still want to pay off the debt on their homes even though they understand that Equity Harvesting is logically a better way to build wealth, I want illustrate that H.E.A.P. also can be used to build your wealth besides paying down the debt on your home.

Once the debt on your home is paid off, can't you still borrow money using your HELOC and do something with it? Sure, you can. At this point, you no longer need to borrow money from your HELOC to pay down the debt on your home; but you can still borrow X amount of dollars from your HELOC and reposition that money into a tax-favorable, wealth-building tool.

Let's look at an example.

Assume Mr. Smith is age 45 and just paid off his house using H.E.A.P. It took him seven years, and he started at age 38. Now he has a $200,000 home that is paid off. Mr. Smith's income is $95,000 a year.

When Mr. Smith used H.E.A.P., he was paying down an extra $20,000 a year on his primary mortgage (he paid down $10,000 in HELOC debt every six months).

Now that the home is paid off, Mr. Smith has an extra $10,000 every six months to do something with now that he does not have to pay down the debt on the HELOC.

Mr. Smith could buy a new car, upgrade his house, travel around the world, etc. Or Mr. Smith could reposition $20,000 a year into a low-expense, cash-building indexed universal life insurance policy (if you have not read the chapters of this book that explain how cash value life insurance works to build wealth, especially through Equity Harvesting, I suggest you read those chapters, which will help you understand this example).

Let's assume Mr. Smith funds $20,000 a year into a low-expense indexed equity universal life insurance policy from ages 45-65. Every year, Mr. Smith will borrow from the HELOC to fund the life insurance policy, and every year he will pay off the $20,000 in debt through H.E.A.P.

How much could Mr. Smith remove income tax free from his life insurance policy from ages 66-85?

$83,596 every year income tax free.

If that amount sounds like a lot, it is; and that's the power of Equity Harvesting.

I assumed a conservative rate of return on the cash in the policy of 7.5% (the policy's growth is pegged to the S&P 500 index).

Using H.E.A.P. as a way to fund tax-favorable, wealth-building tools is not classic Equity Harvesting; but it is a form of Equity Harvesting in that you use the home's equity to build wealth. With pure Equity Harvesting, a borrower utilizes an "interest-only" loan to allow for the maximum amount of money to be borrowed and repositioned for wealth building.

H.E.A.P. is a more conservative way to build wealth because a borrower can feel more comfortable due to the fact that proper budgeting allows him/her to pay off the HELOC by the end of the year.

I suppose to some this is a matter of semantics due to the fact that in my Mr. Smith example Mr. Smith could simply allocate his after-tax income to fund the cash value life insurance policy (which is true). H.E.A.P. funds the life insurance policy quicker (annually or semi-annually instead of monthly); but the real reason to use H.E.A.P., as explained in this example, is to create a systematic plan that a client can follow.

H.E.A.P. is simple to implement and keep in place. If Mr. Smith doesn't have the mindset to use the easy-to-follow H.E.A.P. in some manner, he may never have the discipline to put extra money away for retirement.

WHAT IF A READER HAS "OTHER" DEBT?

Many readers who want to implement H.E.A.P. to pay down the debt on their primary residence also have "other" debt. If you listen to the news, you know that millions of Americans have leveraged themselves not just with debt on a personal residence but also with thousands of dollars of credit card debt. Also, there are many readers who have student loans and loans on automobiles.

Often, the interest rate that is charged on this "other" debt is the same or higher than that of a regular mortgage. If that is the case, then such readers should consider using H.E.A.P. to pay off that other debt before, or in conjunction with, paying down the debt on their personal residence.

Think about it. If you carry a balance on your credit card, the interest rate is probably in excess of 8% (and, many times, over 10%), and the interest on this debt is NOT tax-deductible. However, as you read in Chapter 2, Home Equity Debt is tax deductible up to $100,000 of new debt (limited by the FMV of the home).

Therefore, wouldn't it make sense to use a HELOC to pay off credit card debt? Absolutely. By using H.E.A.P. with a HELOC, the interest on the debt would be tax deductible; and because you are using H.E.A.P., you would systematically pay down the debt on the HELOC much quicker than you would your credit card debt.

The big caveat with credit card debt is to make sure you have the discipline to not run up a bunch of new debt on the credit card after you use the HELOC to pay it off.

Let's consider the following example. Roger and Sherry, married with no children, are in their early thirties. Both have graduated from law school with a substantial amount of student loans and credit card debt that was accumulated during their educations. (I debated whether to put this example in the book as it is a little outrageous, but this is a real life example of people I know.)

Creditor	Balance	Monthly Payment
US Dept Education	$97,007.00	$311.00
Student Loan MA	$34,793.00	$176.00
Student Loan MA	$28,337.00	$143.00
US Dept Education	$37,000.00	$509.00
Key Student Loan	$13,226.00	$133.00
Key Student Loan	$13,226.00	$133.00
Key Student Loan	$12,686.00	$123.00
Citi Card (cc)	$8,031.00	$321.00
Bank of America (cc)	$7,644.00	$285.00
Chase (cc)	$5,535.00	$211.00
Key Bank (cc)	$5,462.00	$52.00
CitiCard (cc)	$871.00	$67.00
Rooms To Go (cc)	$4,805.00	$109.00
USAA (cc)	$4,354.00	$95.00
GM Mortgage	$97,821.00	$858.00
TOTAL	**$370,798.00**	**$3,526.00**

They purchased a home about two-and-a-half years ago with a small down payment; and with a little appreciation, they have accumulated about $18,000 of equity in the property.

They both have secure, good-paying jobs; however, their finance charges are not allowing them to reduce their debt.

They have opted to have $1,000 per month from Sherry's paycheck directly deposited into a regular checking account for their utilities and miscellaneous expenses and to have $3,536.50 direct deposited twice a month into a HELOC to be used solely for debt reduction through H.E.A.P.

Step 1: The Setup

Their current equity allowed them to set up a $15,000 HELOC. Because they have dual incomes, an emergency reserve fund of only $5,000 was established. They also decided to keep the first two credit cards open after they are paid off, which will offer them approximately $10,000 more in emergency reserves. This setup will be maintained until they have built up enough of a cushion to comfortably sustain a potential loss of one income.

A $10,000 withdrawal was made from the HELOC. That money was used to pay off the Chase ($5,535) and Rooms To Go ($4,805) debts (an extra $340 from savings was used to pay off the remaining Rooms To Go balance). This immediately reduced their total monthly payments by $320 to $3,206 ($3,526 was the original total monthly payment to service debts).

The following chart shows the account activity for the first three months:

Date	Transaction	Amount	HELOC Balance	Available HELOC Balance
June 1st	Debt Reduction	-$10,000.00	$10,000.00	$5,000.00
15-Jun	Payroll	$3,536.50	$6,498.43	$8,501.57
1-Jul	Payroll	$3,536.50		
1-Jul	Bills	$3,206.00	$6,190.63	$8,809.37
15-Jul	Payroll	$3,536.50	$2,675.75	$12,324.25
1-Aug	Payroll	$3,536.50		
1-Aug	Bills	$3,206.00	$2,354.60	$12,645.40
15-Aug	Payroll	$3,536.50	-$1,173.68	$16,173.68
16-Aug	Debt Reduction	-$11,173.68	$10,000.00	$5,000.00

On June 1, they eliminated two credit cards using the plan. On August 15, they reduced the debt by another $11,173.68. As the chart indicates, the clients accessed $10,000 again from the HELOC, as well as the $1,173.68 surplus created by the last direct deposit. The $11,173.68 was used to pay off the CitiCard debt ($8,031) and reduce the Bank of America debt down to $4,501. This reduced the total monthly payment to service their total debts by $426 a month. Their new total monthly debt service payment dropped to $2,780.

Because their new monthly payments to service debt dropped to $2,780 from the initial $3,526, more money was able to be applied toward paying down the HELOC. This accelerated the pay down of the HELOC, which, in turn, allowed them to pay down their remaining debt quicker.

As you can see in the following chart, the clients were able to pay down the $10,000 HELOC by November 1. This allowed the clients to continue with H.E.A.P. by accessing $9,232.08 on November 1 ($14,232.08-$5,000, which still left them with their $5,000 emergency fund).

Date	Transaction	Amount	HELOC Balance	Available HELOC Balance
16-Aug	Debt Reduction	$11,173.68	$10,000.00	$5,000.00
1-Sep	Payroll	$3,536.50		
1-Sep	Bills	$2,780.00	$9,278.43	$5,721.57
15-Sep	Payroll	$3,536.50	$5,774.34	$9,225.66
1-Oct	Payroll	$3,536.50		
1-Oct	Bills	$2,780.00	$5,038.01	$9,961.99
15-Oct	Payroll	$3,536.50	$1,519.11	$13,480.89
1-Nov	Payroll	$3,536.50	-$2,012.08	
1-Nov	Bills	$2,780.00	$767.92	$14,232.08

Because of the massive amount of debt, many components were considered when setting up this plan.

For example, the debts with the highest interest rates were the first bills eliminated. Credit card debts usually have the highest interest rates. Student loans typically have lower rates and will follow the credit cards.

The goal is to have everything but the mortgage eliminated within eight years. After that, the mortgage should quickly follow suit.

I understand this is an extreme example, but it is real life; and you should now be able to understand the math behind using H.E.A.P. to pay down non-home mortgage debt.

For clients with "other debt," their focus should be the other debt that is putting the largest burden on them. They should also realize that significant life changes could occur (children, additional job opportunities, etc.), and eliminating their high-cost "bad" debt makes better financial sense to do right now.

Side Note: Student loans sometimes have very low interest rates. If that is the case for your student loan debt, you need to run the numbers to make sure it makes sense to use the HELOC to pay down that debt.

Variables that will affect this calculation are your income tax bracket, the HELOC rate, the student loan interest rate, and the amortization schedule of the student loans. If you are in a low tax bracket and the interest on the student loans is low, then it would make more sense not to pay off the student loans until after the HELOC and primary home loan balances are paid off.

For auto loans, many sales incentive programs are offering no interest or low interest financing. Again, you need to simply run the numbers based on your tax bracket and interest rates of the auto loan and the HELOC to determine if it makes sense to pay down the auto loan prior to focusing on your home mortgage.

WHEN DOES H.E.A.P NOT WORK AS WELL?

H.E.A.P. is less effective in the following circumstances: bruised credit, limited equity, and irregular income.

1) Bruised Credit limits H.E.A.P.'s effectiveness as it is predicated on obtaining a suitable Home Equity Line Of Credit. These loans often require a higher credit standard than some closed-end mortgage programs. Lenders will reserve these accounts for people who have managed their credit well. One of the major factors that affect the effectiveness of H.E.A.P. is your ability to manage credit, so the two go hand in hand.

Some readers have had bruised credit in the past but have been working very hard to clean it all up. In these cases, simple counseling and determining the direction of how to best repair a reader's credit can help him/her get to the point where the program can be used.

2) Limited Equity also poses a problem for the program. Some readers may not have enough available equity to start the program. This may be a result of a recent home purchase with little or no money down. It may also be the result of a recent refinance where cash was obtained to pay off some debt or carry out some home improvements. If either of these is the case, one of the other aforementioned acceleration programs could be utilized until the equity position is substantial enough to enlist the program. Readers need to keep a watchful eye on their local housing market for upward trends that may help improve their home's value, which would increase their equity position.

3) Irregular income can also reduce the effectiveness of the program. As you have learned, one feature of the program is that it reduces daily interest charges by utilizing regular deposits directly into a HELOC. This reduction of interest charges helps reduce the debt more rapidly.

Consider a self-employed individual, like a builder, who receives large sums every couple of months. Although the program can still work, interest charges on the money borrowed from the HELOC will accrue for longer periods of time; and, if the time between deposits is long enough, there may be situations where the available balance of the HELOC may not be sufficient to support regular monthly payments. Also, since the HELOC is a loan, if regular payments are not made to service the loan, the lender may limit the borrower's ability to draw more funds from the HELOC until the late payments are made. In cases of irregular income, a more conservative H.E.A.P. should be implemented.

For the self-employed individual example above, using H.E.A.P. to force the client to allocate more dollars annually to debt reduction still makes sense. When clients use H.E.A.P., they are more aware of the harmful effects of interest and many will curb frivolous spending habits because they know every dollar they take out of their HELOC costs them interest every month.

Although these three examples are the most common variables that make the program ineffective or less effective, for certain clients, the program will not make much sense to use.

For example, the program makes little sense for a high-income/high-net worth client. Sure, the client can use a HELOC to pay off the primary residential mortgage quicker than just making the minimum required mortgage payment each month; however, the question is whether it makes financial sense to do so. In my opinion, the answer is no. Instead, a higher income/net worth client should look at Equity Harvesting as a way to build maximum wealth for retirement.

A FEW THINGS TO WATCH OUT FOR

While H.E.A.P. is relatively simple to understand (although not always the easiest to illustrate), there are a few nuances to the plan that you need to watch out for or follow when you implement it.

1) There is more than one kind of "equity line."

Some equity lines are "closed-end" and do not make the unused or paid portion available for withdrawal to the borrower. You access the line once and then are not allowed to access the remaining balance until the line is paid off. It's basically a one-time draw for a specific amount. This type of loan obviously does not work as you need to use the HELOC as a checking account and access the line of credit every time you write a check to pay your bills (and access large chunks at a time as you pay down your primary mortgage on a periodic basis).

2) The line of credit provided by the institution must be able to accept direct deposit, allow unlimited check writing against the account, and not limit the transactions each month. Hopefully, it also provides some sort of debit card for weekend emergencies.

3) You need to be able to budget yourself properly and have financial discipline when using H.E.A.P. The reason this plans works is because spending habits and miscellaneous spending are budgeted correctly. Although the budget is based on your current spending habits, a stricter budget, if enforced, could speed up the plan even more.

4) You need to keep in mind your ultimate goal. The goal with the H.E.A.P. is to pay off your primary mortgage as quickly as possible. It is not the best plan to build your wealth, but it is the plan many will chose nonetheless. When you keep this goal in

mind and maintain the discipline to stick to it, H.E.A.P. will pay off your home mortgage literally years earlier than you otherwise would be able to.

5) Your "emergency cash fund" needs to be carefully considered and should be able to pay for at least several months of bills in case you have a loss of income.

6) If there is a loss of income and the payments are not made on the HELOC, you need to know whether the bank will allow you to access the remaining line of equity.

Summary of the caveats of the program:

1) You need to have equity in your home.

2) Typical lines of credit are harder to acquire with bruised credit.

3) Local institutions may have limitations on transactions (writing checks), and costs are associated with exceeding the limit.

4) Some lenders may not offer direct deposit.

5) If your home is sold, the equity line would not automatically transfer to the new property. In order to continue the plan on the new home, a new line of credit would need to be obtained and secured by the new property.

6) Many lines of credit have a limited "draw period" or time in which money can freely be taken out. Often, it is as much as ten years. This period should be clearly identified, and a plan should be put in place to pay down the line after the draw period ends. If the plan is maintained, there should always be plenty of available equity; and if scheduled payments are made on time, many institutions will roll the line over into a new one with little or no cost.

HOW CAN YOU RECEIVE SPECIFIC NUMBERS TO DETERMINE IF AND HOW H.E.A.P. WILL WORK FOR YOU?

Great question. I imagine many readers of this book (even those who really understand and believe Equity Harvesting is the way to build maximum wealth) will want to know how H.E.A.P. will work to pay off their home's debt. I don't blame you.

I use Equity Harvesting to build my wealth, but I too was curious to see how much quicker I could pay off my house using H.E.A.P.

As this topic becomes more popular, you will find advisors trying to sell you this concept and software so you can implement it yourself.

Fundamentally, with this book, my goal is to educate you with real world math on home equity management topics so that you can be informed and make the best decisions for yourself. I'd like you to use certified advisors who have taken the CWPP™, CAPP™, and/or MMB™ course and who are "rated" by the Asset Protection Society.

Having said that, many other advisors can also help you with the concepts in this book; and regarding H.E.A.P., many advisors have purchased software to illustrate this concept for their clients.

I'll say this: be very skeptical of an advisor trying to sell you a H.E.A.P.-type software package that costs anything over $1,000, and be outraged if an advisor tries to sell you a package that costs $3,500.

As you now know, this concept is relatively simple but powerful; and advisors are playing on ignorant clients who see the thousands of dollars in savings and are willing to pay upwards of $3,500 to get access to a "program."

There are less expensive programs out there; and because I had the demand from advisors who've taken my certification courses, I, along with my co-author of this chapter, John Steinke, created a simple software program advisors can use and consumers can purchase.

You have heard me rant throughout the book about how authors who put out so-called "educational" books do so in an attempt to sell services and products. Some may accuse me of the same since I am telling you about the software we have created. However, as I've done and will continue to do with my educational institute, when advisors request tools from me so they can provide better advice to their clients, if I'm capable of providing it, I do. That is the case with the H.E.A.P. software.

As I've already stated, you can find several vendors out there with software packages for sale. I can't vouch for them, but they are not complicated software programs to create. I'm not necessarily advocating that you use the software we've created; but, since it has been created, it makes sense to let you know where you can find it.

www.heaplan.com has the software that allows advisors and clients to run illustrations to determine how helpful H.E.A.P. can be when trying to pay down debt.

H.E.A.P SUMMARY

As with anything in life, a game plan is only as good as the follow-through. Certainly, most homeowners, if asked, would say they'd like to pay their home off early. Homeowners who want to pay off the debt on their home as soon as possible should jump at the opportunity to use H.E.A.P. due to the fact that the program can accelerate paying off the debt on a home by several years, thereby saving thousands, and sometimes hundreds of thousands, of dollars in interest payments.

Many homeowners are already using the common debt reduction plans like Rounding Up, Apply the Bonus, and/or Bi-Weekly Payments. While there is nothing wrong with these plans, H.E.A.P. is a much better program in many ways.

H.E.A.P. is a flexible plan that can adjust when you need the plan adjusted. The key to the plan is to always pay down maximum debt as you have your income/paycheck directly deposited into your HELOC.

If you use H.E.A.P. and have the discipline to stick with the program, you will pay off your home early. There is no doubt about it.

Let me go back to my initial statement when I started this chapter:

> "Is it a fair statement to say that there are two types of people in this world? There are those that want to use the equity in their homes to tax-favorably build a retirement nest egg, and there are those that want to pay off the debt on their home as soon as possible."

I believe the above statement to be true; and, hopefully, after reading this entire book, you will determine whether you want to pay off your home early or use the equity in your home to build wealth.

My goal is to give you real world math and examples so that you can make informed decisions. I hope this book has accomplished this goal.

If you can't find a local advisor you feel comfortable working with on the topics discussed in this book or if you simply want to ask a few questions, please feel free to e-mail me at info@thewpi.org, and I will answer your questions or refer you to a local advisor who has been through one of my training courses.

Help From The Author

I hesitated when determining whether to have a section in the book titled "Help From The Author." Why? As you've read in numerous places in this book, I give a hard time to the other authors in the marketplace who have books on the topics covered in this book due to the fact that it is my opinion their books are not "educational" books but instead are "marketing" books with a specific purpose-that purpose being to generate leads from consumers so they can be sold and/or directed to advisors who pay to be trained in the teachings of the books.

I also tout this book as the only unbiased educational book on the topics covered and as such I don't want to taint that with an ad in this book for potential clients to contact me so I can sell them my services.

Having stated the above, I do have to deal with the realities of what will come from this book. Many non-advisor readers will read this book and will want help from someone who is qualified to discuss the topics covered. While I'm the author and I am qualified to help, my business model is set up **not** to have individual non-advisor clients. My clients today are the advisors who take one of the certification courses from The Wealth Preservation Institute (www.thewpi.org). My clients are also those advisors who become "Rated" through The Asset Protection Society (www.assetprotectionsociety.org).

Generally speaking, the topics in this book are not what I consider complicated or advanced. I cover advanced and complicated topics in my certification courses. My point is that, if you had an advisor hand you this book and the advisor studied the topics in this book, the chances are significant that the advisor can help you with the topics covered. Also, after you read this book you should be able to determine for yourself if the advisor who is helping you knows what he/she is talking about.

If you were not given this book by an advisor and would like to ask me questions, I would be happy to answer them and you can feel free to e-mail me at roccy@thewpi.org or give me a call at 269-216-9978.

If you would like individual one-on-one help with one or more of the topics covered in this book, know that I will likely refer you to an advisor who has taken one of the certification courses offered by my educational institute. I will not and do not "sell" leads like other authors who have books in the marketplace, and my intention is not to solicit calls from non-advisors with this book. I simply know from past experience with my other books that this will happen, and this section of the book is an attempt to be open about how I deal with questions from those who purchase the book.

If you are an advisor who purchased this book because you believe by learning the topics covered the "correct" way you will be able to provide better advice to your clients and you would like to learn more about the subject matter, you can contact me at roccy@thewpi.org or 269-216-9978. Before creating this book, I already had an educational program dealing with the subject matter; and as I always advocate, I recommend advisors take one of the courses offered by the Wealth Preservation Institute.